Public Speaking

Public Speaking

A Handbook for Christians

Second Edition

Duane Litfin

BAKER BOOK HOUSE
Grand Rapids, Michigan 49516

Second printing, August 1995

Printed in the United States of America

> **Library of Congress Cataloging-in-Publication Data**
>
> Litfin, A. Duane.
>   Public speaking : a handbook for Christians / A. Duane Litfin. —
> 2nd ed.
>   p.   cm.
>   Includes bibliographical references and index.
>   ISBN 0-8010-5675-6
>   1. Public speaking. 2. Public speaking—Religious aspects —
> Christianity. I. Title.
>   PN4121.L56 1992
>   808.5'1—dc20   91-42786

The author expresses appreciation for permission to reprint

"What People Usually Fear" by Peter Watson, *Sunday Times* (London), 7
October 1973, © Times Newspapers Ltd. 1973.

An excerpt from *At Wit's End* by Erma Bombeck, Field Enterprises, Inc./Field
Newspaper Syndicate.

An excerpt from *C. S. Lewis at the Breakfast Table,* 2d ed., edited by James T.
Como, © Harcourt Brace Jovanovich, 1992.

A question and answer by Dr. Sherwood E. Wirt and C. S. Lewis in the essay
"Cross-Examination," taken from "Decision" magazine, October 1963; © 1963
Billy Graham Evangelistic Association. Used by permission. All rights reserved.

An exerpt from *The Weight of Glory* by C. S. Lewis, by permission of Harper
Collins Religious, an imprint of HarperCollins Publishers.

An Excerpt from *The Art of Persuasion* by Wayne C. Minnick, 2d ed., © 1968
by Houghton Mifflin Company.

An excerpt from *Public Speaking as a Liberal Art* by John F. Wilson and Carroll
C. Arnold, 4th ed., © 1978 by Allyn and Bacon.

The advertisement "On Advertising and Speechmaking," used by permission of
D'Arcy Masius Benton and Bowles, Inc.

An excerpt from *Public Communication* by Roderick P. Hart, Gustav W.
Friedrich, and William D. Brooks.

Excerpts from speeches by Ernest L. Boyer, Waldo Braden, Kenneth Mason,
William H. Webster, Newton N. Minow, and Samuel L. Becker.

Contents

91552

Preface to Second Edition

I have been gratified by the reception *Public Speaking: A Handbook for Christians* has received over the past decade, and I am pleased that this reception has warranted bringing out a second edition.

It was time. In some ways the first edition had become dated. Much had taken place during the decade of its life, and the layout and some of the language and illustrations had begun to show their age.

Yet as I worked on this revision, I was struck by how much did not need to be changed. As I said in the original preface, I wanted to "stick to the basics and avoid the fads that seem contrived only to justify the existence of each new wave of textbooks on public speaking." This strategy has allowed the contents of *Public Speaking* to age gracefully. The principles in the book have not changed over the last decade, nor will they change over the next. Fundamentals tend to remain fundamental.

Several generations of college students have used this textbook in their public-speaking courses, and I have appreciated hearing from quite a few of them. Many seminary students have also used this text, often in conjunction with Haddon Robinson's popular book *Biblical Preaching*. These seminarians too have encouraged me by letting me know how well the two books complement one another. Since I value Haddon and his work so highly, this is especially pleasant to hear. Mrs. Kathy Ethridge and Mrs. Judi DeFranco have provided invaluable contributions to the completion of this second edition. For their always cheerful help I am deeply grateful.

If this second edition proves to be as well received as the first, I will be very gratified indeed.

Preface to First Edition

Perhaps the safest way to begin this book is with the observation that, just as there is no such thing as a Christian theory of driving an automobile, there is no such thing as a Christian theory of public speaking. Sound principles of communication, like sound principles of driving, apply in the same way to those who claim the name of Christ as they do to everyone else.

Why, then, one may ask, a book on public speaking that is directed specifically to Christians? A fair question and one that deserves an answer.

To insist that there is no such thing as a Christian theory of driving does not require us to conclude that being a Christian has no bearing on one's driving habits. Likewise, to insist that there is no such thing as a Christian theory of communication does not require the conclusion that being a Christian has no bearing upon one's communication. Christians who take their faith seriously share a set of values, attitudes, and priorities which are derived from the Scriptures and which inevitably influence their behavior, expanding it in some areas and restricting it in others. In this way a Christian's perspective shapes the manner in which he or she participates in the daily rounds of life. And nowhere is this more true than in the realm of a Christian's communication with others.

Thus, even though sound principles of communication are no different for a Christian than for anyone else, being a Christian does inevitably have an impact upon how, when, and where Christians tend to practice these principles. To help Christians relate to others in a more fully Christian way, then, should be the rationale for any book on communication directed specifically to Christians. At least it is the rationale for this one.

As a result, the book you hold in your hands differs from secular books not so much by saying the same things differently, but by saying *other* things, things one would be quite surprised to find in a standard work on public speaking. For example, throughout this text the reader will encounter explicit references to God, the Bible, and Christian presuppositions, things one would never expect to find in a secular book. As Christians, of course, we might wish to criticize these missing elements, arguing that the omission of such items from any book on communication is a serious flaw. After all, we might say, it is doubtful whether the most human of our capacities—the ability to think rationally and communicate symbolically—can ever be fully appreciated without consulting the original model and designer. But quite apart from whether we would win such an argument (it would depend, of course, upon with whom we were arguing), this book includes such references explicitly and unapologetically. The truth of the Christian worldview is assumed throughout.

Or again, one would be startled to find in a standard work on public speaking more than a passing reference to public address in a religious context. This, too, seems a strange omission since so much public speaking in modern America still occurs in just such a context. Why—except from an inordinate fear of things religious—omit such a discussion? Why, indeed! This book assumes throughout that the reader is a Christian who may want to address both religious and nonreligious subjects, on both religious and nonreligious occasions. So, in presenting sound principles of communication this book endeavors to encourage both "ordinary" speeches and specifically Christian speeches wherein the speaker attempts to set forth a Christian perspective on some topic. Moreover, an entire chapter at the end of the book is devoted to that very special type of speech in which most Christians feel a need for improvement, the exposition of a passage of Scripture.

Or again, the discerning reader will notice that we draw in several key places upon a source that is almost completely avoided by most secular writers: homiletics, the study of preaching. The homiletical literature abounds with some of the most practical advice on speechmaking to be found anywhere. Yet one would look in vain in most secular books on public speaking for the insights and techniques of homileticians. Why? Because secular writers hardly know such homiletical literature exists, much less have studied it. This book will use homiletical insights freely—not out of a desire to make the reader into a preacher, to be sure, but because these insights are genuinely useful to any and all public speakers.

These are the types of characteristics that distinguish this book. It is a handbook designed for Christians in the classroom and beyond. It is for those taking a course in communication or for those merely seeking to improve by doing some reading, for students laboring together with an instructor or for individuals working alone. It is the sort of text that speakers may keep for future reference when their formal work is over, or pass along to others who have never thought of studying public speaking formally.

But above all this book is designed to be practical. A how-to approach is used throughout. I have attempted to stick to the basics and avoid the fads that seem contrived only to justify the existence of each new wave of textbooks on public speaking.

Most writers begin books by acknowledging the debts they owe to others, and then gracefully absolving those others of any blame for what follows. By contrast, Haddon Robinson in his excellent book *Biblical Preaching* cuts against this tradition (as Haddon is wont to do) by citing his creditors and then declaring, "Since all of these and others influenced me deeply, it is only fair that for weaknesses in this volume they should shoulder a large share of the blame!"

Since I am named among Haddon's creditors, I shoulder that burden willingly. Far more praise than blame will accrue from that volume. Furthermore, it also frees me to return the favor by spreading some blame of my own. For over sixteen years, Haddon Robinson has been my teacher, mentor, and friend. To him I owe the largest debt for whatever I may know of public speaking.

But not to him alone. To others who have taught me, most notably Charles Stewart of Purdue University, I owe similar debts. To my students who have asked and forced me to answer questions I would never have posed myself, I am grateful. To the seemingly countless audiences I have addressed over the last twenty years, who were witnessing unbeknownst to them the birth and refinement within my own public speaking of the principles described in this book, I also express my gratitude for their patience and encouragement.

But most of all I want to acknowledge my gratitude to my family, not simply for their long-suffering while I was writing this book, which should be noted, but for their cheerful and patient encouragement to my public-speaking ministry in general. Only the spouse and children of a professional student can know the special frustrations of having someone "home," but "not available," and only the family of a public speaker can understand the regular discipline of listening attentively to a message for the third or fifth time. To my wife, Sherri, and to my children, Bryan, Matthew, and Becky, I express my profound thanks for their support and participation in my work.

Chapter 1

An Introduction to Effective Public Speaking

Effective communication is important for everyone, not just Christians. From a merely pragmatic viewpoint all members of society must get along with others, and effective communication is the best means we have of doing so. The alternative, force or violence, usually causes more problems than it solves, even when it is justified (and it seldom is). So everyone, it would seem, has a vested interest in promoting the study of communication.

Whatever agreement or assent is arrived at in human affairs . . .
is reached by linguistic processes,
or else it is not reached.   Benjamin Lee Wharf

But Christians have an especially high stake in pursuing effective communication. Why? For *theological* reasons. Do not be put off by the term *theological*. The most important truths we know in life are theological truths. Theology is not something for dusty teachers and musty tomes; it is the most useful truth of all since it tells us about ourselves from God's point of view. And when we glimpse ourselves from that perspective, we realize that communication is not just incidental to being human; it is at the very core of life.

Tied to our ability to communicate are all the unique characteristics of the human race. Of all of God's creatures only human beings can use language to think abstractly, name things, ask questions, agree, deny, argue, discuss, or proclaim. Only the human race, modeled after God's own likeness, was created *to communicate*. To be sure, some of the higher animals do display a certain limited capacity to "think" and manipulate their environment through "communication," but their abilities pale into insignificance when compared with humankind's. The contrasts are so vast as to suggest not merely differences in degree, but differences in kind. By God's design only human beings were created physically and mentally to be talkers, communicators.

To be fully human, then, each person must be able somehow to bridge the gap to others as effectively as possible. God has uniquely gifted us to do so, and it should be the desire of every Christian to use these gifts to the full.

God's Original Design

The goal of every Christian is to be as completely human as possible. This may seem to be a strange statement, but do consider it carefully. Every Christian's goal is to be all that God intended him or her to be in the Creator's original design, a design at whose core was this business of communication. Because the Bible teaches the innate sinfulness of the human race, we sometimes lose sight of this goal and begin thinking that our destiny is to escape our humanity. But such thinking reflects a misunderstanding of the Bible.

In the beginning God created the human race to communicate with him and with each other, and he declared the results of his creative act "very good" (Gen. 1:31). God was completely pleased with his design. It was perfect.

Adam and Eve, of course, soon blighted that perfect creation with sin, thereby infecting all the cosmos with their rebellion. Even the image of God in their own selves was marred, and the untainted communication the man and woman had enjoyed with each other and with God was polluted by sin and selfishness. Thus did human beings become quite incapable of fulfilling God's design for the race.

But notice that God's solution to our dilemma was not that we should somehow try to become something other than human beings. Rather, the solution was that God's original design be salvaged through Jesus Christ, the new Adam (Rom. 5:12–21; 1 Cor. 15:20–58). In him human beings can become new creatures; they have the opportunity to become what God intended them to be. In their sin they became something less than fully human, but in Christ each person can recover all that God originally desired for the human race. And again, at the heart of God's original intent was this matter of communication. God

---

Speaking is innate, writing is an invention. George A. Miller

---

designed humans to be like himself, a communicator, one who reaches out, a builder of bridges. God designed people to talk! Thus Christians, who desire all that God has for them, have a heavy stake in becoming the best possible "talkers" they can be.

This book is designed to help you become a better builder of bridges to others, a better talker, so to speak. More specifically, our goal is to zero in on that peculiar form of talking we call public address. But to prepare ourselves for that, let us first think a bit about our broader subject, human communication in general.

The Nature of Communication

What happens when people communicate with one another? The answer is unbelievably involved, and we cannot do it justice here. But let us at least underline some of the especially relevant aspects of the process.

At the simplest level, human communication involves three steps: (1) a source encodes his or her meaning in a signal; (2) this signal is transmitted to a receiver; and (3) the receiver decodes it, attributing meaning to it (see fig. 1). To the extent that the meaning the receiver finds in the signal is similar to the

Figure 1
Steps in Communication

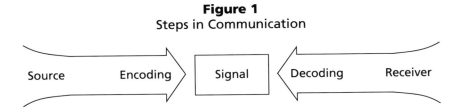

Source   Encoding   Signal   Decoding   Receiver

meaning the source intended, communication has occurred. To the extent that the two meanings do not match, communication has not occurred.

While this sounds simple enough, the real-life process of communication is torturously complex and is subject to a wide array of misunderstandings. Here are three common misunderstandings:

1. *Each act of communication is separate and discrete, and can be studied as such.* This is a common and very tempting misconception because it appears to simplify to a great extent the task of understanding human communication. Unfortunately, communication is a much more complicated *process* than it might seem on the surface.

No act of communication, including a public speech, can be fully appreciated apart from the context in which it occurs. Thus we should view any given act of communication as we would a small eddy in a large river. We can focus our attention on it, but we will never understand it apart from an understanding of the surrounding water of which it is a part. What is the river like as a whole? What specifically gives rise to this whirlpool? What are its characteristics and dimensions? How does it relate to other whirlpools (similar or different) around it? These are just a few of the pertinent questions we would have to ask in order to understand a simple little eddy in a river. They are analogous to the kinds of questions we must ask about any single event in the ongoing process of communication.

2. *Communication is linear in the sense that a message travels one way from a source to a receiver.* This may be true as far as it goes, but it does not go far enough. It represents a vast oversimplification of normal communication. Except in unusual circum-

stances, human communication is always *circular* in nature. We are seldom a source of messages without also becoming a receiver of messages; likewise, in the process of receiving messages we almost always become sources of messages in return. Thus the process is circular, involving both the sending and receiving of messages, often simultaneously.

When we think of a speaker standing before an audience, it is especially tempting to think of the communication as one-way, or unilateral. But every experienced speaker knows better. Certainly the speaker does influence the audience, but the audience also influences the speaker in a wide variety of ways—before, during, and after the speech. In fact, so strong is this bilateral influence that a sensitive speaker often winds up wondering who has had the greater influence, speaker or audience!

3. *The speaker transfers thoughts to the listeners.* This is one of the most common oversimplifications of the communication process. It seems to suggest that we can somehow directly implant our ideas in the mind of another. If mental telepathy were possible, this might be the case; and certainly the Spirit of God can bypass the communication process and reach our minds directly. But apart from such exceptional circumstances, we must depend upon symbols to communicate our ideas, and this introduces gaping opportunities for misunderstanding.

Thoughts can exist only in someone's mind. Technically speaking, they can never be directly transferred. To be communicated, our thoughts must be encoded in some signal, either verbal or nonverbal. This signal is the only element that ever becomes public and observable by others. The receiver decodes or interprets our signal and attributes meaning to it. This decoding process thus prompts the receiver's own thoughts. But notice that neither the sender's nor the receiver's thoughts are ever anywhere but in their respective minds. There is a sense in which the sender's thought exists in the signal, of course, but this is only a secondary existence.

When we want to communicate, then, we attempt to choose the symbols that will prompt our listener to conjure up in his or her mind thoughts that are as close as possible to the thoughts we have in our minds. Thus our choice of symbols must be dominated by considerations of *how the receiver will understand them.* In this way our listener has a profound influence on how we encode our message.

By the same token, when we receive messages from someone else, our primary concern must be not what these symbols mean in some abstract sense, nor how we ourselves typically use these symbols, but *what the source intended them to mean on this particular occasion.* In other words, our goal must be to decode the message exactly as it was encoded. That we can never perfectly accomplish this task must not prevent us from trying. Rather, it should propel us to consider all the relevant data so as to be sure that we have come as close as possible.

So whether we are functioning as senders or receivers, our goal, if we want to promote understanding and effective communication, is to relinquish our own perspective, insofar as it is possible to do so, and adapt ourselves to the other person, to see the world as he or she sees it, to use the symbols as he or she uses them. This does not require us to agree with the other person once we have accurately understood, of course. At that point we are quite free to applaud, protest, or refute. But at least we will be responding to a reasonably accurate version of what our partner in communication actually intended to say.

Even when we have avoided the misconceptions dealt with in this section, our task of understanding human communication has only just begun. The next step in zeroing in upon public speaking is to think about some of the varied types of communication we experience daily.

Nonmediated Communication

Contrast with Mediated Communication

Consider the important differences between mediated and nonmediated communication. *Mediated communication* includes all those ways people transmit messages through some interposing medium. Radio, television, film, and print are all forms of mediated communication. *Nonmediated communication,* on the other hand, is direct, immediate, involving some sort of face-to-face contact. It is *interpersonal*. The two parties are present in the same general area at the same time.

The distinction between mediated and nonmediated communication is an important one because the use of media can have a profound influence on the results. In mediated communication the source and receiver can be far removed from one another in both time and space yet still communicate. This occurs daily as we listen to a tape of a speech, watch a movie, or read a book by a deceased author. What is more, in mediated communication the receiver often has no chance to ask ques-

---

I had many things to write to you, but I am not willing to write them to you with pen and ink; but I hope to see you shortly, and we shall speak face to face.   3 John 13–14 (NASB)

---

tions or to feed back a response to the source. And even if the receiver does, the response is usually indirect. In other words, the feedback itself is usually mediated, if in fact it is possible at all. Mediated communication can often be stored and used again with different audiences (think of a book in a library). Thus, while mediated communication is less direct, a communicator may often use media to speak to a much wider (mass) audience than would be possible without the media.

Nonmediated communication, by contrast, is more direct and personal. It is more attuned to a particular receiver or group of receivers. It is *im-mediate* in the sense that nothing stands between the source and receiver (the prefix *im-* is another form of the Latin prefix *in-*, which here means "no, not, without, non-," as in *impossible* or *immaterial*). Such communication cannot be stored without being transformed into some form of mediated communication, such as a tape recording or transcript. Feedback is often received without delay—indeed, simultaneously. Thus nonmediated communication typically involves a much more direct transaction between the source and receiver than does mediated communication. Nonmediated communication is more narrowly focused, having been personally tailored to fit a much more specific audience.

This book is about that brand of nonmediated communication we call public speaking. Of course a speech can be recorded or written down and so shared by many who were not a part of the original audience, but that is not within the purview of this book. Though the circumstances may sometimes be otherwise (as when the president uses the opportunity of speaking to a relatively small audience to make a nationally televised policy address), the focus of our study will be on a speaker's addressing a limited body of people seated before him as he stands at the podium. His goal will be to communicate first, and usually only, with this particular group of individuals, quite apart from any use of media. (In this case the use of a microphone does not qualify as a "medium," of course.) Thus his speech can and should be narrowly focused and personally tailored for his listeners.

Types of Nonmediated Communication

We have said that one way to analyze the broad subject of human communication is to divide it into two general categories: mediated and nonmediated communication. And we have pointed out that public speaking as we will approach it is a form of communication that belongs in the second category: it is typically an instance of interpersonal, direct, *nonmediated* communication. But to see public speaking in an even clearer light, let us contrast it further with two other common forms of nonmediated communication, dyadic and small-group communication.

Dyadic Communication

Almost all nonmediated communication tends to occur in one of three settings. The first and most common is one-to-one communication, or *dyadic communication* (a dyad is a group of two). Dyadic communication thus includes all interviews or conversations with one other person.

Because dyadic communication involves only one other person, it is typically the most intimate and private of the three forms of nonmediated communication. We position ourselves rather close to the other and engage in direct communication. Usually such conversations are relaxed and familiar; and unless we are acutely shy, we experience little or no speech anxiety ("stage fright"). Our communication task is relatively uncomplicated, since we must make only one other person understand us and we must in turn understand only one other. We can monitor the other person constantly, adapting ourselves step by step as we go. The interchange of ideas is highly unrestricted, and we freely switch roles from source to receiver and back again many times within a short period. What is more, since there are usually no others who hear our conversation, outside influences play a much reduced role.

Small-Group Communication

In small-group settings (from three to, say, fifteen or twenty people) the picture becomes much more complicated. As the number of people in the group increases, the chemistry becomes geometrically more complex. The discussion becomes more public, less intimate; and the distances between people increase. The influence of others begins to take effect so that we find ourselves more concerned with group approval and, therefore, experience a higher level of speech anxiety. Our communication task is much more complicated since now there are numerous others who must be understood, and be made to understand. Our communication becomes multidirectional, balancing the differences among our hearers. Monitoring becomes more difficult simply because there is so much more to keep track of. Problems of adaptation multiply due to the competing needs, abilities, and dispositions of our various listeners. And while the flow of communication in a small group tends to be relatively unrestricted, there are multiple speakers now instead of just two. Thus interaction is more limited, and the average participant spends considerably more time listening than speaking.

Public Address

In the third form of nonmediated communication (speaker-audience), the communication becomes still less private. In fact, it is by definition "public." Intimacy becomes more difficult as the number of participants rises and the distance between speaker and audience grows larger. Because more people are involved, the influence of others on audience and speaker alike increases and stage fright becomes much more pronounced (butterflies in the stomach, dry mouth, weak knees, etc.). Since the speaker faces the difficulty of having to accommodate a still wider range of people, the communication task becomes even more complex, with many more differences to be bridged. Monitoring the audience during the speech, much less adapting to them while speaking, becomes ever more difficult. Hence, pre-analysis, whereby the speaker studies and adapts to the audience's needs during the preparation period, becomes much more important. Interaction is, of course, highly restricted, with the speaker functioning primarily as the source and the audience primarily as the receivers.

Perhaps you can see that there are advantages and disadvantages to each of these three forms of nonmediated communication. Each has its own strengths and weaknesses. Thus there are some communication goals which might be accomplished very well in a dyadic setting, but only poorly in the public-address setting (and vice versa). The small-group setting seems to represent a sort of compromise between the other two. In the small group there is a balanced trade-off of the advantages and disadvantages of the other two settings.

The Public-Address Setting

Advantages of the Public-Address Setting

As we have noted, the communication task becomes increasingly complex as we involve more people in the process. So in several important ways the public-speaking setting is the most difficult of the three, particularly if you are the speaker! Why, then, do we not drop back and simply eliminate the speaker-audience setting, opting instead for either the dyadic or small-group setting?

The answer to this question is that, while there may be distinct disadvantages to the public-address setting, there are also

Speaking Before a Group

Have you any idea what fear was rated No. 1 in a recent survey among adults? Speaking before a group.

That's right, the anxiety of standing before an audience beat out fear of death, fear of failing, fear of heights, and fear of alienation. (Come to think of it, they all mean the same thing.)

It occurred to me that this year a virtual army of amateur speakers will, for the first time, take to the podiums to conduct club meetings, volunteer seminars, and instructional classes.

How do the professionals handle it?

• Demand a podium capable of supporting a dead body (yours) up to 187 pounds. Throw yourself over it, being sure to hook your arm over the microphone so you won't slip away.

• Adhere to the old wives' tale, "Feed a cold crowd, starve a speaker." It cuts down on spitting up.

• Insist on a table near the restroom. For some unexplained reason, speakers have a kidney wish.

• Never read a speech. Use note cards which serve a double purpose. You can rearrange them to fit your audience and in the event the person who introduces you uses the jokes on your first eight cards, use the sharp cutting edges on your wrists.

Believe me, I know what you are going through. A couple of years ago, my son brought home a mimeographed memo from school announcing that the principal was having 12 parents in at a time to "engage in dialogue about the future of the school."

At the beginning of the meeting, he announced that before the session was over he wanted to hear from EVERYONE. If they didn't volunteer, he'd call on them. One by one, I watched them get it over with. Questions on what the administration was doing to raise standards of education . . . could he please interpret the test scores in relation to those given the previous year . . . did he feel that schools were becoming isolated or were they addressing themselves to alternatives, such as technical or vocational classes.

As a professional speaker, I waited until he called upon me. Then I casually poked myself in the eye with a green felt-tipped pen and stood up to reveal the back of my dress which was plastered to my body. I opened my mouth to discover my tongue had dried up, causing my lip to shrink. I cleared my throat, folded my arms over my chest (the green ink would never wash out) and asked, "Yes, do the nuns really shave their heads?"

Erma Bombeck

two primary advantages to this setting that are often so valuable that they more than offset the drawbacks.

First, there is a simple logistical advantage. We regularly face situations in which something must be communicated to a large number of people. To attempt to do so through one-to-one or small-group settings would be unworkable. So we opt for the public-address setting, which has the advantage of reaching an entire group of people simultaneously, while yet avoiding the disadvantages of the various kinds of mediated communication.

A second advantage of the public-address setting is a more subtle but equally important one. The public speaker has the opportunity of programing the sequence of ideas and the parts of the message so that they occur in a relatively organized pattern. Furthermore, the speaker can complete the development of the ideas before receiving overt responses from the listeners. In the communication of many kinds of ideas this can be a great advantage.

It is an almost universal human trait to speak up before we have fully thought through our own ideas or evaluated the best way to communicate them. On the other hand, it is also a common fault to respond to a message too quickly, before we completely understand it. Both of these faults plague the dyadic and small-group settings: the speaker badly articulates ideas which are poorly thought out, and the listener(s) responds in kind. It is just this tendency which prompts some to dismiss such conversations or discussions as a mere "pooling of ignorance."

The public-address setting affords a framework wherein these two faults can be minimized. At the very least, the speaker has the *opportunity* to think through and then structure his or her ideas with a view to effective communication. At the very least, the listeners have the *opportunity* to hear the ideas and postpone responding to them until they are understood fully. That this so seldom occurs does not negate the fact that the public setting provides such potential; it merely underlines the unfortunate state of the art of speaking and listening in our day.

The public-speaking situation is, then, only one of three general settings in which interpersonal communication takes place. Of the three, it is the one most of us probably engage in least. More often we find ourselves in a small-group setting or in a one-to-one setting. What is more, most of us take to these latter two settings with relative ease and expertise; and while there is much we can learn about them, too, we tend to function in them relatively well. In our ordinary conversation and in small groups we do not face the problems encountered when we have to prepare a speech for an audience. Thus, it is precisely because most of us have practiced public speaking so little, and because the task is so much more complicated, that we must study it formally all the more.

Characteristics of a Good Public Speaker

From even this brief discussion we can begin to discern the characteristics of a good public speaker. There are five qualities that every Christian definition should include:

Integrity

Quintilian, the great Roman teacher of rhetoric, said:

> The orator . . . whom I am concerned to form, shall be the orator as defined by Marcus Cato, "a good man skilled in speaking." But above all he must possess the quality which Cato places first and which is in the very nature of things the greatest and most important, that is, he must be a good man.[1]

Quintilian believed it is not possible to promote evil and be great at the same time. Thus, to be a great orator one must first be a person of integrity, committed to what is good and virtuous.

As Christians our definition of virtue would certainly differ from Quintilian's in some important particulars, but we can at least agree with his broad conviction that to be great one must first be good. We can, of course, think of people who have been "effective" in accomplishing evil goals through public speaking. Perhaps Adolf Hitler would be the prime example from modern times. Yet Quintilian would not have thought of Hitler as a great orator, even though Hitler was extremely effective. Nor should we. Any Christian appraisal of public speaking must rise above mere pragmatism by asking whether the goals and means of the speaker are good when measured against the yardstick of Scripture. Is the speaker honest, unselfish, straightforward, and committed to good and virtuous ends? Or is the speaker dishonest, self-serving, manipulative, and out to win regardless of what tactics must be used? From a Christian standpoint, only that speaker whose efforts are characterized by integrity can be considered a good speaker.

Sensitivity

Closely allied to integrity is sensitivity. A good speaker must be both willing and able to respond sensitively to the audience.

A willingness to be sensitive to others stems from a fundamental conviction of their worth. Those who do not value others have few reservations about and experience little difficulty in manipulating them. To such speakers—and there are too many of them at both podium and pulpit—other people are mere sheep, dupes to be shuffled about at will to serve the speakers' own purposes.

But for Christians, who see others through the eyepiece of the Bible, such an attitude is unacceptable. Human beings represent God's finest creation (Ps. 8). As members of the race for whom Christ died, they have infinite worth to God. Thus each person is valuable and deserves to be treated as a responsible individual.

Blessed is the man who, having nothing to say, abstains from giving in words evidence of the fact. George Eliot

---

A good speaker, by any Christian definition of that term, recognizes this and demonstrates it by dealing selflessly with his listeners, putting himself in their place, trying to see as they see, serving their best interests, valuing their ability to choose, and being transparent with them throughout the speech.

Knowledge

But being a sensitive person of integrity is not enough, by itself, to qualify a person as a good speaker. Being willing to serve the people in one's audience does not guarantee the ability to do so. There are no doubt many who would be quite ready to serve others in this way if they could, but they have nothing to say. They lack the necessary knowledge.

A good speaker must obviously have something worthwhile to say. Thus a large part of your speech preparation must be devoted to extensive homework on your topic. There are few shortcuts here. Even the best motives will not compensate for ignorance. If you are already an expert on your subject, then much of your study may be behind you; if you are not an expert, then much study lies ahead. There is no substitute for a knowledge of the subject. You cannot communicate to others what you do not know. To be a good speaker it is imperative that, one way or another, you know what you are talking about.

Desire

A good speaker must also possess a desire to communicate. Many speakers have no such desire, of course, and that is one of the main reasons they are not good speakers. They have no purpose, no goal, nothing that prompts them to excellence.

A good speaker, by contrast, has something that she wants to say to her audience. She may not always begin her study with a sense of purpose, but as she progresses through the preparation process, the ideas of the speech and their relevance to the audience become clear. And with this growing clarity comes an increasing desire—indeed, at times even an urgency—to get up and speak. Without some such desire to speak, the speech will remain flat and perfunctory for both speaker and audience. But with such a desire, the occasion can come alive with interest. The speaker knows the speech is worthwhile and is thereby motivated, in spite of any stage fright, to communicate her ideas. The audience senses the speaker's desire to communicate and is infected by it immediately. In this way a speaker's sense of purpose—or lack of it—can often color the entire effort, marking the line between success and failure.

Skill

The last (but by no means the least important) mark of a good speaker is communicative skill. It is quite possible to be a knowledgeable, sensitive person of integrity who desires to communicate and still be a poor public speaker. We have all heard speakers like this. Why do they fail as speechmakers? Because of a lack of skill in communicating ideas effectively in a public setting.

This book is designed to help you primarily in this last category. If you are not a person of integrity, this text can do little to change that. The book *can* help you become a more sensitive communicator, however (chap. 2), and still more can it aid you in becoming knowledgeable about your subject (chap. 3) and purposeful in communicating that knowledge (chap. 4). But the major contribution of this book will be to help you with the communication skills you need to become an effective public speaker (chaps. 5–10).

Whether you emerge in the end as a good speaker, as we have defined it here, depends wholly, of course, upon your willingness and ability to meld all five of the above characteristics into your every effort. This is something you will have to do for yourself; in the last analysis, no one else can do it for you.

The Public-Speaking Market

But wait, someone may say. Is public speaking really worth studying today? To be sure, during the eighteenth and nine-

---

The art of rhetoric is at best very chancy, only partly amenable to systematic teaching. Wayne Booth

---

teenth centuries, when life was slower and there were fewer distractions, public speaking flourished. But has not that golden age of oratory passed us by? Now that we live in the era of lengthened life spans and shortened attention spans, now that people take for granted space exploration, nuclear bombs, and genetic engineering, now that Americans are so bombarded by the sensory overload of television and film and the dazzle of the advertising industry, are people really interested in hearing public speakers anymore? Other than preachers and politicians (whom we all know no one *ever* listens to anymore), what market is there for a public speaker today, and especially for a Christian public speaker?

Though such questions were common a generation ago, it is curious that they continue to crop up, for the evidence is all on the other side of the ledger. According to Roderick Hart, Gustav Friedrich, and William Brooks in their book *Public Communication,*

> Today, communication is not limited to face-to-face situations—we have worldwide electronic communication, television saturation, and packaged entertainment. And it is understandable why some have said that live, in-person public speaking is as extinct as the dodo bird. Nothing could be further from the truth! Not only is public speaking alive and well, but it is thriving as it never has before despite—and perhaps because of—the coming of the mass media. Per person, public speech consumption is higher today than ever before, including the era of the late 1800s. . . . We, as a people, have not lost our enthusiasm for in-person public speaking as a significant social institution.[2]

In fact, by all accounts public speaking appears to be something of a growth industry in America. According to Hart, Friedrich, and Brooks,

> In 1972 alone, there were upwards of 25,000 professional speaking opportunities in the business and convention fields alone—ranging from closed seminars for a handful of top-echelon executives to the annual open meetings for the National Education Association, which brings out a whopping 10,000 registrants.
>
> The second largest sponsor of paid lecturers is education—from kindergarten assemblies to graduate school forums. About one in five of all elementary and secondary schools have at least one public program annually. The average number of speaking programs is running as high as five per institution. This totals up to 130,000 programs each year. Add to that another 200,000 programs on the junior college, college, and graduate levels, and it seems that the machinery of education is being well lubricated by the juices of eloquence![3]

By 1979, *Parade* was able to claim even more startling figures.

The platform industry, with an annual gross of hundreds of millions of dollars, has come a long way since Ralph Waldo Emerson received a fee of $5 plus oats for his horse for giving lectures. Today, there are over 3,000 platforms on any given day in Los Angeles alone; 30,000 in Chicago, and 50,000 in New York. These include Rotary clubs, universities, women's groups, church groups and conventions.[4]

By 1989, *Fortune* reported that everyone seemed to be joining the bandwagon. So great was the demand for speakers that few celebrities could afford to stay away from the lecture circuit. Ronald Reagan, for example, who in 1990 accepted over $1 million for a brief lecture tour of Japan, was able to post equally high prices for his domestic speeches. His typical fee was $50,000 per occasion, which usually involved speaking for a half-hour and answering questions for fifteen minutes or so. At that rate, one observer calculated, the former president was making about $10 per word. By contrast, Nancy Reagan and Henry Kissinger could command only $30,000 per speech. Author Tom Wolfe and television host Louis Rukeyser, along with network anchors Dan Rather and Tom Brokaw, each earned $25,000 per speech, followed by Gerald Ford, "Tip" O'Neill, and Jeane Kirkpatrick at $20,000. Way down the list were such notables as columnist Ann Landers and, for some reason, ABC's anchor Peter Jennings, at $12,500 per speech.

The market for public speaking today reaches far beyond the typical American desire to see and hear celebrities, however. Even in modern, sophisticated, overstimulated, often cynical American society, people enjoy an effective speaker who has done his or her homework, and they show up again and again in hopes of finding one. Listeners are drawn to and captivated by thoughtful, perceptive, interesting treatments of issues that are relevant to their interests.

Not surprisingly, businesses have caught on to just how important effective public speaking can be in our society, and they are putting their money where it counts. Today more than a few companies employ in-house ghost writers to help executives craft their speeches. One such ghost writer was reported to be earning upwards of $100,000 per year (the average annual income of professional speech writers was cited in one informal survey as $49,000). Companies such as Communispond in New York, Speakeasy in Atlanta, Executive Technique in Chicago, and Decker Communication in San Francisco charge businesses as much as $2,500 per day for personalized, high-tech seminars designed to hone an executive's public-speaking skills.

Everywhere you look today, opportunities for public speaking abound. Whether it be in conference rooms or ballrooms, outdoor amphitheaters or civic auditoriums, churches or college campuses, effective public speakers are in demand.

Opportunities for Christians

The American willingness to listen to public speakers represents a wide range of opportunities for Christians to exercise a witness for Christ. At times you may have the opportunity of explicitly communicating to an audience the gospel of Jesus Christ. On other occasions you may be able to give your personal testimony to the saving power of Christ in your own life or to design a message from some portion of Scripture. In fact, chapter 10 of this book focuses on precisely that.

Often, however, you may also have an opportunity to speak in a Christian way about subjects other than the Christian faith. In such situations your Christianity will be latent, between the lines, but powerful nonetheless. In this way Christians become salt and light in their world, as C. S. Lewis pointed out in appealing for Christian apologists (defenders of the faith):

> I believe that any Christian who is qualified to write a good popular book on any science may do much more by that than by any directly apologetic work. The difficulty we are up against is this. We can make people (often) attend to the Christian point of view for half an hour or so; but the moment they have gone away from our lecture or laid down our article, they are plunged back into a world where the opposite position is taken for granted. As long as that situation exists, widespread success is simply impossible. We must attack the enemy's line of communication. What we want is not more little books about Christianity, but more little books by Christians on other subjects—with their Christianity latent. You can see this most easily if you look at it the other way

The Uses of Eloquence

For since through the art of rhetoric both truth and falsehood are pleaded, who would be so bold as to say that against falsehood, truth as regards its own defenders ought to stand unarmed, so that those who attempt to plead false causes know from the beginning how to make their audience well-disposed, attentive, and docile, while the others remain ignorant of it; so that the former utter their lies concisely, clearly, with the appearance of truth, and the latter state the truth in a way that is wearisome to listen to, not clear to understand, and finally, not pleasant to believe; so that one side, by fallacious arguments, attacks truth and propounds falsehood, the other has no skill either in defending the true, or refuting the false; so that the one, moving and impelling the minds of the audience to error by the force of its oratory, now strikes them with terror, now saddens them, now enlivens them, now ardently arouses them, but the other in the cause of truth is sluggish and cold and falls asleep! Who is so foolish as to be thus wise? Since, therefore, there has been placed equally at our disposal the power of eloquence, which is so efficacious in pleading either for the erroneous cause or the right, why is it not zealously acquired by the good, so as to do service for the truth, if the unrighteous put it to the uses of iniquity and of error for the winning of false and groundless causes?

Saint Augustine

round. Our Faith is not very likely to be shaken by any book on Hinduism. But if whenever we read an elementary book on Geology, Botany, Politics, or Astronomy, we found that its implications were Hindu, that would shake us. It is not the books written in direct defence of Materialism that make the modern man a materialist; it is the materialistic assumptions in all the other books. In the same way, it is not books on Christianity that will really trouble him. But he would be troubled if, whenever he wanted a cheap popular introduction to some science, the best work on the market was always by a Christian.[5]

Christians must be an influence for Christ in a needy world, and there is no better place to exert such an influence than from the public rostrum. Here, in the so-called marketplace of ideas, the goods that are bought and sold have profound implications: What a person believes will determine his eternal destiny. To abandon this public forum to the other side due to a faint heart or lack of ability would be tragic.

The world is looking for people who know what they are talking about. In a time so dependent upon communication, Christians who are willing to think deeply and speak out effectively can have a lasting impact. To help you do so is the goal of this book.

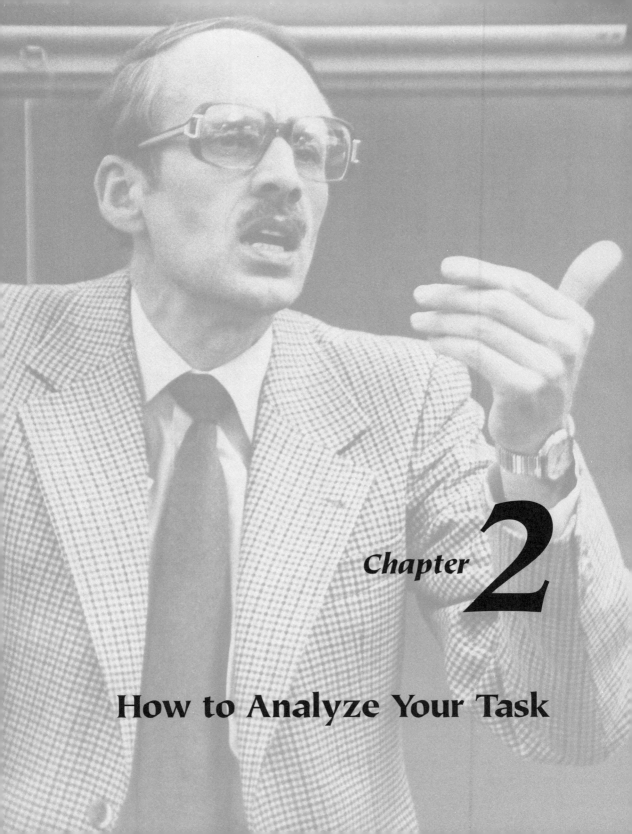

Chapter 2

How to Analyze Your Task

Our goal in this chapter is to present a workable approach to analyzing our speaking task. The reason we place these considerations first is that they are fundamental to all that we are attempting to accomplish as public speakers. We cannot choose well among the flurry of options we face as speakers unless we have a broad conception of what it is we are trying to do and where the many obstacles to our goal may lie. Thus the material we are about to examine is fundamental to the entire process of preparing and delivering a speech, and we will return to it repeatedly.

The Necessity of Adapting to the Audience

Our task, to put it most broadly, is to communicate an idea to an audience. To accomplish this we must make a series of choices about what to say and how to say it so that our message is, to a reasonable degree, accurately received by our audience. How deceptively simple that sounds! The truth is that the process of communicating a message to an audience is a highly complex one and we dare not oversimplify it.

Consider this example: Suppose a speaker is assigned to communicate to an audience the idea, "Because fossil fuels are running out, America needs to look to nuclear power as the energy source of the future." "Simple enough," says the novice. "It shouldn't be too difficult to put together a message that will communicate this idea." And off he runs to the library to begin preparing his speech.

The experienced speaker, by contrast, knows better. He knows that he does not yet have enough information to form an intelligent opinion even about *whether* the idea can be effectively

---

Best rule I know for talkin', is the same as the one for carpenterin': measure twice and saw once.   **Anonymous**

---

communicated, much less about *how* he will begin to approach the subject. The information he lacks has to do with *who his listeners are*. Thus, the question the experienced speaker raises at this point is, To whom am I to communicate this idea?

This question must be answered before you can even begin to shape your speech. Think, for example, of how your handling of the topic of nuclear power might vary with each of these audiences:

1. A group of college students in an ecology class
2. A group of elderly people in a nursing home
3. A class of third-grade children studying a science unit
4. A group of people gathered for a friend's birthday party
5. A group of petroleum-company executives
6. A crowd gathered around a soapbox on a busy street corner
7. A convention of nuclear engineers
8. A group of state or federal legislators

Obviously, each of these audiences would require a tailor-made approach; no single speech would effectively reach any two of them. In fact, with at least a couple of these audiences you would want to think very hard about whether to make the attempt at all!

It is not difficult to see that your primary challenge as a speaker lies in the choices you must make about how to reach *a particular audience* with a given idea. No two audiences are ever the same. To be sure, audiences are all made up of people, and there are certain broad observations we may make which apply generally to every audience. (In fact, we will explore some of them shortly.) But for the most part the variables you must evaluate in an audience are so numerous and complex that the process of audience analysis is one of your most difficult tasks. Yet it is a task you must face and learn to handle effectively, for if the choices are poorly made, your message may well be doomed to go no farther than the podium.

In discussing the necessity of adapting to the audience we are not talking about "pulling our punches" or shading the truth so as to make it palatable. Such practices can be a subtle form of lying to an audience and are unethical. In emphasizing adjusting to the audience we are not suggesting any form of deception whatsoever. We are instead emphasizing the need to take advantage of all the elements within any given speaking situation so that your audience, to the greatest extent possible, will be able to comprehend and willing to act upon your ideas. You can achieve this by (1) understanding your audience, who they are, how they think and feel, what their perceived and unperceived needs are, and then (2) relating your ideas to them in such a way that they can *see* your meaning and its relevance to them. To achieve a similar result with a different audience you might have to rework completely the way you would handle the same basic set of ideas. The difference between the two efforts would be the result of your *audience adaptation*.

One would be hard pressed to find better instances of such audience adaptation than the messages delivered by the apostles that are recorded in the Book of Acts. For example, Donald Sunukjian, who studied in detail the messages of the apostle Paul in Acts 13, 17, and 20, states that one of the most prominent features of these messages is Paul's "total adaptation of his message to the particular audience before him." Says Sunukjian of Paul, "Every aspect of his preaching is deliberately suited to the hopes, needs, and understandings of his immediate listeners."[1] The study then proceeds to demonstrate adjustments in theme, structure, supporting material, style, and mood in each of Paul's messages. Sunukjian concludes, "Every choice [Paul] makes is guided by the nature of his immediate audience, and every aspect of his preaching is suited to their unique needs."[2]

Inevitably, this is one of the marks of any effective communicator, and Paul certainly fits that description. People attend to ideas that are associated with their own needs and goals, and to speakers who show an awareness of these needs and goals. We will do well to follow this apostolic example in our own speaking.

Because understanding and adapting to one's listeners are so crucial to effective communication, this book will take an *audience-centered approach* throughout. This does not mean that other aspects of the communication situation—such as the speaker or the message—will be slighted. Rather, taking an audience-centered approach simply means that we acknowledge that the audience must shape and influence every element of the speaking process if we are interested in communicating effectively. It means that we disallow the basically self-centered atti-

---

Of the three elements in speechmaking—speaker, subject, and persons addressed—it is the last one, the hearer, that determines the speech's end and object.   **Aristotle**

---

tude which says, "If they want to understand, let them get on my wavelength. I've done my part if I merely give out the information." Maintaining an audience-centered approach to public speaking means that we take upon ourselves as speakers the responsibility to do everything we can to promote effective communication by adjusting to our audience. We submit to what someone has called "the tyranny of the audience." To be sure, more often than we like to think, our best efforts will still not be enough to achieve our goals entirely, but this will not be for a lack of trying.

It is not enough, then, merely to combine a speaker with a speech to achieve effective communication. We must have a speaker who has so adapted himself and his speech to the needs of a particular audience that the listeners are both willing and able to assimilate what they receive.

The Nature of Listening

What must you know about your audience to make intelligent adjustments? First, you need to understand something about your audience as listeners. Someone who obviously knew a great deal about human communication once said, "The study of speaking is first and foremost the study of listening." How true! To be an effective speaker you must first understand something about the way people listen. Here are three points you need to keep in mind as you think about your audience as listeners:

1. *Listening is difficult, at least when it is done well.* Listening demands a great deal of concentration and self-discipline. The main reason for this is that we can listen at a much faster pace than anyone can speak. Thus, as we listen to others, our minds are left with large amounts of "spare time." What do we do with this spare time? Most people allow their minds to wander and think about things other than the message to which they are presumably listening. Using all of this spare time wisely, that is, plowing it back into thinking about the matter being discussed, requires a commitment to listening and a discipline of our attention that too few of us possess.

Researchers tell us that we are able to hold our attention continuously on a single stimulus for only a few seconds; then we must break off attending to that stimulus and shift to another. At each of these "breaks" there is a tendency to tune into something other than our speaker. Thus it requires much concentration and mental energy to keep our attention constantly channeled in a single direction for any length of time. To do so is both mentally and emotionally tiring.

2. *Most Americans are relatively poor listeners.* As we have just noted, listening well is a difficult business. It requires an effort that most people in our busy culture seem unwilling to put forth. Western society today is basically an *eye*-oriented rather than an *ear*-oriented culture. In preliterate cultures (i.e., cultures

which have no written language or societies in which only a tiny fraction of the people can read and write) people must depend upon their ears and their memories much more than in a highly literate culture such as our own. Interestingly, a common plea

---

On Writing

Socrates recounts the conversation between the Greek gods Theuth and Thamus, in which Theuth explains his new invention, writing:

"This invention . . . ," said Theuth, "will make [men] wiser and will improve their memories; for it is an elixir of memory and wisdom that I have discovered." But Thamus replied, "Most ingenious Theuth, one man has the ability to beget arts, but the ability to judge of their usefulness or harmfulness to their users belongs to another; and now you, who are the father of letters, have been led by your affection to ascribe to them a power the opposite of that which they really possess. For this invention will produce forgetfulness in the minds of those who learn to use it, because they will not practise their memory. Their trust in writing, produced by external characters which are no part of themselves, will discourage the use of their own memory within them. You have invented an elixir not of memory, but of reminding; and you offer your pupils the appearance of wisdom, not true wisdom, for they will read many things without instruction and will therefore seem to know many things, when they are for the most part ignorant and hard to get along with, since they are not wise, but only appear wise."

Plato *Phaedrus* 274E–275B

---

of modern students is, "Xerox it and let me file it." They prefer reading and storage over having to listen well and then remember what they have heard. This is understandable since today's students are products of a culture which is highly dependent upon the eye. Keep in mind, however, that as this tendency to depend upon the eye has grown, our ability to listen has atrophied from disuse.

Add to this broad cultural problem the barrage of messages the average person meets each day—and through which he or she must sort to separate those that are worth attending to from those that must be discarded—and we can begin to understand why people today are often not very skillful listeners. Since listening requires such discipline; since people in our society are so busy and so inundated by verbal messages that they have learned to tune out much of what they hear; since they are used to having things written down for them rather than having to listen effectively and then remember what they have heard—for all of these reasons we should not expect too many of the people in our audience to be expert listeners. Unfortunately, they are probably no better at this difficult skill than we ourselves are.

3. *People listen differently for different purposes.* Sometimes people listen just for the fun of it. They listen simply for *enjoyment* of what they are hearing. This is perhaps the easiest type of listening because it requires little self-discipline. When people listen to a comedian's humorous monolog, or when they listen to a melodious voice reading light poetry, they hardly have to work at all to pay attention.

A second type of listening, one which usually requires a much greater effort, is listening for *understanding*. This type of listening requires an auditor to interact with a speaker's ideas in a much more active way. As a church member listens to the pastor preach a sermon or as a student listens to a professor give a lecture, much more is required than passive listening for enjoyment. The emphasis here is upon the absorption and retention of the speaker's ideas.

Perhaps the most stringent application of such listening for comprehension is the active listening that is employed by many counselors. A good counselor will often refrain, at least temporarily, from giving answers to a counselee's problems (even when the counselor is certain of the right answers—a rare circumstance) in favor of serving merely as a sounding board. Such active listening requires great effort on the part of the counselor simply to mirror back to the counselee his or her own feelings and thoughts. This will not always be the best approach, and few Christian counselors use it all of the time, but it is one helpful way of encouraging people to come to their own answers to their own problems.

The third and most difficult type of listening is listening for *evaluation*. The reason evaluative listening is the most difficult is that it requires not only the effort of listening for information,

---

He who answers before listening—that is his folly and his shame. Proverbs 18:13 (NIV)

---

but also the additional burden of making a judgment about what is being said. In listening to evaluate, the auditor must be sure that he or she is hearing what the speaker is actually saying. This is not always as easy as it sounds. The listener must be sure that he is not reading into the speaker's words meaning that was not intended and that he has fully and accurately grasped what the speaker has said before he responds. As a teacher of public speaking, and therefore as one who must continually evaluate the speaking of others, I can testify that this is a very delicate balance to maintain. Most often the temptation is to try to evaluate before we have fully understood the speaker's point. The Bible warns us against this error: "He who answers before listening—that is his folly and his shame" (Prov. 18:13 NIV).

The Nature of Attention

Listening is difficult; we are relatively poor listeners; we listen differently for different purposes. Underlying all of these points is the important matter of *attention*. What is attention and how does it work? How can understanding the nature of attention help us understand our listeners better?

We give attention to something when we focus upon it primarily, allowing any other stimuli we are receiving to drift into the background or out of the conscious mind altogether. We may continue to receive these other stimuli, but they are perceived as secondary to that upon which our attention is focused. For instance, as long as we are "paying attention" (an interesting idiom: attention is something we "pay") to a political speaker, our uncomfortable chair, the cigar smoke from a neighbor, the sound of a siren from the street, a flickering light above, the nagging concern that we have left our car unlocked—all of these fade into the background. Our attention is focused upon the one who is speaking.

But suppose the cigar smoke becomes thicker and truly bothersome, or the siren becomes louder and stops right outside the door, or the light above pops and blinks out, or the discomfort of the chair becomes outright pain, or the nagging concern about the car becomes a real worry. In each of these cases our attention will most likely be drawn to the new stimuli and away from the speaker. Though we would continue to receive the sound waves from the speaker's voice, they would now fade into the background as we give our primary focus to something else.

This is the way attention works. It fades in and fades out. It flits from one stimulus to another, incessantly. We can give our primary focus to only one stimulus (or group of stimuli) at a time, and we can hold it there for only a few seconds; then it must shift. So attention is very transient and unstable, moving now to this, now to that, and now to something else. Every moment we are awake, we constantly and inevitably focus our attention upon one thing after another, either within ourselves or within our environment.

It follows, then, that our attention must always be *selective*. Out of the many stimuli we are receiving, from both internal sources (a pain in my hand, a memory, a daydream) and external sources (sights, sounds, tastes, odors, objects we touch), we constantly select those to which we will give our attention, allowing the rest for that moment to recede into the background. But then very soon our primary focus moves on to something else.

Involuntary Attention

Usually our attention shifts quite involuntarily. We do not consciously control it; it simply gravitates to the stimuli in our environment which call most loudly for it. What is it that tends to draw our involuntary attention? Below is a list of characteristics which are likely to command our primary focus. Notice that most are rooted in some form of contrast.

1. *Novelty:* Our attention is drawn to things that are different from what we would expect.
2. *Movement or activity:* When all else is relatively still, movement will capture our attention; likewise, when all else is moving, the stationary will often stand out. It is the contrast that captures our attention.
3. *Proximity:* Of the wide range of stimuli we receive, those which are perceived as being close to us in time and space will claim our involuntary attention.
4. *Concreteness:* That which is specific, vivid, and concrete stands out from the abstract, the general, and the bland.
5. *Familiarity:* In a setting where things are unfamiliar and unknown, that which is familiar stands out.
6. *Conflict:* Where harmony generally prevails, opposition between two or more things tends to grasp our attention.
7. *Suspense:* When we have the entire picture except a few key pieces, we are drawn to the missing pieces to see how the whole fits together.
8. *Intensity:* When something stands out as more intense than its surroundings, we will involuntarily pay attention to it.
9. *Humor:* At the heart of almost all humor is some form of incongruity, something which is not where or what it is supposed to be.
10. *Life-relatedness:* Those things which are related to our "felt needs" in life tend to draw our attention.

Voluntary Attention

But our attention can also be controlled voluntarily. We can to a very significant degree choose what we will attend to and what we will ignore. For example, you may not be altogether excited about paying attention to a boring lecture—that is, the lecture does not claim your *involuntary* attention—but you can *choose* to pay attention to the lecturer anyway if you know that you will later be examined on the material. In this sense your attention is given to the speaker voluntarily. It is under your control, and you can choose to direct it wherever you will. It may require effort and discipline to keep your attention focused upon the lecture instead of competing stimuli, but you can do it if you try.

This point has significant spiritual implications for Christians. What we choose to pay attention to will inevitably shape our thinking and behavior. That is why the Bible instructs Christians to "set your mind on the things above, not on the things that are on earth" (Col. 3:2 NASB; see also Phil. 4:8).

An understanding of how attention works can also be helpful in understanding our audience. Recall our previous observations about listening: Listening is difficult because it requires us to control our attention, and this takes effort and discipline. Americans are often poor listeners because they are inundated by so many competing messages and because they are not used to disciplining their attention effectively. People listen differently for different purposes—listening for enjoyment is largely involuntary, but listening for comprehension and evaluation is usually voluntary, and thus requires more effort and commitment.

All communication begins with attention. Whether you are trying to change your listeners' minds, mobilize them to do something, or simply inform them of something, you must begin by gaining their attention. What is more, you must keep gaining their attention as you proceed and you must gain their attention when you finish. To speak of "holding" the audience's attention can be misleading, since the truth is that *you must win the audience's attention again and again throughout the speech.* The listeners' focus upon you will be constantly slipping away, and you must bring it back repeatedly, regularly, in fact, constantly throughout your message. It is this process of winning and rewinning that is in view when we speak of "holding" the audience's attention.

It is a relatively simple thing to gain your audience's attention once or even twice, but to win it repeatedly throughout the speech is a much more difficult task. The stimuli which potentially may distract your audience's attention away from you are almost infinite in their variety. You must continuously compete with these distractions by designing your efforts from beginning to end so that they are more interesting to the listeners than the many other messages they may be receiving from other sources.

Since listening is such a difficult undertaking, is there any hope that an audience will ever pay attention to your speech? Yes, but not without intelligent and concentrated efforts on your part to shape your message to the audience so as to communicate with the listeners effectively. How can you do this? By understanding *people in general,* and *your audience in particular.*

Understanding Your Audience

Audience Commonalities

There are certain general observations which will be true of any people you may address. Consider, for example, the observation that the human mind craves *unity, order,* and *progress.* This is a fundamental pattern of human thought, and we may reliably assume that any audience to whom we speak will be made up of people who share this pattern in common. Less basic aspects of the thinking process are profoundly affected by cultural factors, a fact that becomes obvious when we compare oriental and occidental views of the world. But the fundamental tendency to look for unity, order, and progress in the stimuli we receive seems to be universally basic to the human mind. We will explore this point at length in the next chapter. For now, let us take a look at some further commonalities we may take for granted.

Theological Commonalities

First, the Bible teaches that human beings are *made in the image of God.* While we may not understand entirely what this means, the *imago Dei* in the human race seems to involve at least four elements. (1) We are rational beings. We are able to think on a level that distinguishes us from all other creatures. We are able to abstract and symbolize, processes without which human communication would not be possible. (2) We are volitional beings. Like God, we possess a will. We are able to choose, and what is more, we are responsible for how and what we choose. (3) We are moral beings. We have a conscience. As one noted theologian puts it, "God has implanted in all men a moral instinct that gives them a sense of right and wrong."[3] No other creature possesses this moral dimension. (4) We are social beings. Even as God is a social being (as seen in the Trinity), so also God created us with social needs. Though Adam enjoyed unhindered fellowship with God and a perfect environment, God decreed that it was not enough (Gen. 2:18); Adam needed a companion like himself because he had been created with a social dimension that even his fellowship with God could not satisfy. This, too, is part of the *imago Dei* (Gen. 1:27).

Second, the Bible also teaches that *human beings possess not simply a material dimension but a spiritual dimension as well.* Many influential philosophers and psychologists today deny that humans have a spiritual dimension. They prefer a strictly material view which is highly deterministic. We are the product of purely materialistic forces in the universe, they say. Any notions of "choice" or "will" or "freedom" are mere illusions. When all else is pared away, we are basically only biological organisms which are responding to the stimuli of our environment in a predetermined, seemingly inevitable way. By contrast, the Scriptures teach that there is more to human nature than the study of biology or any other of the natural sciences can discover. We have a spiritual dimension and, therefore, spiritual needs that only a proper relationship to God can satisfy.

At this point it is important to emphasize that the Scriptures also indicate that *humans are unified beings.* We are not a duality, consisting of two distinct elements which never merge to a unity. This make-up was a common view among the ancient Greek philosophers, but is not the teaching of the Scriptures. In the Bible our nature is portrayed as a complex fusion of parts into a unity. Thus, our every response is a response of the whole person, material and spiritual together, with both dimensions influencing the other. Our material needs affect our spiritual dimension; likewise, our spiritual needs affect our material dimension.

Third, the Bible teaches that *humans are sinful beings.* Apart from Christ, our natural bias is toward evil, away from God. By no means does this require us to conclude that every person is devoid of all qualities that people find pleasing, or that any person commits or is inclined to commit all forms of sin, or that all people are as defiantly opposed to God as it is possible for them to be. Rather, to say that humans are sinful beings means that

> every sinner is totally destitute of that love to God which is the fundamental requirement of the law (Deuteronomy 6:4, 5; Matthew 22:35–38); that he is supremely given to a preference of himself to God (2 Timothy 3:4); that he has an aversion to God which on occasion becomes active enmity to Him (Romans 8:7); that his every faculty is disordered and corrupted (Ephesians 4:18); that he has no thought, feeling, or deed of which God can fully approve (Romans 7:18); and that he has entered upon a line of constant progress in depravity, from which he can no wise turn away in his own strength (Romans 7:18).[4]

While by contemporary standards this is a rather pessimistic view, measured by both the Bible and our history books it is, unfortunately, a *realistic* view of our human nature. Each of

---

. . . With Whom We Deal

The load, or weight, or burden of my neighbour's glory should be laid daily on my back, a load so heavy that only humility can carry it, and the backs of the proud will be broken. It is a serious thing to live in a society of possible gods and goddesses, to remember that the dullest and most uninteresting person you talk to may one day be a creature which, if you saw it now, you would be strongly tempted to worship, or else a horror and a corruption such as you now meet, if at all, only in a nightmare. All day long we are, in some degree, helping each other to one or the other of these destinations. It is in the light of these overwhelming possibilities, it is with the awe and the circumspection proper to them, that we should conduct all our dealings with one another, all friendships, all loves, all play, all politics. There are no ordinary people. You have never talked to a mere mortal. Nations, cultures, arts, civilizations—these are mortal, and their life is to ours as the life of a gnat. But it is immortals whom we joke with, work with, marry, snub, and exploit—immortal horrors or everlasting splendours.

C. S. Lewis
The Weight of Glory

---

these biblical teachings may be assumed about the people in our audiences. Our listeners are complex individuals who can think and feel and act. They are people who are deeply affected by what others are doing around them. They are people who can choose, and what is more, the choices they make will often have moral overtones, lifting them up or carrying them deeper into their rebellion against God. As the image bearers of God, the people to whom we speak are the most valuable of all of God's creations. They must never be manipulated or otherwise abused or taken advantage of. We must appeal to their better rather than their lesser motives. We must treat them for what they are: the crowning glory of God's creation (Ps. 8), even though their exalted position has been tainted and marred by sin.

Psychological Commonalities

There are also some psychological assumptions we may take for granted about the people in our audience. Immediately upon saying this, however, Christians face a problem. As we have already noted, many psychologists' basic view of who and what the human race is, is foreign to a genuinely biblical perspective. Should Christians uncritically accept conclusions about psychology that are generated from a largely erroneous set of presuppositions? Certainly not. This is not to imply that the writings of such psychologists are entirely without merit or that they contain nothing of worth for Christians. It is to say, however, that from a biblical perspective many of these theorists' assumptions and theories about human psychology prove to be highly inadequate, if not downright misleading.

Fortunately, there is a sizable group of psychologists whose underlying presuppositions about human nature much more closely approximate the biblical viewpoint. To be sure, few, if any, of these secular thinkers have come to these presuppositions from a study of God's Word, and their views are seldom entirely biblical. Our point here is merely that these writers' views in certain essentials do agree with the Christian perspective. Thus their theories, which have grown out of quasi-biblical presuppositions, are more likely to be useful to a Christian. Of course, Christians must not accept the conclusions of even this group of theorists before their ideas have been measured against and integrated with biblical teachings. But once this is accomplished and the ideas prove sound, Christians can profit from these secular sources of learning.

As long as we have the Word of God to serve as our plumb line we ought not fear any helpful ideas that measure up.

Some Christians believe that all psychology is worthless. This seems to be an unfortunate overreaction. At the very least, some psychological viewpoints are less worthless than others. Or, to put it more positively, some viewpoints have more value to Christians than do others. As Frank E. Gaebelein has so insistently pointed out, all truth is indeed God's truth.[5] As long as we have the Word of God to serve as our plumb line, we ought not fear any helpful ideas that measure up, regardless of their source.

One helpful source is the writings of the humanistic psychologists, sometimes referred to as the "third force" in contemporary psychology. Rollo May, Carl Rogers, Gordon Allport, Erich Fromm, and numerous others belong to this broad and loosely defined school of thought. Third-force theorists proceed from presuppositions which describe humans as complex but basically wholistic (read "unified") beings who are initiators of their own acts. They are rational-emotional beings who are assumed to have in some real sense the ability to choose. Thus, they also carry an accompanying responsibility for their actions. In addition, humanistic psychologists see human beings as having built-in social needs; that is, they require interpersonal relationships to become what they are capable of being. Thus, in some important ways these theorists are in agreement with the Bible. (It should also be noted, however, that in some other important areas third-force views are not consistent with the Bible at all.

For example, most humanistic psychologists would not hold that people are inherently sinful. They see humans rather as innately good—a clear contradiction of God's evaluation of the human race.)[6]

Abraham H. Maslow is one of the most influential writers in the school of humanistic psychology. His studies of human motivation are helpful to us in formulating general psychological assumptions about the members of our audience.[7] Maslow has theorized that all our behavior is motivated by our attempts to meet a hierarchy of needs. From a Christian perspective, we would say that these needs were placed in us by our Creator. Maslow has five levels of classification for these needs:

1. Physiological needs
2. Safety needs
3. Love needs
4. Esteem needs
5. The need for self-actualization

The *physiological needs* are the most primitive. They involve such fundamental human requirements as the need for food, the need to maintain body temperature, the need to avoid pain and injury, and the need for sensory stimulation. In contemporary Western civilization, most people have little difficulty fulfilling these basic needs.

Safety needs have to do with the human desire for security. As Maslow points out, the human child "generally prefers a safe, orderly, predictable, organized world, which he can count on, and in which unexpected, unmanageable or other dangerous things do not happen."[8] Healthy adults desire much the same thing but on a more sophisticated level. Savings accounts, insurance plans, written contracts, job tenure, welfare, social security, police forces, and the military are all manifestations of our human need for a sense of safety and security.

Love and belonging needs are met by being part of primary groups, such as a family, and secondary groups, such as a club, ethnic group, or nationality. An outgrowth of the fact that we are social beings, such belonging needs also help explain why God instituted the church. One can become a Christian only as an individual, but when one becomes a Christian, God immediately incorporates the individual into a body, the church (1 Cor. 12:13). God designed us so that we cannot be a complete Christian in isolation. In other words, we have certain belonging needs that the Bible teaches can and should be met by association with other believers in a church.

Esteem needs are met through being respected and appreciated by the others in our world. Such needs also stem from our social nature. Human beings cannot prosper in the absence of other persons; we need the recognition and attention of others. Without this an individual has little sense of his or her own worth and therefore lacks self-esteem. It is important to keep in mind that God is the most significant "Other" in a Christian's life and his evaluation of us should become the primary (and sometimes the solitary) source of our own self-esteem and worth, even in the face of rejection from other people. But saying this does not contradict the fact that we do have basic needs for esteem that can legitimately be met by recognition and attention from our fellow humans. Again, we need to keep in mind that it was God himself who pronounced Adam's condition of being the only one of his kind as "not good," and then proceeded to create a partner "suitable" for him (Gen. 2:18).

The *need for self-actualization* is the most complex of the five levels. Maslow argues that within every human being there is the desire for "something higher." There is a need to fulfill all of one's potential. As Maslow puts it, "What man can be, he must be."[9] From a Christian perspective, we must understand such needs as stemming from the magnificent potential God designed within the human race, a potential that was impaired by sin in the fall but not eradicated. Our inherent desire to be more than we are, to reach our fullest potential, is thus a remnant of God's creative work in the human race, the crowning glory of all creation.

If self-actualization needs seem dormant in most people at most times, it is because the list of needs we just examined constitutes a *hierarchy* and the self-actualization needs come to the fore only as the other needs are being reasonably satisfied. Obviously, if a person is dying of thirst or sitting in the midst of an artillery bombardment, the needs for safety take priority. In these situations, belonging, esteem, and self-actualization needs are quite beside the point. Likewise, fulfilling the need for a sense of belonging takes precedence over esteem and self-actu-

---

The mind is a mismatch detector.   George A. Miller

---

alization and becomes almost a precondition or means of meeting those higher needs. It is only when our physical and safety needs are satisfied (a condition taken for granted in our culture but not in others) and we have come to a reasonable sense of belonging and self-worth that the matter of self-actualization becomes a motivating force in our lives. It is probably not an overstatement to assert that most people in most places at most times in the history of the human race have been so preoccupied with meeting their more basic needs that they seldom, if ever, have found themselves pressed by their needs for self-actualization.

Our point in all of this is a very simple one. In attempting to formulate valid generalizations about the psychology of the people in our audience, people who in all essentials are just like us, we are limited to only a few broad statements. But the first and one of the most important for our purposes in this book is that *we are all, at the core, need-fulfillers.* Our attitudes and behavior are motivated by the desire to satisfy various needs that God has designed into our very nature. Maslow's hierarchy is one way of thinking about those needs. It is not the only way, nor is it an exhaustive way. Maslow has not explicitly acknowledged, for example, our spiritual dimension and the role our spiritual needs play in interacting with the hierarchy of our physiological and psychological needs. Nor would Maslow have much time for the assertion that in the final analysis one must look to God for the supply of all five of these levels of need. Nevertheless, Maslow's

---

How the Mind Works

I truly believe that's the way the mind works. You have your conclusion to begin with, and you are very clever at searching for evidence that either directly—or indirectly, by arguments you cleverly invent—leads to your conclusion. I think it's very important to understand how the undisciplined mind operates. The scientific way of thinking is supposed to be an antidote to that.

George A. Miller

---

hierarchy is useful in helping us to see that our basic nature shapes us into need-fulfillers who choose and act in ways that are designed to meet certain fundamental requirements (unfortunately, much of our effort in all this is often futile or even counterproductive). An understanding of this basic fact, combined with a feel for what a human being's basic needs are, is one of the first steps toward becoming an effective public speaker.

But we not only attempt to fulfill our needs; we also strive to maintain "cognitive consistency."[10] This is the second major psychological assumption we may make about our audience, an insight that comes not from the third-force psychologists alone, but from a wide consensus of psychological theorists.

Cognitive consistency is a technical term used to describe the tendency within almost all of us to keep our attitudes, behaviors, and perceptions consistent. The theorists variously describe this state of consistency as "balance," "congruence," "harmony," or "symmetry." And Leon Festinger, perhaps the most famous cognitive-consistency theorist, calls an inconsistent state of mind "cognitive dissonance."[11]

The cognitive-consistency theorists hold that there exists within most people a strong desire for consistency. We bring our attitudes, behaviors, and perceptions of the world in line with one another. As long as all is balanced, congruent, or symmetrical, we are psychologically comfortable. But suppose something

---

interferes with our harmony by changing one of the elements in the system, thereby creating inconsistency. The theory holds that such a change produces psychological tension which we seek to reduce by either distorting the new message or by changing some other part of the system. This response is motivated by our strong desire to regain a state of consistency.

For example, suppose there is a book which you intensely disliked. You tossed it aside halfway through and refused to pick it up again. Suppose also that you have a friend whose literary insight you deeply admire. So far, no inconsistency exists. But now suppose you overhear your respected friend telling someone that the book you disliked is the finest book she has ever read, a first-rate piece of literature which anyone with any literary taste at all could not fail to appreciate. Suddenly you have been confronted with a stark inconsistency. Your dislike for the book, your respect for your friend, and your friend's view of the book are not congruent with one another. What will you do?

The cognitive-consistency theorists all agree that you will not simply tolerate the inconsistency. Such inconsistency creates a psychological tension which is uncomfortable. Instead you will seek to reduce the tension by somehow changing the parts of the pattern. Most likely you will decide to try the book again, since it cannot be as bad as you thought if your friend liked it so much. Or, you might decide that your friend does not know as much about literary matters as you thought, since if she did, she would surely not endorse that book. Or, you might even decide that your friend had ulterior motives for what she said and that she did not actually like the book as much as she claimed. Which of these options (or others) you choose will depend on a very complex set of factors, but one thing is almost certain: you will not simply tolerate the inconsistency. Rather, you will find some way to reduce it so as to recover your psychological balance.

This basic desire for consistency stems from the *rational* dimension of our natures built into us from the beginning by God. But it is quite interesting to see how *irrational* people can be in attempting to maintain their cognitive consistency. For example, the heavy smoker who dismisses all of the connections between smoking and lung cancer as "lies of the government" is responding quite irrationally—in order to maintain her rationality. She cannot admit that the research findings are true without being forced by her desire for consistency to conclude that she should quit smoking, something she desperately does not want to do. So, she must discredit the information instead. Likewise, the man who cheats on his income tax cannot admit to himself that he is a thief, so he rationalizes that "everyone does it" and "the government expects a certain amount of cheating." By any objective standard, of course, this is an irrational response, but it enables the individual to retain his cognitive consistency.

Our desire for a balanced system also explains the phenomenon of "selective perception." It is commonly recognized that people tend to listen best to messages which are consistent with their own views and tend to avoid messages which contradict their views. They select from the many messages available to them those which support their own ideas and refuse to open themselves to those messages which do not. The reason for this is that contrary messages tend to arouse the tension which stems from inconsistency. Since the easiest way to deal with this tension is to prevent it from arising in the first place, people commonly listen only to those with whom they already agree. In this way a comfortable balance can be maintained.

There are few postulates of modern psychology which are as widely accepted and as solidly based as this assertion: *people desire mental consistency and strive to maintain it, often at the expense of the truth.* You may assume that this characteristic will be true of the members of your audience. As we shall see, an understanding of this concept will aid you in your attempt to communicate your ideas to them.

Audience Variables

Having observed the theological and psychological commonalities about all audiences, we still have not learned much about our *particular* audience. These broad observations are of little use to us except as a framework for thinking about the characteristics of the specific group to whom we will be speaking. Such observations about audiences in general serve mainly to focus upon some of the questions we must answer about our audience in particular. Furthermore, alongside the questions raised by these general observations there are others which stem from additional variables we may confront in the speaking situation.

External Variables

In attempting to analyze an audience, we must consider a whole series of variables which reflect external aspects of the speech setting:

OCCASION. Each occasion has its own rules, so to speak. These rules grow out of both the traditions and the expectations of the listeners. Many settings (particularly ceremonial occasions, such as weddings, inaugurations, or worship services) have rather firm rules; these are the more *formal* settings. Many other speaking situations (such as after-dinner addresses, picnics, or impromptu speeches) are governed by a much looser and less stringent set of rules; these are the more *informal* settings. But in each case there will be some rules that you can ignore only to your own peril. Considerations of the occasion are significant in shaping everything from the initial choice of subject matter (to the extent that this is an option for you) to the style in which the speech is delivered.

SIZE OF THE AUDIENCE. Large audiences are generally more difficult to address than small audiences. Larger numbers inevitably bring greater diversity, and the more diverse the audience, the more difficult it is to focus clearly upon the common needs of the auditors. Indeed, in a large audience one often discovers several subaudiences with distinct differences. When this diversity is combined with the increased anxiety many speakers experience when they face a sizable group of people, it is not difficult to see why many speakers try to avoid large groups.

On the other hand, experienced speakers often prefer large audiences because of the effect members of the audience have upon one another during the speech itself. Experienced speakers know that members of any audience, but particularly larger audiences, are influenced constantly by the others in the group. The key question seems to be, Do the members of the audience see themselves as part of a group or as individuals? The evidence seems to indicate that to the extent the group feeling predominates over the individualistic feeling, the auditors are more susceptible to the influence of the speaker. Since in larger audiences the influence of audience members upon one another is multiplied and the feeling of being submerged in a group is enhanced, persuasibility increases. Experienced speakers often make use of this phenomenon.

Another reason some speakers prefer a larger audience is that in larger groups intimacy decreases. It is actually easier to "hide" psychologically from a larger audience than a smaller one. As the group grows, both physical and emotional distance tend to increase. In the smaller setting the level of closeness and intimacy between speaker and audience is so high as to be almost intolerable to some speakers. Thus, some people actually prefer a larger audience.

These reasons for preferring a larger audience are not presented here to encourage you to manipulate the persuasibility of your audience or the level of intimacy. Rather, we simply need to note the effects of audience size so that we can adapt to them intelligently in our attempt to communicate our ideas well.

LOCATION. Where will the speech take place? This is a crucial question in most speaking situations. The audience will often be profoundly influenced by its surroundings, and you need to analyze what that environmental influence will be in order to understand your audience.

Some questions relating to the location are merely common sense: Can your audience see you clearly? Is there enough lighting? Is it proper lighting? Are some people behind a post? Will you be high enough for people in the back to see? Can people hear you clearly? How are the acoustics? Is a public-address system available? Is it a reliable public-address system, or is it likely to fail during your speech? Do you need it at all, or will it merely get in the way?

To these very practical questions you should add the matter of the audience's seating arrangement. Is there an intimate half circle or a long, narrow tunnel effect? How far from the podium are the most distant auditors? How close to the podium are the nearest auditors? How close are people seated to one another? Are they so cramped that they will be uncomfortable? Are they so dispersed as to be isolated from one another with little sense of being part of an audience? Knowledgeable speakers generally avoid a widely dispersed audience. Indeed, 50 people crowded into a room designed for 40 is far better than those same 50 people spread all over an auditorium with seating for 250. In cases where an oversized facility is unavoidable, people should be comfortably seated as a unit near the speaker.

A still more subtle factor concerning the location is the matter of *atmosphere*. How formal or informal is the setting? A church basement, for instance, is generally much less formal than the sanctuary. Factors such as architecture, colors, and interior decor all have an impact upon an audience. To illustrate, think of how differently you would feel as a listener if you were seated in a college classroom, a funeral parlor, a plush banquet room of an expensive private club, a Gothic cathedral, a living room in someone else's home, your own living room. In each of these locations the colors, decor, lighting, and architecture will shape the atmosphere, which in turn will influence how you might respond. As a general rule, your goal should be to schedule your speeches in settings your audience will find as pleasant as possible.

Your final—but in one sense your first—concern about the setting should be the physical comfort of your audience. Usually the comfort of an audience depends upon having enough (but not too much) space, decent seating, an appropriate temperature range, fresh air, and enough (but again, not too much) lighting and sound. If these basic needs are not met, the audience may have a difficult time attending to your message.

Internal Variables

Along with these external considerations, you must confront an intricate system of internal variables at work in your audience. These factors are so numerous and complex that it is difficult to discuss them in a brief space. The prime requirement here is to weigh carefully the composition of your audience. Is your audience heterogeneous or homogeneous? Generally, the more alike your auditors are, the easier your task of analysis and adaptation will be. The more mixed your audience is, the more difficult your task will be.

There are several dimensions in which audience homogeneity/heterogeneity will vary:

SEX. Gender-based differences are social as well as biological. In both cases, biological as well as social, the needs, interests, and values of men and women are often shaped differently. While it is possible to overemphasize sex differences, the wisest course is to give serious weight to the sex of your audience.

The importance of sex differences in an audience will vary, of course, with the subject matter of your speech. With some subjects (e.g., "how a computer works") the matter of sex is virtually irrelevant; with others it is paramount ("the problem of date rape on American campuses"). You need to weigh whether the subject is such that gender-based differences are significant.

You also need to keep in mind that even in mixed audiences where neither sex predominates, the matter of the auditor's sex will affect how he or she hears your message. Thus in mixed audiences, when you are dealing with material that is affected by sex differences, the best course of action may be to think in terms of two "audiences" and attempt to adapt to the needs of both throughout the speech.

AGE. Generalizations about age differences are every bit as precarious as generalizations about sex differences. Yet it is plain that people's interests do vary with their age. The common wisdom has it that older people tend to be more conservative and cautious than younger people. Moreover, recent research on the stages of adult life demonstrates that there are certain patterns of crises and needs that people tend to face at fairly specific periods in their progress from adolescence to old age. Not all of the evidence is in by any means, and this is not the place to go into great detail even about what we do know. We need conclude only that age differences will affect how people listen to many, if not most, messages. Where a particular age group predominates, you should try to adapt your message accordingly. Where the audience is mixed, you may be forced to adjust to the several age groups you face.

SOCIAL STATUS. Social status is a term that refers to the complex of roles an individual plays relative to the others in his or her culture. There is little question that people from different strata of society often see things differently from one another. For instance, several interesting studies have shown high levels of correlation between certain social classes and the membership of respective Christian denominations. Those designated as belonging to upper social groups tend to be attracted to one brand of Christianity; those who are designated as belonging to the lower echelons are drawn to another. As disconcerting as this may be to contemplate—since such "classes" have no business in the church (James 2:1–7)—it seems unrealistic to think that such differences do not exist. Thus, social status appears to be another of the dimensions in which people of our audience may vary. For better or for worse, such differences tend to affect how people think and feel, and there seems to be little virtue in ignoring this fact in our audience analysis.

CULTURAL AND ETHNIC BACKGROUND. One of the ongoing points of tension in our culture is that the lines distinguishing social classes tend to correspond to the lines distinguishing American ethnic cultures. Thus, when we think of status roles in our society, we are to some extent inevitably thinking about cultural and ethnic backgrounds as well. The American upper class continues to consist heavily of WASPs—the familiar acronym which stands for white, Anglo-Saxon, Protestant—and the lower classes continue to reflect high percentages of blacks and Hispanics. But these socioeconomic realities are breaking down gradually. Increasingly we should be able to think about cultural and ethnic factors quite apart from the matter of social class. This can be only for the better, both for society in general as well as for our speech preparation in particular.

Where members of the audience belong to an identifiable ethnic group, you need to weigh carefully what you know about that group. Not a few white people have failed to communicate to blacks in their audience because they failed to wrestle with the distinctives of a black perspective on the subject—and vice versa. Sometimes the chasm seems almost too wide to be bridged. Consider, for example, the task you would have in trying to produce within an audience of Israeli citizens a clear understanding of a Palestinian Arab's perspective on the city of Jerusalem. The emotional commitments of the two sides seem almost to preclude any mutual understanding.

Fortunately, differences in cultural perspectives are not always so pronounced. Yet each cultural group maintains some unique aspects in its way of viewing the world; you should strive to understand this uniqueness as a part of your preparation.

EDUCATIONAL LEVEL AND INTELLIGENCE. Another way in which members of your audience may vary is in their intelligence and their educational level. These two factors are often related, but

---

> ### *People do not usually try to disprove their own ideas.* George A. Miller

---

they are not to be equated. One speaker evaluated a group of farmers to whom he was to speak as being of low intelligence because they sported few academic credentials. What he found instead was an extremely competent group of people who had some strong and very well-thought-out views on the subject of the speech.

The most relevant aspect of the audience's educational level has to do, not so much with their level of knowledge in general (though this is significant), but with their knowledge of your subject matter in particular. Are there large differences in the levels of the audience's knowledge about your subject (perhaps because of training, sex, age, or cultural differences)? If not, your task is much simplified. Keeping in mind the general principle that more intelligent and better-educated people tend to comprehend ideas more easily but are more difficult to persuade than those of lower intellectual ability or training, you need strive only to adapt your message to the mental level of your audience. If, however, your audience consists of people with widely divergent levels of knowledge, your task is a much more difficult one. In this case you may have to gear your message to one level or another, thus to some extent leaving out the others. While this is distasteful because it involves talking either beyond or beneath the capacities of certain members of your audience, sometimes it is unavoidable. At other times you may want to aim for the middle so that your message can reach the largest possible group. However, if you choose this option, be careful lest you wind up pleasing no one and in fact missing everyone.

BELIEF SYSTEM OF THE AUDIENCE. There are probably few areas of human psychology that are more complex than the material dealing with how people come to believe and feel about things as they do. The matter is far too complicated to permit a detailed treatment of it here. Moreover, it is probably not necessary to do so since most of the theories are too abstruse to be of direct practical use to the average public speaker. Nevertheless, it will be helpful to make some general observations about three key ingredients of our belief system: *values, attitudes,* and *beliefs.*

A *belief* is a conviction or assertion that a certain something is true. Examples: "My desk is made of wood"; "The world is round"; "God loves me"; "All men are sinners." An *attitude* is a reflection of positive or negative feelings about a belief or some other object of attention. Thus attitudes involve evaluative, subjective, personal responses. Examples: "I like you"; "I am glad my desk is made of wood"; "I prefer taking a train over flying"; "Preparing an effective speech is not an easy job." The term *values* refers to structured clusters of related beliefs toward which we have an attitude. Thus values tend to be broader than beliefs, more abstract, and more difficult to pin down. Some prevalent values among contemporary Americans include intelligence, ambition, sociability, responsibility, perseverance, honesty, sincerity, friendliness, trustworthiness, kindness, generosity, and loyalty.[12]

The picture is further complicated by the fact that beliefs and attitudes exist in widely varying strengths, from strongly positive to strongly negative. The evidence seems to suggest that views people have stated publicly tend to be stronger and more resistant to change than views which have been kept private; views which have been acted upon will be stronger still. What is more, in any given situation a person's attitudes may temporarily conflict with one another. For example, a listener may strongly support a speaker's point but find the speaker himself repugnant. How, then, will the auditor respond to the message? Good question, and a very difficult one to answer.

In any case, it is not difficult to see that an auditor's belief system will influence how he or she perceives both speaker and speech. Thus you should attempt to take the belief systems of your audience into consideration in shaping your speech. Of course this is easier to say than it is to implement, but the potential benefits are worth the effort.

At the broadest level you should consider the general elements of the belief system people within your culture tend to share. But this is not as easy as it sounds. A society's belief system is constantly changing. How well do you suppose you are aware of the belief system of your own culture? The following is an exercise that will help you think about the belief system of the typical audience in America today.

In 1968 Wayne C. Minnick published the following summary of the belief system of the "average" American.[13] At the time, it was notably accurate. As you read through it, take a pencil and mark those items you believe still apply with a *y* for yes. Mark those items which no longer accurately describe the America you know with an *n* for no. Then, for each of the "no" items, think how you would word the description today. This exercise will help you better understand your own culture and reinforce your awareness of just how quickly belief systems of an entire society can change over just a few decades.

I. Theoretic values of contemporary Americans
  1. Americans respect the scientific method and things labelled scientific.
  2. They express a desire to be reasonable, to get the facts and make rational choices.
  3. They prefer, in meeting problems, to use traditional approaches to problems, or means that have been tried

previously. Americans don't like innovations, but, perversely, they think change generally means progress.

4. They prefer quantitative rather than qualitative means of evaluation. Size (bigness) and numbers are the most frequent measuring sticks.
5. They respect common sense.
6. They think learning should be "practical" and that higher education tends to make a man visionary.
7. They think everyone should have a college education.

II. Economic values of contemporary Americans
1. Americans measure success chiefly by economic means. Wealth is prized and Americans think everyone should aspire and have the opportunity to get rich.
2. They think success is the product of hard work and perseverance.
3. They respect efficiency.
4. They think one should be thrifty and save money in order to get ahead.
5. Competition is to them the most important aspect of American economic life.
6. Business can run its own affairs best, they believe, but some government regulation is required.
7. They distrust economic royalists and big business in general.

III. Aesthetic values of contemporary Americans
1. Americans prefer the useful arts—landscaping, auto designing, interior decorating, dress designing, etc.
2. They feel that pure aesthetics (theatre, concerts, painting, sculpture) is more feminine than masculine and tend to relegate the encouragement of them to women.
3. They prefer physical activities—sports, hunting, fishing, and the like—to art, music, literature.
4. They respect neatness and cleanliness.
5. They admire grace and coordination, especially in sports and physical contests.
6. They admire beauty in women, good grooming and neat appearance in both sexes.
7. They think many artists and writers are queer or immoral.
8. They tend to emphasize the material rather than the aesthetic value of art objects.

IV. Social values of contemporary Americans
  1. Americans think that people should be honest, sincere, kind, generous, friendly, and straightforward.
  2. They think a man should be a good mixer, able to get along well with other people.
  3. They respect a good sport; they think a man should know how to play the game, to meet success or failure.
  4. They admire fairness and justice.
  5. They believe a man should be aggressive and ambitious, should want to get ahead and be willing to work hard at it.
  6. They admire "a regular guy" (i.e., one who does not try to stand off from his group because of intellectual, financial, or other superiority).
  7. They like people who are dependable and steady, not mercurial.
  8. They like a good family man. They think a man should marry, love his wife, have children, love them, educate them, and sacrifice for his family. He should not spoil his children but he should be indulgent with his wife. He should love his parents. He should own his own home if possible.
  9. They think people should conform to the social expectations for the roles they occupy.

V. Political values of contemporary Americans
  1. Americans prize loyalty to community, state, and nation. They think the American way of doing things is better than foreign ways.
  2. They think American democracy is the best of all possible governments.
  3. They prize the individual above the state. They think government exists for the benefit of the individual.
  4. The Constitution to the American is a sacred document, the guardian of his liberties.
  5. Communism is believed to be the greatest existing menace to America.
  6. Americans believe the two-party system is best and should be preserved.
  7. They think government ownership in general is undesirable.
  8. They believe government is naturally inefficient.

9. They think a certain amount of corruption is inevitable in government.
10. They think equality of opportunity should be extended to minority groups (with notable minority dissent).

VI. Religious values of contemporary Americans
   1. Americans believe Christianity is the best of all possible religions, but that one should be tolerant of other religions.
   2. They think good works are more important than one's religious beliefs.
   3. They believe one should belong to and support a church.
   4. God, to most Americans, is real and is acknowledged to be the creator of the universe.
   5. They think religion and politics should not be mixed; ministers should stay out of politics, politicians out of religious matters.
   6. Americans are charitable. They feel sympathy for the poor and the unfortunate and are ready to offer material help.
   7. They tend to judge people and events moralistically.

We have seen that the composition of the audience should be carefully considered. Such factors as age, sex, and cultural background are helpful indicators of values and attitudes. Further, if the message is to deal at all with spiritual issues, the religious background of the group members will be crucial. Are they Christians or non-Christians? If non-Christians, are they members of another religious group? Are they agnostics? Atheists? If the audience members are Christians, are they of a particular denomination? Where do they fit in the theological spectrum, conservative to liberal? You may not be able to bridge all of the gaps you discover, but neither will it do to ignore them.

Another important means of discovering relevant aspects of your audience's belief system is to ask, What is my audience's attitude toward the subject matter of my message? The most likely answers are that your listeners will be to some extent *supportive* (they already agree with you), *apathetic* (they don't really care), *doubtful* (they have serious reservations), or *hostile* (they are actively opposed); they may be *knowledgeable* (they already know a great deal about your subject), *unlearned* (they know little or nothing about your subject), or *indifferent* (they have never thought about it). Often these characteristics will exist in combination. For example, ignorance of and apathy toward a subject often occur in tandem; likewise, high levels of knowledge often produce stronger support of or hostility toward an idea. Captive audiences, made up of individuals who would rather be elsewhere but who are required for some reason to listen to your message, are often both apathetic and resistant. Voluntary audiences almost by definition will be more interested, though not necessarily more receptive.

The belief system of a single person, much less of any combination of people, is so intricate as to virtually defy any final description. Nevertheless, a thoughtful analysis of how an audience thinks and feels—based, as it must be, upon certain informed but often intuitive guesses and inferences—is an important part of trying to understand our listeners so as to communicate more fully with them.

Adapting to Your Audience

We have said that the first step in shaping a speech to fit your listeners is to understand them. Such understanding is not an end in itself. Rather, it is merely a *means to an end*. The goal of audience analysis is to use this understanding of your listeners *to adjust* to them and thereby maximize your potential for reaching them with your message. It is for this reason that you strive to discover the factors that are already affecting your auditors' ability and readiness to understand, accept, and act upon what you have to say. Thinking carefully about the relevant characteristics of the audience enables you to discover the problems you will face and the possible advantages you can utilize to communicate effectively with this particular group of people.

Attempts to adjust to your audience will influence at least eight important aspects of your speech:

Subject Matter

You will not always be able to choose your own topic. Sometimes it will be assigned to you. In such cases your subject matter becomes a given, and you are free to adapt to your audience only in the manner in which you deal with your topic. In most cases, though, you will have the freedom to choose what you want to talk about. How do you make such a choice? Certainly it should be made in the light of your own interests and abilities; you do not want to be stuck with a topic you care or know nothing about. But your choice should also weigh heavily the needs, interests, expectations, and intellectual abilities of your audience. Ignoring these factors in your choice and insisting upon pursuing your own interests alone is not only selfish; it is tantamount to committing rhetorical suicide. Your speech may perish before it has ever had the chance to live.

Statement of Purpose

We have not yet discussed the nature or role of purpose statements, general and specific, in the preparation of your speech. Let us note here only that each speech should have a clear sense of purpose. You should try to articulate exactly what you are trying to accomplish, both broadly and more specifically.

Audience analysis helps us formulate relevant and appropriate purposes. The same speech content might be used with two different audiences for two completely different purposes. An obvious example is the gospel: to a group of unbelievers we might communicate the gospel with one purpose in mind (salvation), but with a group of Christians our purpose for discussing the gospel would probably be quite different (reinforcement and edification). Thus our purpose for discussing any particular subject matter will be shaped by our understanding of the needs of our audience. We will address this point in detail in chapter 4.

The Organization of the Message

Different audiences and occasions often require different ways of handling the content of a speech. Ceremonial events often have their own built-in rules that you must respect. Whether an audience is receptive or hostile to your proposition is another factor. Which points should be included and which would be better left out? Should the strongest argument be presented first or kept until the last? Is the material of the speech familiar enough to the audience for you to move through it quickly, or must you take only "baby steps" so as not to leave your audience behind? These and numerous other questions of organization can be answered only after you have taken the time to analyze your audience.

Supporting Material

In chapter 6 we will deal at length with the various types of supporting material speakers typically have available. What we shall discover is that one of the limiting factors as to what can be used effectively and what cannot is the nature of the audience. A quotation from a well-known environmentalist might carry weight with a group of college students but would probably be less than useful before an audience of lumber company executives. An illustration that would touch a responsive chord in parents might miss a group of teenagers altogether, and vice versa.

Introduction and Conclusion

Of all the several parts of your speech, few will be so dramatically affected by audience considerations as your introduction. If a basic principle of communicating to an audience is to begin where they are and take them to where you want them to go, then the introduction will be shaped to a very large extent by your understanding of who your auditors are and where you will have to begin in order to make contact with them. While this is less true of your conclusion, the way you tie together the many parts of your speech at the end will nevertheless be significantly influenced by the requirements of your audience.

Language

The choice of wording for a speech is another factor that is affected by our understanding of the audience and occasion. In a more formal setting, more formal language is appropriate. Since serious occasions require serious language, slang and colloquial language will generally be avoided in favor of more dignified and respectful wording. Conversely, on more informal occasions, lighter and more natural words are often not simply allowed but required. In either case, appropriate wording can be chosen only in the light of the makeup and expectations of the audience.

Delivery

The nonverbal aspects of the speech are influenced as much by our audience as are the verbal elements. At this point we need observe only that we would not use the same style of delivery to communicate to a group of fifty that we would use to reach an audience of five thousand. The demands upon our ability to deliver a message would be quite different. Or again, the dignified delivery of a eulogy at a funeral would vary greatly from the delivery of a humorous after-dinner speech. These examples simply indicate that delivery is another element that is significantly affected by our understanding of the characteristics of our audience and their needs.

Length of the Message

How long should your speech be? This question can be answered only in light of the requirements of the particular occasion. Often, of course, a time limit is assigned. But on other occasions you will have more flexibility and must decide for yourself (within reasonable limits) how long to speak. An analysis of the interests, abilities, and expectations of the audience will help you make the appropriate decision.

Finding Information about Your Audience

As valuable as information about your audience may be, it is not always readily available. Sometimes it is not available at all. In such cases you must make do with broad assumptions and proceed accordingly. But usually you will not be limited to such meager information. There are almost always some avenues available for gaining additional insight about an audience. Here are some of the most common:

Past Experience

In most speaking situations you will have had some previous contact with the audience. In fact, you may know the audience intimately. Perhaps you are even a member of the group you will be addressing, such as a student speaking to her class. If so, thinking about the various aspects of the audience's needs, abilities, and expectations will not be difficult at all. You need only review, with your subject matter in mind, what you know of your audience to pinpoint the relevant information. But what if you have little or no previous experience with this particular audience? Some benefit can be gained in such cases from a consideration of *similar kinds* of speaking situations you may have observed in the past. But for the most part you will want to rely on some of the following sources of information for your analysis.

Interviews

In one way or another you should attempt to question knowledgeable people to gain the information you lack. Perhaps you have access to certain members of the audience. Try to find out as much as you can about them and their fellow listeners through the use of appropriate questions. If the audience represents some sort of organized group, one of the leaders would be an excellent source of information. A conversation with others who have addressed the group in the past would be another way of learning pertinent information about it.

Records

Sometimes written documents can be of help in obtaining information about an audience and speaking situation. Such documents as a constitution, bylaws, or charter can give valuable insight into the nature of an organization. Minutes of past meetings, where available, or brochures, leaflets, pamphlets, and other documents published by the group can also be useful. Writings of representative group members are still another potential source of insight. Membership lists may provide a picture of the makeup of the group, and invitation lists, if such exist, can tell you about the particular audience you will face. Even the nature of the announcements that brought the group together can provide insight into what the audience's expectations may involve.

Observation

Do you have access to the efforts of past speakers to this group? Perhaps there are manuscripts, notes, or tape recordings available. In an attempt to sensitize your own feel for the group, try exposing yourself to what these previous speakers have done. This is a common tactic of professional public speakers. Where the necessary materials are available, it can be a profitable use of your time.

The process we have outlined for analyzing your audience is a rigorous one. If the job is done thoroughly, it will often occupy a significant amount of your speech preparation time. Yet it is time well spent. Few other activities can contribute more toward the preparation of a successful speech. The simple truth is that the better you know your audience, the more likely it is that you will be able to reach them with your message.

Exercises

1. Examine Paul's speech on Mars Hill in Acts 17:22–31. Find out everything you can about the occasion and audience. Then examine Paul's address for signs of audience adaptation. Write an analysis of how Paul adjusted his speech to this situation.

2. Observe a speaker addressing a live audience—teacher, preacher, lecturer, politician, lawyer, for example. Make a record of all the ways the speaker attempted to adapt to the audience. Were the speaker's attempts successful? Why or why not? In what other ways might the speaker have adapted to the audience?

3. Consider some group of which you are a part, perhaps a church, club, class, or civic organization. Think of a specific occasion in the future when a speaker will be addressing this group on an announced topic. Then put yourself in the place of the speaker and write an analysis of the speaking situation. Be sure to include all of the relevant data—the internal and external characteristics of both the occasion and audience.

4. Suppose you had to teach a course in public speaking to a class of high-school students. Using the content of

this chapter and any other help you can find through your own research, put together an outline for a ten-minute lecture on one of the following topics: the importance of adapting to your audience, why good listening is difficult, or how attention works.

Chapter 3

How to Discover an Idea for Your Speech

There exists a remarkable consensus among those who have studied and practiced public speaking over the last twenty-five hundred years that the most effective way to structure a speech is to build it around a single significant thought. From the ancient Greek and Roman rhetoricians to the latest communication theorists, from the preaching in the Bible to the sermons heard in pulpits today, from the political oratory of democracies long past to the persuasive messages of our own times, the history of public speaking and the lessons we have learned from that history unite to argue forcefully that *a speech, to be maximally effective, ought to attempt to develop more or less fully only one major proposition.*

The Need for a Central Idea

The reason for this consensus stems from the way God has designed our minds. The human mind craves *unity.* Conversely, the thing we find most difficult to tolerate is chaos or randomness. For example, we look into the heavens and see a seemingly random mass of stars. But we are uncomfortable with such disorder, so we seek to discover patterns or "constellations." We try to organize what we see into a unity or series of unities. Or again, we observe the phenomena of nature, including human nature, and find them on the surface to be complex and unrelated. Unhappy with this, we immediately begin looking deeper to construct a theory or hypothesis that will organize what we see into some sort of unified whole. This is the process we call "science." Or again, we consider the seemingly chaotic, unrelated details of the Kennedy and Martin Luther King assassinations. Such randomness is inherently dissatisfying, so there exists a natural tendency to arrange the events into some unifying pattern or "conspiracy." This is as it always has been. The human mind is constantly seeking to discover unity in the stimuli it receives, to separate those items that seem to be related to one thing from those that are related to another.

Further, our minds also seek *order*. This is intimately involved with our desire for unity. It is not enough to discover which parts are related to which whole; we also seek to discover orderly relationships between and among the parts. For example, all the various pieces of a jigsaw puzzle or a carburetor combine to make a unified whole—but only when they are arranged in their proper order, with each part appropriately related to the other. Apart from these proper relationships the parts do not work together to form a larger unity at all. They are merely a jumble of individual parts. Thus, to grasp the unity of diverse parts, to discover *e pluribus unum* (out of many, one), we must also discover the proper relationships or order among the many parts. And our minds are ever seeking to do so.

There is also the matter of *progress*. Not all unities are like a jigsaw puzzle or a carburetor. Some entities have a chronological dimension to them. A symphony, for example, is made up of thousands of notes played on perhaps scores of different instruments. Yet the composer has so designed the symphony that it organizes all of these many notes into a unified whole. In this the symphony is not unlike the puzzle or carburetor.

On another level, however, the symphony is very different. We may lay out the pieces of the puzzle or the carburetor so that we can see them all at once, but with the symphony we can hear only one part at a time. All we have of the symphony is what we are hearing at the moment (combined, of course, with what we can recall of the past and what we may be able to anticipate of the future). Thus, for us to make sense of a symphony—or any "unity" that has a time dimension, such as a play, a novel, or a speech— the matter of progress becomes significant. As we try to sort out the pieces we are perceiving, to discover their relationships, we are looking for an order consisting largely of some sort of *progression,* one thing following another in an appropriate chronological relationship. Thus a symphony performed backwards would be a cacophony. We would find it unpleasant, jarring, and frustrating. Likewise, a play with the acts and scenes jumbled out of sequence would be unintelligible. (But notice that our minds would attempt to

---

We cannot do everything at once, but we can do something at once. **Anonymous**

---

rearrange the parts into some sort of sensible progression, order, and therefore unity.) In a time-dependent entity progress contributes to the order and thus the unity our minds need.

Because our minds—and our listeners' minds, too—seek unity in what we perceive, a speech, to be maximally effective, ought to be the embodiment of one major idea. *Having a central idea tends to build unity into a speech,* allowing us to work in conjunction with the natural tendencies of our listeners' minds. By limiting ourselves to the development of one main idea—and thus striving to eliminate anything, regardless of how impressive, interesting, or entertaining it may be, that does not in some way directly or indirectly support that idea—we can produce a finished product that hangs together and carries a unified communicative thrust. It is an entity that draws its unifying power from the central thesis that serves as its core. Like the hub of a wheel or the trunk of a tree, the central idea becomes that which relates all the parts to one another and gives coherence to the whole.

A central idea within a speech promotes not only unity, but order and progress as well. Obviously, it is difficult to proceed in an orderly way if we do not know where we are going. It is nonsense to speak of making progress when we have no destination.

But with a central idea, we know where we want to go and thus we can take the appropriate steps to arrive there.

Unfortunately, many speeches suffer from a lack of direction. The speaker has no clear destination even in his or her own mind, and so the speech falls dead in the water. The only movement we perceive is a sort of wallowing in the troughs, rather than real progress. In contrast to this, an effective speech will be one that has a destination. It seems clearly to be going somewhere.

As we have said, building a speech around a central idea promotes this sort of headway. Since you know precisely what you are trying to communicate to your audience—that is, you know the main idea you are seeking to drive home—you may then

---

Form is the creation of an appetite in the mind of the auditor, and the adequate satisfying of that appetite. Kenneth Burke

---

begin to ask yourself such pertinent questions as: Where is my audience relative to this idea? Where do I need to begin in order to introduce this idea effectively? What subideas will I need to develop to provide my audience with the complete picture by the time I am finished? In what order should these ideas be handled so as to maintain a clear progression of thought toward my destination? Only the speaker whose message is the embodiment of a single significant idea can answer such questions satisfactorily.

Having a central idea, then, tends to promote the important characteristics of *unity, order,* and *progress* in your speech. These characteristics in turn work in conjunction with the natural processes of your listeners' minds to promote effective communication.

Anatomy of an Idea

We have been using the term *idea* as if everyone understands *what an idea is.* In one sense, of course, this is a valid assumption. The word *idea* is a common one, and we all use it regularly in everyday conversation. Thus almost everyone, upon hearing the dictionary definition of an idea as "a thought; mental conception; mental image; notion," would reply, "Why, of course. That's what I mean when I use the word *idea*."

On a deeper level, however, most people have probably never stopped to think more carefully about what an idea really is, about what it takes to constitute an idea, about the basic building blocks of which an idea is constructed. This is certainly understandable, and one might argue that it is not really necessary for most people to analyze ideas in this fashion. However, for those who desire to engage in the public communication of ideas to others, such an oversight becomes a very expensive luxury, one that can seldom be afforded. When we take upon ourselves the role of public speaker, we automatically acquire with that mantle the responsibility to think well and communicate clearly. To do so, we must first understand the *nature of thought, how it works,* and *where its pitfalls lie.*

Subject and Complement

The first step in the process of understanding thought—and, therefore, in learning how to communicate our ideas to others— is to understand the two basic building blocks of an idea: *subject* and *complement*. Every complete idea is made up of these two elements. It is not possible to have a complete idea if either of these components is missing. The *subject*, very simply, is the answer to the question, What am I talking about? The *complement*, equally simply, is the answer to the question, What am I saying about my subject?

The concepts of subject and complement are elegantly simple and easy to understand. But we should never think that because the concepts are simple they are therefore unimportant. A speech is inevitably made up of a pattern of ideas. Further, some subject and some complement together make up each of the ideas of our speech, including the central idea. So subjects and their complements are at the heart of our effort to communicate to an audience. Until we grasp this, we probably do not yet understand the way ideas work in our thought or in our communication.

To have a complete idea we must assert or predicate something about something else. As long as we have merely a "something" (a subject), we do not yet have an idea. It is only the assertion of "another thing" (a complement) about the subject that gives birth to a complete idea.

For example, suppose we choose "desk" as our subject. All we have is a *part of an idea,* a "something," a topic, without anything being asserted about it. So far, "desk" is not an idea. Even if we add qualifiers to the subject—thereby *narrowing* the sub-

---

Churchill reports that the most valuable training he ever received in rhetoric was in the diagraming of the sentences. Wayne Booth

---

ject, not broadening it!—such as "my desk" or "my desk upon which I am now writing," there is still only a narrowed subject, not an idea. This merely delineates more specifically which "something" is being referred to in the subject.

But now let us add a *complement* to construct a complete idea. Suppose something is asserted or predicated about "my desk" as follows: "My desk [subject] is made of wood." In this case "is made of wood" is the *complement* portion of the idea. It is the assertion being made about the subject. When these two come together, we have a complete thought or idea composed of (1) a "something" about which an assertion is to be made (a subject) and (2) the assertion about that "something" (a complement). Remember: until we have both, we do not yet have a complete idea.

It is important to understand at the outset that the term *subject* is being used here in a nongrammatical sense. This means that the subject of the idea and the grammatical subject are not necessarily identical. To be sure, sometimes the subject of the idea and the grammatical subject are the same. This is the case in the statement, "My desk is made of wood." The word *desk* is both the grammatical subject and the subject of the idea. But we must remember that, whereas the grammatical subject is determined on the basis of the rules of syntax and grammar, *the subject of the idea is determined on the basis of thought and meaning.* The grammatical subject is pinpointed more or less mechanically, but the detection of the subject of the idea is a far more subtle, complex, and delicate process.

For example, if we examine the idea "I like my desk," what do we find? The grammatical subject is easy to detect; it is the word *I*. But what is the subject of the idea? Remember that the subject of the idea is the answer to the question, What am I talking about? (or, if the idea is someone else's, What is the speaker talking about?). Obviously the answer to this question would not be simply "I." Rather, what is being talked about in the statement "I like my desk" is *how I feel about my desk*. This is the subject. The complement is, "I like it." Together this subject and this complement make up the idea "I like my desk." We can display the dissected idea in this way:

Subject: *How I feel about my desk*
Complement: *I like it*
Idea: "I like my desk."

Notice several things about this example. First, observe that the subject is actually an entire clause. This is often the case. A subject may be a single word or a phrase, of course, but it will often have to be longer so as to be sufficiently narrow. Simple, single-word subjects (such as "I" in the above example) are usually too broad and therefore do not specify clearly enough our *exact* subject. Additional words function as qualifiers which narrow the statement of what we are actually talking about.

Second, notice that the subject "how I feel about my desk" is incomplete in itself. It is not a full idea. It needs to be "completed" by the addition of a *complement;* that is, some assertion about the subject.

A subject, by definition, must *always* be incomplete in itself. Thus a full sentence cannot be a subject, for a full sentence is by definition *complete*. If it were not inherently a finished thought, it could not be stated in full-sentence form. Sometimes a full sentence can be changed into a subject by the addition of a single word, but only because the full sentence is thus transformed into a clause that needs a complement to become a full thought. Thus, "Jesus died on the cross" is a full sentence and a complete idea, but "*why* Jesus died on the cross" is a clause that needs a complement to become a full idea. The former is not a subject, but the latter is.

Third, notice that if we change the complement, we change the complete idea. The main thrust of an idea is carried in its complement, the assertion about the subject. If we change the assertion, we change the entire idea. For instance, if we change the complement in our sample idea "I like my desk" to "I hate it" or "I am apathetic toward it," the entire thrust of the idea shifts dramatically.

Here are some examples of ideas with their subjects and complements:

Idea:	*What this country needs is a new president.*
Subject:	what this country needs
Complement:	is a new president
Idea:	*The garbage disposal service in our city needs to be improved.*
Subject:	the garbage disposal service in our city
Complement:	it needs to be improved
Idea:	*To be maximally effective, a speech ought to be the embodiment of one main idea.*
Subject:	a primary characteristic of a speech that is to be maximally effective
Complement:	it should be the embodiment of one main idea
Idea:	*Jesus Christ died on the cross to save humankind from their sin.*
Subject:	the reason Christ died on the cross
Complement:	to save humankind from their sin

Multiple-Complement Ideas

We have said that every idea consists of a subject and a complement. Here we need to add one more observation to that statement. There are some ideas which involve *more than a single complement;* that is, they have *multiple* complements. Reasonably enough, we will call this type of idea a *multiple-complement idea.*

Multiple-complement ideas are those whose subjects inherently involve a plurality. For example, the statement "The elements of an idea are its subject and its complement" is a multi-

---

There is no sense in trying to do anything unless you give it your maximum effort.   John F. Kennedy

---

ple-complement idea. The subject of the idea (answering the question, What is being talked about?) is "the elements of an idea." Obviously, there is a plurality inherent in "elements," so it should not be surprising to see a twofold complement—"are (1) its subject and (2) its complement."

The reason this statement remains a single idea instead of two is that there is only one assertion being set forth. To be sure, it is a *multifaceted* assertion (complement), but it is nevertheless a single assertion about the plural "elements" of the subject. The multiple facets required by the plural subject, combined with the multiple complements, do not require us to conclude that we have two ideas. We simply have plural aspects of a single idea.

This point may be clarified by comparison with a *two-idea* statement. It is quite possible to build two ideas into a single sentence. For example, examine the sentence "My desk is made of wood and is quite sturdy." Here we have two ideas joined into a single sentence. The subject is "my desk." But as we examine the sentence, we find two different assertions being posited about my desk: (1) it is made of wood and (2) it is quite sturdy. These are clearly two different complements, not two facets of a single complement explaining some plurality inherent in the subject. Thus we have two complete ideas built into a single sentence.

As we have noted, the multiple-complement idea is different. It is not several ideas combined, but rather a single multifaceted assertion. Its complements are always an attempt to bring out some inherent plurality within the subject. Here are some examples of multiple-complement ideas:

Idea:	*The three spatial dimensions are height, width, and depth.*
Subject:	the three spatial dimensions
Complement:	are (1) height, (2) width, and (3) depth
Idea:	*To be a good tennis player one must possess dedication as well as natural ability.*
Subject:	the requirements to be a good tennis player
Complement:	one must have (1) dedication and (2) natural ability
Idea:	*Let everyone be quick to hear, slow to speak, and slow to anger.*
Subject:	what should characterize all Christians
Complement:	they should be (1) quick to hear, (2) slow to speak, and (3) slow to anger

The matter of ideas with their subjects and complements is so basic that we will not be free of it anywhere in the process of preparing a speech. We will return to it again and again.

Characteristics of a Good Speech Idea

Not all ideas are good speech ideas. A good idea for a speech is one which successfully balances two sets of sometimes opposing requirements: First, the idea must meet the needs of both the speaker and the audience; second, the idea must be broad enough to be significant, but also narrow enough to be handled in a relevant way (see fig. 2).

Figure 2
Qualities of Good Speech Ideas

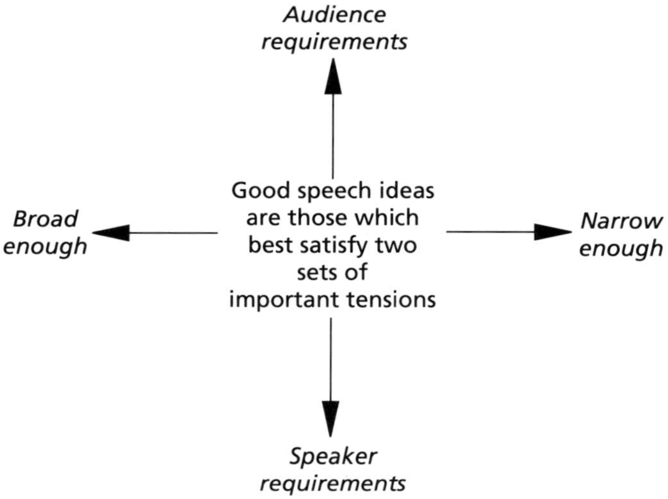

*Audience
requirements*

↑

*Broad
enough* ← Good speech ideas
are those which
best satisfy two
sets of
important tensions → *Narrow
enough*

↓

*Speaker
requirements*

The Audience-Speaker Tension

We have already discussed the fact that a speaker should adjust to his audience in every way possible. One important area of adjustment is in the choice of subject matter. If your topic is not assigned, you must choose what it is you will talk about. How do you make this choice?

First, choice of subject matter should be made in the light of the interests, attitudes, needs, and expectations of your audience. Thus your audience exerts a very strong tension upon your choice of topic.

Speakers too commonly fail to respond to this pull of the audience. Students in particular sometimes take the easiest path by settling for some subject that is suitable for them, but relatively inappropriate for their audience. Their goal seems to be to choose whatever will require the least amount of work. An honest appraisal of the matter would have to acknowledge that by taking this option a speaker can indeed reduce significantly the amount of labor he must expend. But we should also point out that a speaker who chooses this option ought not expect much of significance to occur as a result of his message. In most cases such a speech will become simply one more of those irrelevancies which give public speaking a bad name. An effective speaker will never settle for such low aim, but will rather make every effort to choose a topic which takes into consideration the requirements of the audience.

Having emphasized the *audience's* requirements, however, we must also note *the requirements of the speaker.* These requirements include both knowledge and interest. Put simply, a suitable speech idea is one in which the speaker is interested and

---

No tears in the writer, no tears in the reader. **Robert Frost**

---

about which she knows something (or at least can become knowledgeable by the time she must speak).

There are subjects which may interest you, but which you know little about. In addition, you may realize that despite your interest you would not be able to become knowledgeable enough by the time of your speech to treat the subject well. Such topics would be poor ones for your speech for obvious reasons. Likewise, there may be other subjects about which you are knowledgeable, but which no longer hold your interest. Such topics would also be poor choices even though they might be convenient ones. If you as the speaker are bored with your subject, what chance is there that the audience will be interested?

This matter of speaker interest is a far more important consideration than most beginning speakers realize. Those who often speak to audiences know that one's motivational level is a crucial determinant of the success of a speech. Without a sizable desire to speak to a given audience about a particular subject, the preparation and delivery of a speech can be sheer drudgery, a mere going-through-the-motions. The speech becomes simply a spiel, a chore to be gotten over as quickly as possible. And such an attitude in the speaker quickly permeates the audience as well. But the opposite is also true. When you truly desire to reach your audience with your ideas, a sense of purpose and even excitement often percolates through the entire process and is infectiously communicated to the audience.

Sometimes the needs and interests of the audience and speaker work against one another. They are different enough that the speaker must strive to find some compromise or middle ground between the two tensions. But it is also true that in the hands of a sensitive and gifted communicator these two tensions can actually feed one another. You consider your audience's needs and interests. Out of this analysis you may discover an area or areas to which you believe you can make a contribution. Such a realization in turn furnishes you with the incentive and enthusiasm you need to pursue the project to completion. The audience's requirements thus merge with your requirements in a happy synthesis for all.

In any case, we may conclude that *one measure of a good speech idea is how well it satisfies the requirements of both the audience and the speaker.*

The Broad-Narrow Tension

A second tension an idea must satisfy to be considered a good one is that which exists between significance and relevance, or what we will call the *broad* and the *narrow*.

In one way or another, virtually all human thought is either *inductive* or *deductive*, both of which grapple with the relationship between the general and the particular. For the moment let us observe only that the further we move in the direction of the particular, the closer we come to individual things, whereas the further we move in the direction of the general, the closer we come to the abstract, universal ideas which categorize and give meaning to particular things. Thus we might think of a hypothetical ladder of ideas, with the inconsequential and trivial at the bottom giving way to the increasingly inclusive and therefore significant as we move to the top. This is inevitably an oversimplification, but a useful one for our purposes here.

Our point is that a good speech idea must be broad enough (that is, high enough on the ladder) to have some substance to it. Ideas that are too narrow (that is, too close to the bottom of the ladder) are insignificant and unworthy of your time and that of your audience. Such ideas should be avoided in favor of thoughts which have more weight to them, thoughts which rise above the trivial to stimulate and challenge your audience in some way.

Remember that the entire speech is to be built around the development of your speech idea. Thus the idea must be expansive enough to allow for development. Ideas that are too narrow cannot be expanded or developed. For example, consider our previous example, "My desk is made of wood." Even if the state-

---

Power to expand is generated by compression.   H. Grady Davis

---

ment is true, it is also inconsequential. It is a statement about one very ordinary particular. As an idea it would rank low on our ladder of ideas. Thus it would make a very poor candidate for a speech idea. Intuitively we realize that a speech built around this idea would be trivial, with its major points still more trivial than the main idea ("The surface of the desk is made of solid oak"; "The sides of the desk are covered with pecan veneer"; etc.). By contrast, a good speech idea must be broad enough to allow expansion without falling victim to irrelevance.

"All great thoughts are general," said Samuel Johnson, and so they are. H. Grady Davis provides some excellent examples:

> The power to make generalizations is one of the most astounding faculties of the mind, the power to distill a million facts into a single meaning. Take Thoreau's, "The mass of men lead lives of quiet desperation." Take a kindred generalization, Blaise Pascal's, describing life in the face of misery and death: "It is enough, without examining particular occupations, to group them all under the

heading of diversion." Take Shakespeare's, "We are such stuff as dreams are made on, and our little life is rounded with a sleep." Take any household word or memorable saying; they are all generalizations. This consideration of much in little is the mark of all great poetry and art. The ability to make significant generalizations is the test of intellectual power. The labor of trying to make them is the most constructive of all mental disciplines.

As another example, the American historian, Charles A. Beard, was once asked if he could sum up the lessons of history in a short book. He replied that he could do it in four sentences, and he chose four familiar generalizations. History teaches that:

1. Whom the gods would destroy, they first make mad with power.
2. The mills of God grind slowly, yet they grind exceeding small.
3. The bee fertilizes the flower it robs.
4. When it is dark enough you can see the stars.[1]

To be sure, few of our speech ideas will be profound metaphysical truths. The more general and powerful an idea is, the more difficult it is to manage well within a given time limit, so that even if we are capable of speaking on such a lofty level, we often have to refrain from doing so for pragmatic reasons. Our point here is not that we should limit ourselves to sweeping syntheses of accrued wisdom. Rather, it is that we should at least respond to a tug in this direction in the choice of our subject matter so as to avoid trivial, mediocre, inconsequential speeches. We have all heard too many of these already, and we should strive not to add to the pool.

On the other hand, it is also possible to choose ideas that are *too broad*. A good speech idea is one that has been honed and sharpened for a particular target, your audience. It needs to be narrow enough that your audience can identify with it. While broad ideas may be profound, they, for this very reason, may also leave people cold. An idea may say so much that, even though it may be truthful, a kind of "overload" occurs and the audience is not able to assimilate it all. The audience is confronted with so much, so compactly packaged, that the magnitude of what they are hearing is lost on them. Thus the idea remains at a distance. It remains an idea for someone else, somewhere else. The audience fails to get involved with the idea because they are overwhelmed by it.

Some of our Lord's teachings strike modern man in just this way. Consider, for example, Jesus' repeated teaching that the way to gain one's life is by losing it for Christ's sake (Matt. 10:39; 16:25; Mark 8:35; Luke 9:24). The truth of this paradox is so profound, so all-encompassing, so demanding that modern man seems incapable of comprehending it. It is a truth that, if it were grasped and acted upon, would call into question deeply ingrained aspects of our whole culture. So, modern man, while not rejecting the idea outright but rather giving it proper lip service, conveniently keeps it at bay, refusing to become involved with it. Our culture does applaud certain of the idea's particulars (e.g., Christians serving others in Christ's name), but neglects to interact with the idea itself. What we need to see is that it is the very broadness of the idea, its profundity and inclusiveness, that allows contemporary man the luxury of keeping it at a distance.

This phenomenon, while a strange one, is not an uncommon one. We all practice it. We may read, for example, an account of the deaths of over twenty-five thousand people in an earthquake. Instead of being horrified by such statistics, most people are left strangely unmoved by them. The reason is that the tragedy is too large to become involved with. The report of a neighbor's dog being hit by an automobile, not to mention the loss of a friend or loved one, causes grief that is both real and often very deep. But twenty-five thousand people dying violent deaths in an earthquake is too much to comprehend, so we keep it at an emotional arm's length.

Thus, ideas that are *too broad* (unless we have the time to "concretize" them in such a way as to allow our audience to get involved) should probably be avoided in favor of thoughts that are narrow enough for an audience to comprehend. The idea should be sharp enough that by the time you are through you have been able to unfold it in all its relevant aspects. The audience has had time to consider it in some detail, to chew on it, and then digest it.

We have made several references to the speaker's time limit. This is a key factor in determining how broad or narrow an idea to choose, but not the only one. Other considerations which might influence your choice include the intellectual abilities of the audience, their expectations for the occasion, and the nature of the location.

A second measure of a good speech idea, then, is that it will be broad enough to be significant, but narrow enough to be made relevant to the audience.

Finding an Idea

Outside the classroom you will often have your subject chosen for you. In such cases the matter of how to discover an idea becomes academic. You must decide only how to handle the idea for a particular audience. We will assume for our purposes here, however, that no subject matter has been assigned. In such a situation, how can you discover a good idea for a speech? The answer involves at least four steps.

Before looking at these steps, however, we should be careful to note that they do not always occur in a tidy chronological order. They represent the four major stages in the development of an idea, but they will often occur simultaneously, or out of order, or in some other unorthodox way. We can lay them out logically here, and you may find that you will sometimes follow this logical order in your own preparation. But on other occasions you will find an idea has suddenly popped up ready for your use. Should you pause to submit your idea to the following steps? Yes, if only to be sure you fully understand your own thought. Take the idea apart into its subject and complement to be certain you know both what you are talking about and what you want to say about it. You may even find during this process that you want in some way to revise this idea which seemed so workable at first. You will in any case be sure to have a firmer grasp on your own point if you take the trouble to analyze it a bit. However, if you do not trip so fortuitously over a good speech idea, here are the steps you must travel to find one:

Find a Subject You Want to Talk About

Subjects come in all sorts of sizes, shapes, and colors. In fact the list of potential subjects for a speech would be, if we could enumerate them all, virtually endless. Yet subjects also tend to fall into several broad categories.

Types of Subjects

First, there are *nominal subjects.* "Dating in American culture," "penal reform," "situation ethics," "ecology," and "jogging as a means of keeping fit" are all examples of nominal subjects. They simply name some person, place, or thing as the object of attention. Such subjects usually include some modifier(s) to narrow their focus sufficiently.

Second, there are *adverbial subjects.* These types of subjects are usually clauses which begin with an interrogative pronoun or adverb: who, which, what, why, when, where, or how. Examples: "who would make the best mayor," "what you need to know about the oil companies," "why Jesus had to die on the cross," "when to write your senators," "where to find the best supporting material for a speech," and "how to influence the content of television programing."

Third, there are *relational subjects.* This kind of subject focuses attention upon the *relationship between* two things. "You and the military," "sex and the single Christian," and "welfare and the hard-core unemployed" are all examples of relational subjects.

Fourth, there are *multiple-complement subjects.* As we have already seen, in multiple-complement ideas the various complements trace out some inherent plurality within the subject. Thus multiple-complement subjects will always encompass more than a single dimension; otherwise, they would be simple nominal subjects. Furthermore, multiple-complement subjects are always *equational.* The subject and complements always function as a quasi-equation. Consider one of our previous examples: "To be a good tennis player one must possess dedication as well as natural ability." The implied equation in this idea is as follows: The requirements to be a good tennis player (subject) equals (1) dedication plus (2) natural ability (complements). Multiple-complement subjects *always* lead to equational ideas of this sort. Other examples of multiple-complement subjects: "the benefits of keeping physically fit," "the potential dangers of genetic engineering," and "four reasons Christians need each other."

Finally, there are *predicating subjects*. This type of subject carries within it some implied form of the verb *to be*. Consider, for example, a subject such as "the wisdom of living for Christ." Technically there is no assertion offered here, but as Davis states, "Rhetorically—or semantically, if you prefer—[such a subject] nevertheless has the force of an assertion. It suggests a predicate so plainly that it is actually felt."[2] In our example the implied assertion is that *there is* wisdom in living for Christ. "Indeed," says Davis, "the suggestion of this predicate, 'there is,' is stronger here than the words themselves would be. Like other forms of the verb *to be*, *is* is here so readily understood that it would be pedantic to say it."[3]

Notice that these different types of subjects are often little more than different ways of saying the same thing. Thus a *relational subject* such as "inflation and interest rates in the American economy" can become a *nominal subject*, "the relationship between inflation and interest rates in the American economy"; or an *adverbial subject*, "how inflation and interest rates relate to one another in the American economy"; or a *multiple-complement subject*, "the three primary ways inflation and interest rates relate to one another in the American economy."

Narrowing Your Subject

In wording your subject, choose the type which best suits your purpose. Try to be as concise as possible, but yet full enough to be exact. If accuracy requires some extra (or even clumsy) wording at this point, do not hesitate to add it. You can always polish your wording as you go (and you will usually need to do so). But it is important that you state early on *exactly* what you want to talk about, with wording that neither leaves out anything important, nor includes extraneous aspects you do not want to cover.

One of the most common pitfalls of beginning speakers is that they tend to choose subjects which are too broad. One student, for example, decided that he wanted to speak on the subject "crime." This was not merely his general topic area; it was his final speech subject! But such a topic is far too all-encompassing for any one speech. Even such narrowed subjects as "the increase of crime" or "the increase of crime in our city" would probably be too broad for the average speech. Perhaps "the reason for the increase of crime in our city during the past year" would be narrow enough to be manageable. The wording could be honed during further preparation (perhaps to "why crime increased in our city last year"), but at least the speaker would know from the outset *exactly* what he wants to talk about, and the subject would be narrow enough to support a reasonable hope that he could actually manage it in a single speech.

Sources of Subjects

Figure 3 represents the relationship between speech subjects and you the speaker. In the *inner circle* of personal experience are included all those things you have directly encountered in your life. The *second ring* represents the various areas of your knowledge. All the subjects you have studied throughout the

Figure 3
The Relationship between Speech Subjects and the Speaker

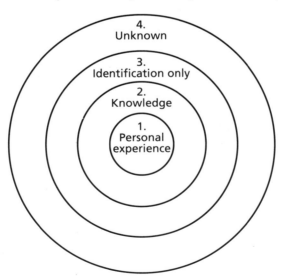

years of your education (both formal and informal) are included here. This ring is obviously much wider than your own direct experience. Broader still is the *third ring*, which includes all those things that you can only identify; that is, you know *of* them but not much *about* them. You have no substantive grasp on them, but you do know they exist. The *fourth ring* represents a large uncharted category of unknown subjects which you do not yet know exist. Only through further research will you be able to discover these.

Note that as you move toward the outer rings of the diagram the number of potential subjects increases dramatically. Your personal experience is relatively limited, but as you move outward you soon come to a virtually unlimited pool of potential subjects. But note too that as you move outward, the amount of effort required also increases. Subjects you have experienced or studied previously will require less effort than those you have not yet studied or even discovered.

The only workable way to sort through the multitude of subjects represented by these four circles is to begin preparing a list of possibilities. With your own and your audience's requirements in mind *generally*, begin to brainstorm about topics you might use. The ideas you produce in this way will probably have to be focused more specifically for your audience after this preliminary process of discovery. The next chapter will examine in some detail how this may be accomplished. But for now you are looking merely for a potential list of ideas that are at least "in the ballpark" of usefulness.

Do not be too quick to judge here. Let your mind range freely and list as many possibilities as you can. Undoubtedly, some subjects will prove to be unworkable for one reason or another, but you will be able to sift them out later. At this point you are simply trying to generate potentially useful topics, a process illustrated by John F. Wilson and Carroll C. Arnold:

> It happens that this paragraph was originally written in the spring, in a motel apartment. That fact will affect the thoughts that come to mind [the power of suggestion; hotel-motel-hostelry operations]. The highway is visible from the window [mass transportation problems, highway construction, auto and truck licens-

ing, highway safety, scenic routes]. Across the highway is a row of shrubs [horticulture, landscaping, plant breeding, land use, plant pathology]. The storm windows are still on the motel [insulating materials and properties, maintenance industries, glass making, fabricating for the construction industries, custom building vs. prefabrication]. A school bus passes [the topic of education calls up too many possibilities to enumerate]. The typewriter is before me [mechanisms of communication, the publishing industry, business machines, automation]. A bookshelf is at my side. On it stands *The Ugly American* [foreign policy, diplomacy, the responsibility of the press], a murder mystery [escapist reading, paperbacks, censorship], Chaim Perelman's *Traite de L'Argumentation* [foreign language study, foreign travel, methods of persuasion, the study of philosophy, the relative merits of different academic subjects].[4]

Using this approach you can generate dozens of potential topics in just a few moments. Let your thoughts range freely and jot down each topic that occurs to you. Try not to evaluate the topics yet, since this will tend to stifle your creativity. You can screen them later. For now just concentrate on recording as many potential topics as come to mind.

Another way to direct your brainstorming is to move through the general subject headings found in leading news magazines such as *Time* or *Newsweek*. General headings such as the following are almost inexhaustible as sources of speech subjects: international affairs, domestic affairs, business and the economy, labor, the arts, education, medicine, law, the sciences, books, people, sports, and show business. What do you know about these general topic areas? Where do your interests lie? Let your mind run freely and list everything that seems useful.

Categories of personal experience you may find suggestive include places you have been, jobs you have held, hobbies you have taken up, events you have witnessed, problems you have faced, sports you have played, people you have met, and new experiences you have tried.

Still another group of potential subjects is practical explanations of "how to do it" (buying a car, refinishing an antique, thinking reflectively, speed-reading, studying for an exam, caring for indoor plants, etc.) or "how it works" (a cuckoo clock, a gas turbine engine, Boyle's law, a pendulum, the DNA code, etc.).

As a Christian you may want to speak from time to time about spiritual and moral issues. Here are some broad categories to prompt your thinking:

adversity	criticism	guilt	labor	reason
affliction	the cross of	happiness	life	resurrection
ambition	Christ	heaven	love	self-love
atheism	death	hell	lust	sex
authority	the devil	holiness	marriage	sin
beauty	discipline	honesty	mercy	suffering
belief	doctrine	hope	miracles	superstition
Bible	duty	hospitality	modesty	temptation
bigotry	eternity	human nature	morality	thankfulness
blessings	evil	human rights	motherhood	theology
boasting	failure	immorality	motives	the tongue
brotherhood	the fool	injustice	obedience	(James 3:5)
character	freedom	intolerance	opportunity	truth
compassion	friendship	jealousy	patience	values
complaining	God	Jesus Christ	peace	violence
compromise	the gospel	justice	persecution	war
courtesy	gossip	kindness	power	wealth
creation	grief	knowledge	pride	wisdom

Closing In

After you have compiled a list of potential subjects, go over the list and eliminate any that are obviously unusable. Perhaps on second thought they do not meet either your requirements or your audience's in some important way. Or perhaps they are subjects which have been badly overworked recently and need to be left alone for a while. Or perhaps the necessary research materials are not available. Let us think for a moment about this last case.

One of the obvious limitations you may face in choosing a speech subject is availability of research materials. You ought not settle finally on any subject until availability of such materials has been confirmed. There are many intriguing topics which must be rejected as speech subjects because the required materials either do not exist or are not available to the speaker. Consider, for example, the subject "the influence of the CIA in the last presidential election." This is certainly a captivating subject, but two questions arise: First, did the CIA influence the last presidential election? (probably not), and second, would the materials necessary to research the subject be available to you? (certainly not). Or again, "the attitude of Christian college professors toward abortion" might make an interesting topic for a casual conversation, but as a speech subject it would suffer from the same shortcomings. Thus in each case, the speaker must ask, (1) does the necessary material exist and (2) is it available to me?

Once the unusable topics have been eliminated from your list, you must begin to zero in upon the subject you will use for your speech. This will generally involve a kind of mental ranking of the most likely prospects. Usually one or two of the possibilities will emerge as the ones which best meet the tension between your needs and the needs of the audience. In some cases you will face a "toss-up" situation and will simply have to make an arbitrary choice.

There is no such thing as an uninteresting subject; there are only uninterested people.

Once you have your subject, you will want to test it to see whether it is at once broad enough to be significant but narrow enough to be manageable. If your full idea must meet these requirements in the end, your subject must meet them at the beginning.

In this regard remember that most of the suggested subject areas listed heretofore are just that—*areas* which encompass a myriad of speech subjects. They are designed to be broad suggestive categories for your brainstorming, not speech topics in themselves. They would have to be significantly narrowed to become usable speech subjects. On the other hand, be sure you do not squeeze all significance out of your subject by limiting it too much. Either of these extremes is costly. If your subject is too broad, your speech may be doomed to vagueness; if it is too narrow, the speech will probably suffer from triviality. Both of these problems can be avoided by giving careful attention to the breadth of your subject at this point in your preparation.

A word of caution is in order before we proceed. It is not uncommon for beginning speakers to spend so much time looking for their subject that they are left with too little time for the rest of their speech preparation. This can be a painful mistake. Few who have had to speak to an audience without adequate preparation have been willing to repeat the experience. You will generally be well advised to place firm limitations on the amount of time you give the process of subject selection. Make it your goal to have chosen a subject by a certain deadline and then push yourself to meet that deadline.

Furthermore, be decisive. Once you have chosen your subject, resist most of the temptations to move to greener grass. Chances are that the same kinds of problems you may be having with the subject you have chosen (and problems of some sort almost always crop up) would plague you equally as much with a different subject—only now you would be further behind in your schedule of preparation. On occasion you will find that despite your best efforts you have chosen poorly. Or you may run across an idea that is clearly and significantly superior to the one you have chosen. In such cases you may want to switch subjects, but you should do so reluctantly, and even then only when you are *certain* it is the better option. Weigh the time and effort you will lose in the switch. Usually you will find it is better to proceed with your initial choice since the disadvantages of switching outweigh the advantages.

Research Your Subject

Your next task is to find out as much as you can about the subject you have chosen. And in the broadest sense, there are only two places you can search to discover this information: inside yourself (brainstorming) and outside yourself (investigation).

Brainstorming

The more personal your subject, the more likely it is that your main source of information will be your own mind. You could hardly go to the encyclopedia to discover information about a subject such as "my primary goal in life." Clearly, you would have to generate most of the information about such a subject from your own thoughts and feelings. Or suppose you choose as a subject "playing the trombone" or "collecting stamps as a hobby" because you have been playing the trombone or collecting stamps for years. Again you would presumably have within yourself much of the necessary information for the speech.

Even with less personal subjects your own mind can often be a key source of information. You may know more about the subject than you think. Try sitting down with paper and pencil for a fifteen-minute brainstorming session. You may be amazed at how much you know.

One helpful tool for generating such information is the topical system devised by Wilson and Arnold. This system represents an attempt to categorize the most common ways that we talk and think about things. It is a sort of checklist of universal topics you may be able to use to pry out what you already know about a subject, or at least to help you focus clearly on the kind of information that you want to find out. Somewhere on this list almost anything you can say about a subject will find a place. This sort of exercise can be a crucial one in your effort to zero in on the appropriate complement for your speech idea. Here is what Wilson and Arnold call a "tolerably complete list" of universal topics:

1. *Existence* or nonexistence of things.
2. *Degree* or quantity of things, forces, etc.
3. *Spatial* attributes, including adjacency, distribution, place.
4. Attributes of *time*.
5. *Motion* or activity.
6. *Form*, either physical or abstract.
7. *Substance:* physical, abstract, or psychophysical.

8. *Capacity* to change, including predictability.
9. *Potency:* power or energy, including capacity to further or hinder anything.
10. *Desirability* in terms of rewards or punishments.
11. *Feasibility:* workability or practicability.
12. *Causality:* the relation of causes to effects, effects to causes, effects to effects, adequacy of causes, etc.
13. *Correlation:* coexistence or coordination of things, forces, etc.
14. *Genus-species* relationships.
15. *Similarity* or *dissimilarity.*
16. *Possibility* or *impossibility.*[5]

To illustrate how this list of universal topics might be used, let us consider a subject that crops up in the news periodically: "the possibility of a recession next year." How might the universal topics help you retrieve what you already know about this subject? Here are some examples of the kinds of things that might appear under the various topics:

1. *Existence:* Experts say there is a 70 percent possibility of a recession during the next twelve months.
2. *Degree:* Inflation will drop from 5.5 percent to 3.5 percent; production growth rate will fall from around 4 percent to a mere 2 percent; interest rates will continue to rise to approximately 12 percent and then drop to about 10 percent by the end of the year; unemployment will go up from 5.8 percent to about 7 percent.
3. *Space:* Some parts of the country will be harder hit by the recession than others: the industrial North the hardest, the Sun Belt states the least.
4. *Time:* The recession will not be a very long one, probably not over six to nine months in duration.
5. *Motion:* The entire economy has been too active for too long. To halt inflation we need a period when everything slows down.
6. *Form:* This will be only a recession, which is defined as two or more quarters of zero growth in the economy; it

will not be a depression, which is characterized by a period of deflation.

7. *Substance:* Some feel this recession will be only a minor correction leading to great growth in the years ahead. Others, primarily the doomsayers, see it as a harbinger of economic collapse in the United States.

8. *Capacity to change:* The government must be very careful as to how it responds to the recession. It must, for example, tighten federal spending, interest rates, and the money supply enough to bring down inflation, but not so much as to bring on a far more serious recession. With any wrong moves on the part of the government the recession could become much worse.

9. *Potency:* By rejecting the president's wage guidelines, organized labor has the power to stymie the administration's entire economic plan.

10. *Desirability:* A year ago few thought that a recession was desirable, but today most agree that such a slowdown is just what the economy needs.

11. *Feasibility:* Is it possible for economists to fine-tune the economy, or are the problems so complex that no one really understands them well enough to solve them?

12. *Causality:* Huge deficit spending by the federal government and an unfavorable balance of trade are the primary causes of inflation in the economy.

13. *Correlation:* In the past, as interest rates have gone up, people have stopped buying new housing. With inflation so high, however, this correlation seems to be breaking down, making estimates of housing starts next year very difficult.

14. *Genus-species:* Some of the key items that are included in figuring the consumer price index or the rate of inflation are the costs of housing, food, energy, and basic commodities such as steel and aluminum.

15. *Similarity-dissimilarity:* This recession will not be as pronounced as the recession of 1974, when the Dow-Jones Average fell by 40 percent.

16. *Possibility:* It is not possible to predict with certainty what will take place in the economy next year.

Notice three things about our examples: First, by the time you read this, all of the points listed above will be out of date. But you could generate an entirely new set of ideas by thinking about the current economic prospects. Second, many more points could have been listed under most of these topics since we are dealing with an enormously complex subject, the economy. With a less complex subject, certain topics would inevitably prove unproductive. If this should happen, simply move on to the next topic. Third, keep in mind that this is a system to promote your brainstorming. Not everything that comes to your mind will be useful for your speech. The main purpose of the system is to help you think through what *might be* said about your subject, from which you will then sift out *the most appropriate* for your speech.

Investigation

When you have exhausted your own store of knowledge, you will often find it necessary to begin a program of investigation. This may take many forms. It may include interviews with experts, eyewitnesses, or others who can contribute to your knowledge of the subject. It may involve attending meetings (student senate, public hearings, court proceedings, etc.) or checking through public records at the courthouse. It might include sending for materials through the mail or otherwise corresponding with key people. But most often it will require several trips to the library.

What a laboratory is to a scientist, a library is to one who would make speeches. We cannot provide here a course in how to do library research, but listed below are at least some of the sources of information you will find most useful in a library:

BOOKS. Every library contains books, books on all sorts of subjects, probably including yours. Go to the card catalog and look up your subject. Most card catalogs list each book under three separate headings: author, title, and subject. If there is no listing for your specific subject, look for related subjects. Check the various cross-references for additional information. For example, if your subject is "breeding cocker spaniels," you might look first under the primary heading "cocker spaniels." But you

---

A Fatal Mistake

If the matter is one that can be settled by observation, make the observation yourself. Aristotle could have avoided the mistake of thinking that women have fewer teeth than men by the simple device of asking Mrs. Aristotle to keep her mouth open while he counted. He did not do so because he thought he knew. Thinking you know when in fact you don't is a fatal mistake to which we are all prone.

Bertrand Russell

---

would also want to look under the headings "dogs," "pets," and "breeding," or "animals, breeding of."

Increasingly you can use the computer to do much of your library searching for you. Many libraries are now cataloged on computers instead of cards. You can search the library's entire holdings by author, title, or subject. In some libraries, when you call the entry up on your screen, the computer will tell you, not only all the bibliographic information you need, but also whether the item is on the shelf or checked out. Larger libraries also sometimes have other computer resources available which allow you to tap into additional banks of information, such as the well-known system called ERIC (Educational Resources Information Center). Your librarian will be happy to help you make the best of these resources.

PERIODICALS. Magazines and journals are another important source of information you can find in a library. To discover useful information in periodicals you will need to check the appropriate indices. The broadest and most useful index for most subjects is the *Readers' Guide to Periodical Literature*. Any library worth the name carries this important tool. The *Readers' Guide* lists by both subject and author all articles that appear in a wide range of over a hundred popular publications. The *Readers' Guide* is published in volumes that reach back to 1900. By examining a particular volume, you can discover all the articles on your subject that appeared during this period. Again, be sure to check all appropriate cross-references to your subject. More specialized indices are also available in better libraries. Moreover, many periodicals (*Christianity Today*, for one) publish a complete index of their contents at the end of each year. Such indices can be very useful for finding contemporary discussions of pertinent subjects.

NEWSPAPERS. Every day a prodigious amount of up-to-date information on an incredibly wide range of subjects is published in newspapers across the country. These, too, can be useful sources of information about your subject. The difficulty with newspapers, however, lies in wading through the great mass of material to find just the information you desire. Perhaps the best way to search, then, is to use the index to the *New York Times,* a detailed categorization of virtually all the information published in what is generally conceded to be the finest newspaper in the United States. Not all libraries will carry this index, or microfilm copies of the *Times* to go along with it, but where it is available, it can be a gold mine of relevant, up-to-date information.

REFERENCE WORKS. Among the handiest places to look for various kinds of information are the standard reference works. Encyclopedias such as the *Britannica, Americana, Collier's,* or the *World Book* are invaluable sources for the speaker. Information about famous people can also be found in such works as *Who's Who, The Dictionary of National Biography,* and *Current Biography.* Helpful sources of facts are the *World Almanac, Facts on File,* the *Guinness Book of World Records,* and the *Statistical Abstract of the United States.* Information about the government can also be found in such works as the *Congressional Record* and the *Congressional Quarterly Almanac.* Information about the Bible or theology can be discovered in a wide range of commentaries, dictionaries, lexicons, Bible encyclopedias, atlases, handbooks, and works on systematic theology. These and many other more specialized reference works populate the shelves of almost every good library.

UNIQUE SOURCES OF INFORMATION. Every library has its unique sources of information, such as a standing file of pamphlets or brochures. No one knows these sources better than does the librarian. In most cases the librarian will be a friendly professional who is trained to help people do just what you are attempting. Check with this key person for any additional sources of aid.

ON-LINE COMPUTER SEARCHES. Today you can "take a trip to the library" without ever leaving home. For those with a personal computer and modem, huge libraries (called *databases*) of books, periodicals, newspapers, newsletters, and other sources of information—many of them offering "full text," not just bibliographical information—are available on-line over your phone. Using this technology can still be expensive, but for those who can afford to take the plunge, the rewards are well worth it. The computer can revolutionize your hunt for information. To make the best use of such resources, a manual such as Alfred Glossbrenner's *How to Look It Up Online: Get the Information Edge with Your Personal Computer*[6] is highly recommended.

On Speechwriting

This is a very convenient time to be a speech writer, in terms of the technology and tools available. Two major technical innovations have revolutionized our craft. The first innovation, word processing, took much of the drudgery out of revision, and made it possible for us to turn out a better product, in less time. The second innovation, online full text database services, put a megalibrary at our fingertips.

Charles Parnell, Professional Speech Writer

Recording Your Research

In doing your research, you will inevitably need to take notes. Otherwise the information you uncover will slip through your fingers like sand. What form should your notes take? Essentially this is an individual decision since what works for one person may not necessarily work for another. But here are some standard time-savers that have proven so useful as to become conventional practice among those who research speeches regularly.

1. Do take notes. It requires more time to stop and write your discoveries down, but if you do not do so, you will usually lose them altogether.

2. Record your notes on cards, preferably three-by-five or four-by-six. Cards are much easier to handle and shuffle than ordinary paper.

3. Restrict each card to a single idea or point. Again, this takes more time at the outset, but once you start sorting your cards, it really pays off.

4. Always list the source of the material on the card. Be specific, including the page number. If you have to go back to the source for any reason or if you need to document the point, you will have the required information readily at hand.

5. Settle on some basic format for the card (for example, topic at the top left, information in the middle, bibliographic information at the bottom or on the back). Stick with this format throughout. Uniform cards are much easier and less confusing to use.

6. Always use quotation marks to set off quoted material. This prevents coming back to a card and wondering whether you paraphrased the material or quoted it verbatim.

7. Be sure to make explicit on each card why you recorded this material if there might be any possible question later on. Perhaps you will decide not to use it after all, but at least you will know what it was for.

8. Record too much material rather than too little. You will be much more comfortable if you have more information than you need rather than not enough.

Avoiding Plagiarism

As one humorist put it, stealing your ideas from a single source is plagiarism, while stealing them from a variety of sources is research. At least the humorist was half right: taking someone else's ideas or writings and passing them off as your own is indeed plagiarism.

Plagiarism is a form of theft. As such, Christians above all should take it seriously and work to avoid it. All you need to do to avoid plagiarism is to follow three simple rules:

1. *Cite your sources.* Seldom will all the content of your speech be original to you. Usually you will depend upon other sources. This is perfectly appropriate provided you let your audience know when you are using someone else's material. You

need not and usually should not try to give your audience full bibliographic details. It is usually sufficient to use such phrases as:

"The lead article in last week's issue of *Newsweek* stated that . . ."

"Peggy Wilson, the director of the local Planned Parenthood office, states . . ."

"According to the *Handbook of Social Psychology* . . . "

"Senator Smith has said that . . ."

2. *Use a variety of sources.* You will sometimes be tempted to take your speech from a single source—say, a well-written, concise article in the *Reader's Digest.* But too much dependence on a single work is a prescription for plagiarism. Seek out a variety of sources rather than merely summarize some other person's material.

3. *Make an original contribution.* The best way to avoid plagiarism is to make your speech an original contribution. You may well be drawing upon a variety of other sources or authorities, along with your own ideas, but the way you organize and build this material together into a single speech can be original to you. This will make your speech more than just a rehash of what others have said.

Decide What You Want to Say about Your Subject

You now have a subject that you have researched. But as it stands, it is not a complete thought. It is simply a statement of what you want to talk *about.* Your next task is to decide (again, keeping your own and your audience's needs generally in mind) what one major thing you want to say about it out of all the possible things you *could* say about it. The result of this decision will be your complement. Together your subject and complement will constitute the main idea of your speech.

Need for a Complement

We have said that a speech, to be maximally effective, should function as a unit. We have also said that the finest way of promoting such *unit*-y is to construct the speech around a single, generative idea; this idea will inevitably consist of both subject and complement(s). Let us acknowledge here at least a partial qualification to these points.

It must be conceded that a speech that is built around a single *subject* will demonstrate a certain degree of unity, and the more narrow the subject, the more that unity will become evident. Such a speech would at least be *more* unified than a speech which consisted merely of a series of statements about different subjects. Thus, it would be possible to take your subject as it now stands, decide upon several different things you want to say about it, and then make these the main points in your message,

---

Eloquence consists in saying all that should be, not all that could be said.

---

even though these several different points do not combine to drive home any single *central* idea. Many speeches we hear are nothing more than this, and we must acknowledge that this type of organization is at least one possible way of designing a speech.

Let it also be said, however, that it is an inferior way. We can do better, go further, work harder to give our speeches more communicative thrust. We can refuse to settle for the semiunity a central *subject* may provide and push on to the more rigorous but more effective approach which requires us to design a speech around a complete *idea*, including both subject and complement. Virtually all the experts—practitioners, theorists, and researchers alike—agree that this is the type of speech that, other things being equal, will communicate with maximum effectiveness.

So, a properly narrowed subject is not sufficient. You need a complement, a statement of the main point you want to assert *about* your subject. This complement will govern virtually all the rest of the material of the speech. Thus it is very important that it be stated clearly and concisely.

"Mode" of the Complement

Almost all complements will be in the *indicative, imperative,* or *conditional* mode. The *indicative* mode, first, simply asserts that something *is* (or *was,* or *will be*) the case. These ideas are all examples of the indicative mode: "Vegetarianism is increasing in the United States"; "Vegetarianism promotes better health"; "There are three different types of vegetarians: strict 'vegans,' lactovegetarians, and ovolactovegetarians." Each of these ideas holds some particular thing or state to be the case. The *imperative* mode, by contrast, asserts that something *ought to be the case.* Examples: "Vegetarianism should be banned in the United States"; "Everyone ought to give vegetarianism a try"; "Refuse all meat in your diet." Note that in each of these statements there is the assertion that something ought to be the case. In the command "Refuse all meat in your diet," the words "you should" are only implied, but they propel the idea nonetheless. Third, the *conditional* mode (sometimes called the *subjunctive* mode) allows some question as to whether something is (was, will be) or ought to be the case. For example, "Vegetarian diets may be dangerous to your health" is in the conditional mode. So also is: "At some point in life everyone should probably consider becoming a vegetarian." Both of these statements are qualified ("may be," "probably"), suggesting that under certain circumstances their validity would be less certain.

"Dictated" Complements

Many subjects dictate to some degree what their complement(s) must be. For example, the subject in a multiple-complement idea generally requires certain specific complements to finish it. Thus, if your subject is "the benefits of jogging," the complements will obviously have to spell out what those benefits are. In much the same way adverbial subjects tend to carry implicit limitations upon your choice of complement. If your subject is "why stocks are a better long-term investment than bonds," your complement(s) must constitute some sort of reason(s). Thus your complement is again dictated to a significant degree by the way you have stated your subject.

As a general rule, the *more narrow* your subject, the more likely it is that your complement will be dictated by it. The *broader* the subject, the more likely it is that you will have a broader range of complements from which to choose. What this amounts to, then, is that sooner or later your idea must be *limited*. If this is not accomplished early on, in the choice of your subject, it must be done later in the choice of your complement.

Whereas both adverbial and multiple-complement subjects tend to be inherently more narrow, thus dictating to a large extent what the complement(s) must be, nominal subjects generally offer a wider range of possibilities. Consider, for example, the nominal subject "black holes." There is no hint here as to what the complement might be. One might add the complement "Black holes *are the figments of astronomers' imaginations.*" Or, "Black holes *are one of the great scientific mysteries of the universe.*" Or, "Black holes *may one day be harnessed to supply all the energy man will ever need.*" These are only three of an almost endless range of possible assertions about black holes. In any

---

In speech making, as in life, not failure, but low aim, is crime.
W. M. Parish

---

case, settling upon one such complement narrows the idea so that it becomes manageable.

Note that we might have narrowed the scope of the idea by limiting the subject. Suppose, for example, that instead of the relatively general nominal subject "black holes," we had chosen the adverbial subject "how black holes are formed" or the multiple-complement subject "the potential benefits of black holes to humankind." In both cases the subject would have been greatly narrowed and the choice of complements would have been restricted proportionately.

State Your Complete Idea

How broad is your subject? Have you narrowed it to such an extent that your complement is already indicated? If so, you need only state your complement clearly to have the central idea of your speech. If not, then you must narrow your idea appropriately through the choice of your complement. Once you have done this, combine your complement with your subject so that you have a single declarative sentence. This statement is the *first draft* of the central idea of your speech.

The reason this statement is only a first draft of your speech idea is that in most cases the thought will need to be refined considerably to be maximally effective. Up to now you have probably had your audience in mind only very generally. This is quite acceptable. But now you need to focus the idea very specifically to the needs of your listeners. As part of this focusing process, you will need to analyze thoroughly your own purposes: Why are you presenting this idea to this audience? What do you hope to accomplish? This analysis, as we shall see, will frequently require that you revise your preliminary idea considerably. Moreover, up to this point you have been concerned only with articulating your thought accurately, for *your own* understanding. Now you must also address the question, *What wording will communicate the idea most clearly and effectively to my auditors?* This sort of focusing will usually require a rigorous reworking of the statement as it now stands.

Exercises

1. Choose ten sentences at random from this book, being careful to avoid compound sentences. Then divide each full sentence into its subject and complement(s). Remember, do not simply look for the *grammatical* subject. Ask yourself in each case, What is he talking about? (subject), and What is he saying about it? (complement).

2. Think of some group of which you are a part. Then for each of the following categories come up with three subjects which might be worked into a speech to your

group: (a) nominal subject, (b) adverbial subject, (c) relational subject, (d) multiple-complement subject, and (e) predicating subject.

3. Choose a speech subject with which you are familiar. Then use Wilson and Arnold's list of universal topics to brainstorm about your subject. Try to discover from your own mind something under each of the universal topics.

4. As the teacher of a course in public speaking for a group of high-school students, you must give a ten-minute lecture on one of these subjects: the importance of having a central idea in a speech, using a library effectively, or how to take notes when doing research. Using the material in this chapter and any other help you can find, put together an outline of that lecture.

Chapter **4**

How to Focus Your Idea

You now have a preliminary statement of the idea which will form the hub of your speech. It is still a *tentative* statement because you have until now kept your audience only very generally in mind. You believe that the idea will meet your audience's basic requirements, but you have not yet thought through clearly just *how* this may be the case. Where exactly does your audience stand in regard to this idea? What are you trying to accomplish by communicating this idea to your audience? How must the idea be focused to reach the audience and meet whatever their need for the idea may be? These are the questions you must answer to discover a true "rhetorical stance."

Taking a Stance

"Rhetorical stance" is a term coined by Wayne Booth, a professor of English at the University of Chicago, in an article in the journal *College Composition and Communication*.[1] Though the article mainly addresses the task of writing, Booth's point concerns public speakers as well. Several of his illustrations are actually drawn from speeches delivered orally, indicating that the thrust of the article is as applicable to the spoken word as to the written. Booth's ideas are so pertinent to our purposes here, in fact, that they deserve our careful attention.

Booth begins his article with this story:

> Last fall I had an advanced graduate student, bright, energetic, well-informed, whose papers were almost unreadable. He managed to be pretentious, dull, and disorganized in his paper on

Emma, and pretentious, dull, and disorganized on *Madame Bovary.* On *The Golden Bowl* he was all these and obscure as well. Then one day, toward the end of the term, he cornered me after class and said, "You know, I think you were all wrong about Robbe-Grillet's *Jealousy* today." We didn't have time to discuss it, so I suggested that he write me a note about it. Five hours later I found in my faculty box a four-page polemic, unpretentious, stimulating, organized, convincing. Here was a man who had taught freshmen composition for several years and who was incapable of committing any of the more obvious errors that we think of as characteristic of bad writing. Yet he could not write a decent sentence, paragraph, or paper until his rhetorical problem was solved—until, that is, he had found a definition of his audience, his argument, and his own proper tone of voice.[2]

The difference between the student's previous efforts and the note that caught Booth's attention was that in the former the

---

The habit of common and continuous speech is a symptom of mental deficiency.   Walter Bagehot

---

student was merely going through the motions of communicating to his "audience" without any clear understanding of *why* he was doing so. But in the note to his professor he had a *goal* in his writing, a *purpose* which propelled him, a *reason* that motivated his communication. In short, he discovered a "rhetorical stance" and it transformed his entire effort.

According to Booth, an appropriate rhetorical stance always involves "discovering and maintaining a . . . proper balance among the three elements that are at work in any communicative effort: the available arguments about the subject itself, the interests and peculiarities of the audience, and the voice, the implied character of the speaker." Though we may never come to the point where discovering and maintaining this balance is easy, we nevertheless need to see that it is just this balance that "makes the difference between effective communication and mere wasted effort."

Losing Your Balance

To clarify his point, Booth discusses three frequent *corruptions* of the balance required for a true "rhetorical stance." The first he calls the "pedant's stance." This approach

> consists of ignoring or underplaying the personal relationship of speaker and audience and depending entirely on statements about a subject—that is, the notion of a job to be done for a particular audience is left out. It is a virtue, of course, to respect the bare truth of one's subject, and there may be even some subjects which in their very nature define an audience and a rhetorical purpose so that adequacy to the subject can be the whole art of presentation. For example, an article on "the relation of the ontological and teleological proofs," in a recent *Journal of Religion*, requires a minimum of adaptation of argument to audience. But most subjects do not in themselves imply in any necessary way a purpose and an audience and hence a speaker's tone. The writer who assumes that it is enough merely to write an exposition of what he happens to know on the subject will produce the kind of essay that soils our scholarly journals, written not for readers, but for bibliographies.[3]

Booth calls this kind of communication "empty fencing," an approach that characterizes much of the writing of his own students. Actually Booth puts part of the blame for this on himself as teacher because, as he notes, the student has "not been led to see a question which he considers worth answering, or an audience that could possibly care one way or the other." As a result, the typical paper "is worse than no paper at all, even though it has no grammatical or spelling errors and is organized right down the line, one, two, three." Agreeing with Jacques Barzun in *Teacher in America,* Booth states: "Students should be made to feel that unless they have said something to someone, they have failed; to bore the teacher is a worse form of failure than to anger him."

If the pedant's stance stems from ignoring the audience or relying too much upon the subject, Booth argues, secondly, that the "advertiser's stance" comes from "*under*valuing the subject and *over*valuing pure effect." Those taking this stance do not hesitate to shade the truth of the matter in favor of accomplishing a certain result.

The advertiser's stance is to be distinguished from valid audience adaptation, of course, a point that is sometimes difficult for beginners to comprehend. As Booth says, "Having told them that good writers always to some degree accommodate their arguments to the audience, it is hard to explain the difference between justified accommodation—*say* changing point one to the final position—and the kind of accommodation that fills our popular magazines, in which the very substance of what is said is accommodated to some preconception of what will sell." Yet as difficult as the line may be to draw, it is nevertheless a valid and necessary one. Taking the advertiser's stance is tantamount to abdicating one's responsibility as speaker or writer, a responsibility which springs from the fact that as communicators we have "a purpose concerning a subject which itself cannot be fundamentally modified by the desire to persuade." Inevitably, says Booth, the products of such an abdication are ignoble, as illustrated by these two examples from the realm of spoken discourse:

> If Edmund Burke had decided that he could win more votes in Parliament by choosing the other side—as he most certainly could have done—we'd hardly hail this party-switch as a master stroke of rhetoric. If Churchill had offered the British "peace in our time," with some laughs thrown in, because opinion polls had shown that more Britishers were "grabbed" by these than by blood, sweat, and tears, we could hardly call his decision a sign of rhetorical skill.[4]

Booth also deals briefly with a third perversion of the rhetorical stance. This he calls the "entertainer's stance": "the willingness to sacrifice substance to personality and charm." Here the gifted speaker who has learned to manipulate an audience by the sheer power of his charisma and ability with words, at the expense of both the subject matter and the autonomy of the people in his audience, is likewise perverting a true "rhetorical stance."

If we were to liken maintaining the balance of Booth's rhetorical stance to walking a tightrope, it would probably be accurate to say that the pedant's stance would represent the danger of falling to the one side while the advertiser's and the entertainer's stances would represent the dangers of falling to the other. The pedant's stance involves the *failure to think through one's purpose* in communicating, while the other two involve *so overvaluing one's purpose* that the truth of the matter is lost in the shuffle.

Avoiding Pedantry

Beginning speakers will generally be more likely to fall into the pedant's stance than either of the other two. Obviously we cannot be guilty of letting our purpose wrongly dominate our efforts until we have at least chosen some purpose. Only when we have set our goals for a speech is it possible that those goals can improperly influence our work. The novice will more often be guilty of failing to focus his goals sufficiently, or of failing to follow through on those goals sufficiently, than of running with those goals beyond proper limits.

Letters dropped into the post office without addresses go to the dead-letter box, and are of no use to anybody.   John Hall

---

To be sure, once we have formulated our goals in communication, the dangers on the other side of the tightrope become real. While it is the temptation especially of the gifted and experienced speaker to fall into the entertainer's stance, the advertiser's stance poses a danger to almost everyone, *especially those who are required to fulfill some assigned goal or purpose.* But for now let us think about how to avoid the *pitfall of pedantry.*

The problem of the pedant, as Booth describes him, is that he has not thought through his *purpose* for communication. He has no *goal*. Why? Because he has ignored his audience. He has become so caught up in his subject matter that he has misplaced the whole point of communication: to reach a particular audience with a message. As we have already emphasized, in any effective communication the audience must inevitably be a *determining factor,* a point that pedants seem not to understand.

The way to avoid pedantry is to give due weight to the audience. (I say *due weight* because to allow the audience to *overin*fluence our efforts is to slip off into the advertiser's or entertainer's stance. That tightrope again!) Now that we have the subject matter of our speech and we know the general direction in which we want to move with it, we must turn to our audience and put to use the analysis we have struggled to accumulate. Our goal in all of this will be a clear and specific purpose for the speech. This purpose will then govern both the final wording of our speech idea and the overall development of the speech itself. If arrived at properly, the purpose can save us from the pitfall of pedantry.

Discovering Your Purpose

Sometimes the purpose for your speech will lie handily about on the surface, and you will need to do little more than pick it up, dust it off, and word it accurately. Purpose statements are not always difficult to come by. On most occasions, however, coming up with a clear and worthwhile purpose will require a more stringent process. Either way, to be an effective speaker you need to understand the nature of the various purposes which speeches may have, what your options are, and how choosing among these options will influence your speech. What follows, then, is an analysis of the most common purposes, with some direction as to how you may go about discovering which is the most appropriate for your speech.

There are essentially only three things you can do with an idea: (1) you can explain it, (2) you can prove it, or (3) you can demonstrate the implications of it. In one way or another almost everything you may do with your idea will fall into one of these three categories: *explanation, proof,* or *implication.*

In most speeches two or even all three of these will be present. At one point you may be defining, at another point you may be offering evidence, and at another you may be developing implications. But in most effective speeches *only one of these categories will dominate.* The others become merely means to an end, rather than ends in themselves.

Notice that these three categories represent a progression. Understanding precedes belief, and both understanding and belief precede acting upon what we believe. Thus we might settle for trying to explain something without proving it, but we cannot settle for proving something our audience does not yet understand. In the same way, showing the implications of something requires that we first explain what it is and prove it to be true. Of course, if our audience already understands something we want to prove, we need not first belabor the definition; likewise, if our audience already understands and accepts as true some point, we do not have to spend a great deal of time explaining and proving before we get on with the business of demonstrating its implications. Why use a battering ram on an open door? The important point to note here is that we may settle for one step of the process without proceeding to the next, but we cannot decide to focus on a subsequent step while ignoring the prior one(s).

Step One: The Audience's Need

The above analysis leads us to the first step in deciding upon the purpose of your speech. The first step is to determine the audience's need for your idea. Do not be confused by the term *need.* We are not necessarily speaking here of some deep craving of your audience's heart that this speech is designed to satisfy (although we sometimes do deal on this level, especially if we are grappling with spiritual issues). We are using the term much more broadly to seek out the point of *relevance* for your audience. If you were to conclude that the audience has no need for your idea, you would in fact be saying that the speech would be irrelevant to them, in which case you should by all means cease working on the project. But if, on the other hand, the choice of subject and complement has been made with your audience generally in mind, the problem will usually lie not so much in deciding *whether* the idea is relevant but rather in deciding *how* it is relevant. *In what way* is this idea pertinent to your audience? What must you as a speaker do with this subject matter *to show* its pertinence to your audience?

Inevitably the need grows out of a consideration of both (1) the subject matter and (2) the audience. Obviously, the need of the *same audience* will vary with *different subjects;* just as certainly *different audiences* will have different needs with respect to the *same subject.* Only when both the audience and the subject matter have been given their full weight can we come to an adequate understanding of the pertinence of our material.

To demonstrate this point, let us consider a specific example. Suppose your tentative idea is "America needs to look to nuclear power as the energy source of the future." Given this idea, let us think through how the need would vary from audience to audi-

---

When a man does not know what harbor he is making for, no wind is the right wind. Seneca

---

ence. Suppose that your audience is a group of people gathered for a friend's birthday party. Almost certainly we would conclude that this idea is a poor, if not hopeless, choice for this audience. Remember that the concept of an "audience" includes not merely the people you are speaking to but the setting and the occasion as well. Regardless of who these people might be, it is almost inconceivable that they would find a speech on nuclear power relevant to their birthday celebration. Thus, for this audience *in this situation,* little or no need would exist for your idea. At best, the speech would produce boredom; at worst, it might produce outright hostility. Obviously, a more appropriate idea should be chosen for this occasion.

Now let us change the picture. Suppose that the audience is a group of elderly people in a nursing home. While this would be a very different audience from the first one, the subject would probably be equally irrelevant to them, albeit for a different reason. Although we can conceive of a particularly lively group of elderly citizens finding such a speech pertinent, in most cases this audience would simply tune the speaker out. They would perceive no need for this speech. Again, for this audience the topic would probably be a poor one.

But now, a bit more realistically, suppose the audience is a group of third-grade children studying a science unit. What is the need of this audience for our idea? One would probably have to do a great deal of *explaining.* In such cases information would dominate the speech, so much so that the idea itself would have to be reworked, perhaps to "An important source of energy in America is nuclear power." Notice how the idea has been softened for this audience. It is not as strongly worded, and it is limited to merely *informing* the audience. The speech might include simple explanations of how a nuclear reactor works, statistics on how much of our energy presently comes from nuclear power, and even, perhaps, authoritative predictions about the growth of the industry. It probably would *not* include persuasive arguments about whether nuclear power should be abandoned or stepped up. It would no doubt be irresponsible to expose children at this level to the force of the persuasive arguments surrounding this hotly debated public issue. Thus, a speaker would probably want to limit herself to providing *information* for the children rather than trying to prove a point to them, much less trying to mobilize them into action. Though we might again think of exceptional cases, for the most part the need of a group of third-grade children would lie more in the realm of *explanation* than either *proof* or *implication.*

But suppose the audience is a class of not third graders but college students taking an elective ecology course. Now the situation changes dramatically. The need for information would probably be lessened, but the need for proof would be much greater. The same would be true if the audience is, say, a group of petroleum-company executives. In both cases we could perhaps assume *a relatively knowledgeable but unconvinced* group. Thus, the need of these two audiences would probably lie in the realm of proof.

Suppose, once more, that our idea was to be communicated to a group of state or federal legislators. It is conceivable that such an audience would have needs in all three areas: they might require information, proof, and implications. The speaker might have to *explain* the alternatives, *prove* that nuclear power is the best alternative, and then *mobilize* the audience, say, to vote in a particular way on a bill that is coming before the legislature. The same tasks might face a speaker who wishes to communicate our idea to a group of people gathered around a soapbox out on a busy street corner, but in this case the vote would be at the ballot box rather than in the legislature. Notice that in these two situations, while the speaker would be required to *explain* and *prove*, both are but means used to motivate the audience to behave in a particular way. Thus, the dominating thrust of the speech would be to *demonstrate implications* (i.e., so to move the audience that they not only *know* or *believe* a particular something, but *behave* in a particular way).

Finally, consider the need which a convention of nuclear engineers might have for our idea. The need would certainly not lie in the realm of *information*. The audience might well know more about nuclear power than does the speaker. Nor, most likely, would the need lie in the area of *proof* (although it is conceivable that a speaker might desire to *reinforce* some belief the audience already holds). Probably the thrust of the speech would lie in the third area, tracing out some sort of *implications for the audience,* helping them to see what their knowledge and belief about the matter require of them. For example, the speaker might attempt to move the audience to begin a concerted lobbying effort in the legislature, thus implementing what they already know and believe about nuclear power in America.

What this analysis demonstrates is that the need for a given idea will vary with the audience. The opposite is also true; the need of a given audience will vary with the subject matter, a point we could demonstrate through a similar analysis. But let us make do with a single example: Suppose the audience is a group of stu-

Figure 4
The Need of the Audience

Tentative Idea: America needs to look to nuclear power as the energy source of the future.

	Explanation	Proof	Implication
Third graders studying a science unit	Entire emphasis	None	None
College students taking an elective ecology course	Some	Main emphasis	None
A group of state or federal legislators	Some	Much	Ultimate emphasis
A crowd gathered around a soapbox on a street corner	Some	Much	Ultimate emphasis
A convention of nuclear engineers	Little	Little	Almost the entire emphasis

dents enrolled in a college speech class. Suppose also that the speaker has chosen the idea "Black holes in outer space represent the most extreme form of matter known to science." The need of the audience in regard to this idea would probably lie in the realm of *explanation.* But suppose the idea is "Divorce is the single greatest danger to the family in America." Here the need of the same audience would probably lie in the realm of *proof,* and any information the speaker provides will be a *means* of prompting the audience to believe. Or again, suppose that the speaker's idea is "We as students should help shoulder the burden of financing the new student-union building." Clearly the weight here falls in the area of *implication,* with any information or proof serving mainly as a *means* to moving the audience to action.

It is not difficult to see that the need you must address can be discovered only in the light of *both the subject matter and the audience.* Thus the first step toward determining a clear purpose for your speech is to weigh the idea you have chosen and the audience you will address and then to decide which of the three types of material will dominate your message: explanation, proof, or implication. If your answer is *explanation,* then your speech probably will not include much proof or motivational material. You have decided that what your audience needs is information about your subject, and the speech will be designed to communicate it to them in a clear, interesting, and orderly fashion. If your answer is *proof,* then your speech may or may not include substantial amounts of explanatory material, de-pending on how well your audience understands your subject. What is certain, though, is that whatever information you pre-sent will be basically a necessary preliminary to the primary thrust of your speech, which lies in the realm of proof. If your answer is *implication,* then your speech may or may not deal with explanation and proof, depending upon the requirements of the audience. But if it includes explanation and proof, both of these will function primarily as a means to demonstrating the implications of your idea for the behavior of your audience.

Step Two: The Desired Response

The second step toward coming up with a purpose for your speech is to decide upon what *response* you desire from your audi-ence. This is not something separate from the consideration of your audience's *need,* but in fact is the natural outgrowth of it. The response you desire from your audience can be expressed through the use of infinitives which correspond to the three categories of need: "I want my audience *to understand how* . . . " (explanation); "I want my audience *to believe that* . . . " (proof); "I want my audi-ence *to behave [in some particular way]*" (implication).

Figure 5
The Response Desired

Tentative Idea: America needs to look to nuclear power as the energy source of the future.

	To understand	To believe	To behave in some particular way
Third graders studying a science unit	*To understand that nuclear power is one of the important sources of energy in America*	None	None
College students taking an elective ecology course	Some, as a basis for belief	*To accept nuclear power as one useful source of energy in America's future, despite its potential hazards*	None
A group of state or federal legislators	Some, as a basis for action	Much, as a basis for action	*To vote yes on a bill which limits environmental controls on nuclear power*
A crowd gathered around a soapbox on a street corner	Some, as a basis for action	Much, as a basis for action	*To vote in favor of allowing a nuclear-power plant to be built locally*
A convention of nuclear engineers	Little	Little, and only as a reinforcement	*To initiate an organized lobbying effort in Congress*

It would not be an overstatement to say that the main idea of this whole section is that you should always be seeking *some* response from your audience. Indeed, the pitfall of pedantry lies just here: the pedant merely goes through the motions without any thought of what response he seeks from his audience. But this is an oversight you cannot afford if you want to be an effective communicator. You must always attempt to elicit a response of some sort from your audience, and it is always helpful to pin down just what that response is to be.

Figure 5 is a chart of potential responses a speaker might seek from several of the audiences we have examined. The tentative statement of the speech idea is "America needs to look to nuclear power as the energy source of the future." (Notice that the speaker's *preliminary* statement of the idea, as it stands, is *already inadequate* for all but the college audience, and even here it will probably have to be softened to something like "America should look to nuclear power as one useful energy source for the future." We will deal with the matter of reformulating the statement of the speech idea later in this chapter.)

Step Three: Wording the Purpose of the Speech

The third step is to put into words the *purpose* of the speech. Having focused upon the audience's need and, from that, having pinned down the response that you desire to elicit from them, you are now prepared to articulate in a single, clear, concise sentence what you hope to accomplish through the speech. Like the statement of the desired response, this purpose statement will usually be built around one of three infinitives which correspond to the three categories of need: "My purpose is *to inform* my audience how . . . " (explanation); "My purpose is *to persuade* my audience that . . . " (proof); "My purpose is *to motivate* my audience *to behave [in some particular way]*" (implication).

The Three Types of Speeches

The three types of purposes we have examined correspond to the three primary types of speeches: (1) the informative speech, (2) the persuasive speech, (3) the speech to actuate. But notice

Figure 6
The Purpose for the Speech

Tentative Idea: America needs to look to nuclear power as the energy source of the future.

	To understand	To believe	To behave in some particular way
Third graders studying a science unit	*To inform the audience that nuclear power is one of the important sources of energy in America*	None	None
College students taking an elective ecology course	Some, as a step for belief	*To persuade the audience that nuclear power can be accepted as one important source of energy in America's future without hazarding the ecology*	None
A group of state or federal legislators	Some, as a step for action	Much, as a necessary preliminary to moving the audience to action	*To mobilize the audience to vote yes on a bill which limits environmental controls on nuclear power*
A crowd gathered around a soapbox on a street corner	Some, as a step for action	Much, as a necessary preliminary to moving the audience to action	*To mobilize the audience to vote in favor of allowing a nuclear-power plant to be built locally*
A convention of nuclear engineers	Little	Little	*To mobilize the audience to begin an organized lobbying effort in Congress*

that these purposes are not so much something which you bring to the situation as they are something that you *discover within the situation*. In a very real sense it is the audience that determines the purpose of the speech, not you the speaker. Let us look more closely at each of these three types of speeches.

The Speech to Inform

Informative speeches are common, everyday occurrences. In business, education, the military, the church, and in many social settings, speeches that are designed to accomplish little more than inform an audience about some particular subject abound.

The distinguishing mark of the informative speech is its *limited objective*. The sole purpose of the speech is to clarify, explain, describe, define, report, or otherwise broaden the audience's knowledge about some concept, term, process, relationship, or other subject. The speaker's goal is simply to enable the audience to grasp and then retain the material.

Because of the nature of this goal, informative speeches consist largely, if not entirely, of *factual material*. Factual materials are those which are independently verifiable, such as historical events, statistics, scientific laws or principles, and other settled, noncontroversial, demonstrable observations. Hence, by their very nature, informative speeches call for *understanding* from the audience, not *belief* or *debate*. Your prime responsibilities when you give an informative speech are to present the material honestly (separating fact from opinion), completely (not leaving out pertinent aspects of the subject), clearly (so that the material can be understood), and accurately (so that the result is not misleading).

While informative speeches seem simple enough at first glance, there are several obstacles they must typically hurdle. The first is the *difficulty of being clear*. The explanation of a complex process, relationship, or concept is not easy. You must work to keep the structure of the message simple. This can be accomplished by (1) limiting the number of major points in the structure of the outline; (2) keeping the transitions clear; (3) including abundant internal summaries; (4) using simple, nontechnical language; (5) defining any ambiguous terms; and (6) making the abstract concrete through the use of analogies, comparisons, contrasts, examples, and even visual aids (see chap. 6).

The second major difficulty of the informative speech is the *problem of gaining and holding the attention of the audience*. Factual material in itself is seldom very exciting. Thus informative speeches can easily become drab and boring. But drabness can usually be replaced with color by employing (1) vivid language, (2) concrete and specific illustrations, (3) hypothetical examples, and (4) human-interest narrative. Each of these should be used in such a way as to relate the new ideas of the speech to the existing knowledge of the audience.

The third obstacle for the informative speech is the *tendency of speakers to cover too much material too quickly*. It is far better to limit the subject and cover it well than to take on a broader subject and then swamp the audience with more information than they can assimilate. The tendency to attempt too much within a given time limit, which is a common one, usually stems from naiveté. We assume that because something is clear to us it will therefore be equally clear to our audience. This unfortunate assumption has doomed many an informative speech! At other times the tendency to cover too much material may stem from a desire to impress the audience with all that we know. Such a temptation must be resisted if we intend to communicate effectively. Once again we must adapt ourselves to our audience, to their capacity to receive information, so that we do not overload them and thereby undermine the effectiveness of the entire speech.

The Speech to Persuade

Persuasive speeches are even more prevalent in our society than informative speeches. Whether politicians, salespersons, philosophers, scientists, or ministers, in countless ways persuaders on every side of us compete for our endorsement of their ideas, even as we compete for their endorsement of ours. In a free society this is the way the business of living is carried on.

The persuasive speech involves a dimension not found in the informative speech. Instead of seeking merely to engender *comprehension* in an audience, the persuasive speaker is seeking to induce his audience to believe, to accept, *to yield to some particular point of view.* The goal is fundamentally to win approval or secure a favorable attitude toward some specific position, or, at the very least, to deepen or reinforce some belief the audience already holds. Thus the persuasive speech will always grapple with issues which have at least two sides to them. Unlike the informative speech, which deals largely with noncontroversial material, a persuasive speech will always attempt to influence the audience toward one side or another of an issue that is debatable in some way.

Suppose, for example, that one could range the viewpoints concerning a given subject on a continuum from -10 to +10. In this case, -10 would indicate a strongly negative view, +10 a strongly positive view, and the midpoint of 0 a position of neutrality. Supposing that you are advocating a position hovering around +9, you might settle for attempting to move a hostile

---

The most powerful stimulus for changing a person's mind is not a chemical. It's not an electric shock. It's not a baseball bat. It's a word. George A. Miller

---

audience (-8) to neutrality (0); or you might attempt to move a neutral audience (0) to a positive position (+8); or you might attempt *to reinforce* in a positively disposed audience (+7) the views they already hold. But in each of these examples you would be intent upon moving the audience to some point on the spectrum and then strengthening their beliefs so as to keep them there.

Thus persuasion may be defined as the use of the various resources of discourse to influence the beliefs of an audience in some predetermined way. To accomplish this goal you may attempt to refute opposing views as well as to inculcate your own. In either case, however, you will in some way identify the ideas you are discussing with the existing attitudes, beliefs, and values of your audience. What you want to refute will be related to the negative elements of the audience's belief system, while the ideas you want to advance will be related to the positive elements of their belief system. In its simplest form this is the way persuasion works.

The Speech to Actuate

As the persuasive speech represents a step beyond the informative, so also the speech to actuate represents a step beyond simple persuasion. In the persuasive speech the goal is to change some belief or attitude of the audience in some predetermined way. In the *speech to actuate* the goal is *to mobilize* the audience; to impel them to action of some sort; to move them to begin, continue, or cease some behavior. This goal will normally require some preliminary attention to both information and persuasion, but the overall thrust of the speech will be to move the audience to *behave* in some particular way. The desired behavior might be voting, giving money, making a purchase, joining a cause, signing a petition, instituting some program, accepting Christ, or any other specific action. It is this additional dimension of action that distinguishes the speech to actuate from the persuasive speech.

The line we are drawing between a speech to persuade and a speech to actuate may be illustrated by this example:

> A great many public speeches are made to the electorate, even in non-election years, about the foreign policy of the administration. The actual authority for controlling this policy lies with the President and with Congress, yet speakers outside the administration attempt to influence the beliefs of the ordinary citizen. Why? Because these beliefs, through the influence they can assert upon public opinion, ultimately will affect the government's foreign policies and help shape the nation's future course of action abroad. The immediate purpose of the speakers, however, is not to prompt performance, not to gain action in the form of a vote, but merely to win agreement and belief. Later, of course, the candidates for President and Congress may speak on the same subjects in an attempt to actuate—to urge or impel people to exert a direct influence on foreign policy by voting in a cer-

tain way at the next election. In the first case, the speaker's purpose is merely to persuade the audience; in the second, the purpose is to secure action based upon persuasion.[5]

We need to acknowledge here that the distinctions we are suggesting between informing, persuading, and actuating are in some ways arbitrary distinctions. Mainly the issue revolves around how one chooses to define "persuasion."

According to the broadest definition of this flexible term, all of language is "persuasive." Every time we attempt to communicate we are trying to influence someone in some way. In this broadest usage, therefore, even speeches to inform would be considered attempts to "persuade."

Defined somewhat more narrowly (but still not in the way we are using the term in this book), the word *persuasion* may also be used to describe a process that *always* includes action as the goal. Thus "persuasion" is broken down into the five theoretical steps of *attention, comprehension, yielding, retention,* and *action.* Each of these steps must occur, with each building upon the last, for "persuasion" to take place. Thus, by this definition all speeches to "persuade" would also be speeches to actuate.

But we are using the term *persuasion* still more narrowly here. The five-step process we have just mentioned will be helpful in making the distinction. We are using the term *inform* to designate only the first two steps in the process: *attention* and *comprehension.* The speaker who sets out to deliver an informative speech limits his focus primarily to these first two goals. The persuasive speaker, by contrast, is a bit more ambitious. His goal is to induce not only *attention* and *comprehension,* but also *yielding* to some particular proposal. More ambitious still is the speaker who decides that actuation is her goal. She has before her the difficult task of inducing in her audience all five of the steps, including *retention* and *action.*

Thus the primary difference between the informative, persuasive, and actuating speeches is how far through the five-step process the speaker attempts to carry the audience. With certain subjects and audiences you may wish to settle for simply getting the audience started in the process by providing basic, noncontroversial information for them. On other occasions, per-

Figure 7
The Persuasive Process

	1. Attention	2. Comprehension	3. Yielding	4. Retention	5. Action
Need	Explanation		Proof	Implication	
Response	To understand		To believe	To behave in a particular way	
Purpose	To inform		To persuade	To actuate	

haps with a different subject or audience, you will want to attempt the more ambitious goal of influencing the audience, not merely to understand, but to yield to (that is, to accept) some debatable proposition about the subject. And on still other occasions you may want to set the goal of not merely inducing comprehension and yielding in the audience, but of advocating some particular way of responding to the subject being presented. When you decide that this most ambitious of goals is the appropriate one, the message will become a speech to actuate.

The five-step process thus becomes a helpful tool for thinking about the three major purposes which speeches may have. These three purposes represent successive stages upon which you may decide to concentrate. The informative speech, concentrating only on the early stages, represents your decision to limit your objectives. The persuasive speech, which concentrates on the middle step of yielding, represents a more ambitious but still limited undertaking. The speech to actuate represents the attempt to carry the audience through the entire process. Where in the process you stop, and therefore which of these purposes you choose to emphasize, is a decision that can be made only in the light of your specific audience and your specific subject matter. You can discover which is the most appropriate choice for your speech by following the approach outlined earlier in this chapter.

Entertaining Speeches

Before we move on, we should also discuss briefly another purpose that sometimes confronts a speaker: *to entertain.* How does this purpose relate to the other purposes we have already discussed? Again, we must first deal with the matter of definition.

In its more narrow definition "entertainment" often carries the idea of amusement, comedy, and laughter. A speech to "entertain" in this sense would have to be funny, comic, and humorous.

The greatest sin is to be dull.
Jack Paar

In a broader sense, however, every speech ought to be entertaining. We are using "entertainment" in this wider sense to refer to anything that is interesting, enchanting, vivid, alive, colorful, charming, and otherwise easy to listen to. We do not have to labor to stay tuned to such a speech; we find listening easy because the speech is in the widest sense "entertaining."

What we need to see is that in this broader sense the purpose to "entertain" does not supplant the other major purposes which a speech may have; *it complements them.* Whether our goal is to inform, persuade, or actuate matters little. In each of these cases we can and should attempt to make our speech broadly entertaining to our audience so that they are captivated by it.

On the other hand, when we attempt to entertain in the more narrow sense, these other purposes *are* affected. As humor or laughter per se gains priority in our efforts, the informative, persuasive, or actuational goals are diminished. In fact, a truly funny speech may often distort fact and be little more than nonsense. Not much informing, persuading, or actu-

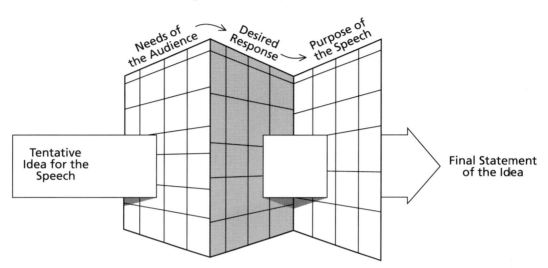

Figure 8
Arriving at a Final Statement of the Idea

ating may be accomplished; but if people laugh, our purpose has been achieved.

Of such humorous speeches we may make four brief observations: First, not everyone can produce effective humorous speeches, since the ability to do so seems to depend more on gift than on hard work. To be sure, writing comedic material does require hard work, but hard work in itself will seldom suffice. Second, few speeches that are solely comedic are effective. In most cases humor will work best in conjunction with (and subordinate to) the goals of informing, persuading, or actuating. Third, even the speech whose goal is simply to make people laugh will best be built around a central idea. Unity, order, and progress are as useful in humorous communication as they are in any other type. Fourth, we will not give much attention to speeches of this type in this book. Our goal is not to develop comedians but to provide help in communicating ideas. It is perfectly legitimate to settle for tickling an audience's funny bone,

Figure 9
The Final Idea

Tentative Idea: America needs to look to nuclear power as the energy source of the future.

	What was, is, or will be	What the audience should think or feel	What the audience should do
Third graders studying a science unit	Nuclear power is one of the important sources of energy in America today		
College students taking an elective ecology course		We in America should look to nuclear power as one potential energy source for the future	
A group of state or federal legislators			You should vote yes on Bill 743D, which will limit environmental controls on nuclear power
A crowd gathered around a soapbox on a street corner			You should vote yes on Proposition 3, which will allow the nuclear-power plant to be built locally
A convention of nuclear engineers			You should organize a concentrated lobbying effort in Congress in favor of nuclear-power plant construction

On Advertising and Speechmaking

An advertising agency placed the following in *Fortune* magazine. Examine the characteristics of a good advertisement. How do they compare or contrast with the characteristics of a good speech?

Six questions
to ask before you
approve
an advertisement.

---

1. Is there a big idea?

Nothing else is so important to the success of an advertisement. A genuine selling idea transcends execution. Before you approve any advertisement, ask yourself if it really has a big idea and if that idea emerges clearly, emphatically, and single-mindedly. Ask yourself: Is it an important idea—such as Scope's "medicine breath," the positioning of Pledge furniture polish as a dusting aid, or AMF's "We make weekends."

2. Is there a theme line?

A theme line that presents your selling idea in a memorable set of words can be worth millions of dollars of extra mileage to your advertising. Provocative lines like "When E. F. Hutton talks, people listen," "Please don't squeeze the Charmin," "We really move our tail for you" (Continental Airlines) make it easy for the customer to remember your selling message. Incidentally, when you get a great one, treasure it and use it prominently in every print ad and television commercial you run.

of course, but our goal here will be to center our attention on those occasions when we desire more significant results.

What we are saying, therefore, is that our concern will be for "entertainment" in the broader sense. While our speeches should always be interesting, absorbing, alive, vivid, often providing pleasure and even laughter, all of these will be viewed as *subservient* to

3. Is it relevant?

If your advertising is remembered but your product forgotten, you might as well run "compliments of a friend." Jokes that steal attention from the selling idea, inappropriate entertainment devices, celebrities who have no logical connection with your product, and other irrelevancies can be devastating. Look for relevance in every advertising execution.

4. Is it hackneyed?

Is the advertisement fresh, innovative, and original or is it merely a pale carbon copy of somebody else's advertising? Too much advertising is look-alike, sound-alike advertising. These advertisements are often costly failures. Don't run the risk of being mistaken for your competitor. Demand an execution that is all your own.

5. Does it demonstrate?

Nothing works harder or sells better than a demonstration of your product's superiority, especially in television. Look for every opportunity to demonstrate. If you can't demonstrate, at least show the product in use. Demonstrations—such as the simple exposition of how the Trac II razor works or the coating action of Pepto-Bismol—are convincing ways to sell.

6. Is it believable?

Does the advertising overpromise? Does the selling idea sound a false note? An advertisement can be totally truthful, yet sound unbelievable. Better to underpromise and be believable than to overpromise and lose credibility.

the overall purpose of the speech. The question must always be, What will best accomplish my purpose of informing, persuading, or actuating my audience? Where humor, parody, satire, exaggeration, wit, or comedy will usefully serve our purpose, they should be readily included. But they should never be included for their own sake.

The idea and the purpose are the only autonomous aspects of the speech, and all else must be marshaled so as to serve them.

In this broader sense, then, all speeches should be entertaining. The organization of the speech, the supporting material used, the wording chosen to convey the idea, the manner of delivery—all of these can and should be designed to hold the interest of the listener so as to make it easy for him or her to attend to your ideas. In this way the pleasure of the audience becomes an important means to an end, though not an end in itself.

Stating Your Idea

To recapitulate, we began this chapter by discussing the formulation of a tentative statement of the idea we want to communicate. We saw that our task is to focus the idea so that it is maximally appropriate for the requirements of our particular audience. To do this we proposed a three-step process: First, we analyze the need our audience may have for the idea. Second, from that need we state the response we desire our audience to make to the speech. Third, out of these first two steps we then state the predominant purpose for the speech. Broadly, this purpose will be to inform, persuade, or actuate and should be stated in terms of the content of the idea we are attempting to communicate.

Our task now is to state the idea in its final form, taking into consideration our predominant purpose. If the purpose is to inform, the idea will be basically a *factual statement of what was, is, or will be.* If the purpose is to persuade, the idea will be basically a *value judgment concerning how the audience should think or feel about something.* If the purpose is to actuate, the idea will be basically *a value judgment about how the audience should behave.* Stating the idea in this way and then allowing it to dictate the rest of the speech will lead to the fulfillment of the speech's purpose.

Notice in figure 9 how the needs of the audience, the desired response, and the purpose have shaped the idea. These are only hypothetical examples, of course, but they demonstrate how the relationship of the subject matter to the audience dictates the direction of the speech and therefore the shape of the final statement of the idea. With a different audience we might develop a different (but, of course, related) idea. With a different starting idea the entire grid would change. Think, for example, of how the picture would be transformed by beginning with the tentative idea: "America *should not* look to nuclear power as an energy source for the future!"

The product of your labor should be an accurate statement of your idea focused specifically for the audience to whom you will be speaking. You may rework the statement somewhat as your speech preparation progresses, but from this point on the revisions will be stylistic rather than substantive. You may be able to improve *how* you state your idea, but *what* you are attempting to communicate is now basically fixed. Of course, the unforeseen can always occur: some misjudgment about your audience or about the availability of research materials, for example. Such things can cause a speaker to have to return to the drawing board and move through the process once more with a different or revised idea. But barring such unforeseen events you now have in hand the proposition you will attempt to communicate to your audience.

In chapter 8 we will make some suggestions that may be helpful in wording your central idea. You may want to consult that portion of the book now as you attempt to word your idea effectively. In any case, here is a checklist of practical suggestions to assist you in stating your idea effectively.

1. Be sure your statement contains only one idea.
2. Be sure your idea is stated in one well-constructed sentence.
3. Be sure your idea is significant enough to be worthy of your audience's time.
4. Try to state your idea positively rather than negatively.
5. Use good grammar.
6. Make your idea concise and to the point. Avoid excess wordiness.
7. State your idea as forcefully, memorably, and interestingly as you can. Beware of boredom.
8. Avoid the vague. Work on making your meaning come through clearly in the statement of your idea.

9. Beware of abstract terms that you have not clearly defined. Work on making your idea as concrete and specific as you can, while still spanning the content of your speech.
10. Avoid metaphorical language in the statement of your idea.
11. Beware of dangling participles, clauses, and phrases that leave the meaning of your idea ambiguous.

Exercises

1. Study a real-life speaking situation. Try to decide which purpose—to inform, to persuade, to actuate—dominated the speaker's efforts. Do you think the speaker was aware of a clear purpose? Was the content of the speech suited to the purpose? Why or why not?
2. By adding appropriate complements, come up with three different ideas for the subject "television in America": one to inform, one to persuade, and one to actuate. Your audience is a group of thirty parents from the local Parent-Teachers Association gathered for a seminar broadly entitled "Contemporary Society."
3. "The Bible is the most important book ever written." Analyze how this idea would have to be adjusted for (a) a class of university students in a public-speaking course, (b) a meeting of the local atheists' association, (c) an adult Sunday-school class in your church, and (d) a class of sixth-grade students in a public school who are studying great literature.
4. As the teacher of a high-school course in public speaking you must give a ten-minute lecture on one of these topics: the importance of having a clear purpose in a speech, the three types of purposes which speeches may have, or how to make a speech entertaining. Using the material of this chapter and any other help you can find, construct a complete outline of your lecture.

Chapter 5

How to Develop Your Idea into a Speech

You know what you want to say to your audience. You have chosen a *subject*, researched it enough to know what can and what cannot be said about it, and have chosen from among the many options exactly what *you* want to say about it, your *complement*. Thus you have your *idea*.

Furthermore, you have measured your idea and cut it to fit. You have a thesis that is tailor-made for your audience. As a result, you have a clear destination: you want to communicate *this* idea to *this* audience.

The question now is, How are you going to reach this destination? It is time to begin mapping out your journey, to begin working on the *development* of the idea within your speech.

Major Speech Divisions

The major divisions in your speech will not be difficult to come by. With few exceptions you will want to abide by the centuries-old overall structure represented by the terms *introduction, body,* and *conclusion.* It was Plato who said, through Socrates, "Every speech should be put together like a living thing, . . . [having] both a middle and extremities, composed proportionately to each other and to the whole."[1] The wisdom of this advice has been echoed by public speakers ever since. It is the exhortation of both common wisdom ("Tell 'em what you're gonna say, say it, and tell 'em what you said") and modern scientific research alike. As an overall pattern, the threefold structure of introduction, body, and conclusion has never really been improved upon, and we will generally abide by it here.

Thus your first and most basic developmental decision can almost be assumed. Until you discover good reasons to depart from this pattern (and there are some), you should probably take for granted that you will be producing an introduction, body, and conclusion for your speech. The proportion of time you assign to each of these will vary according to the subject matter, audience, and occasion, but in most speeches, these three sections will be evident.

Every speech should be put together like a living thing, . . . [having] both a middle and extremities, composed proportionately to each other and to the whole. Socrates

We will postpone discussion of two of these sections (introduction and conclusion) to chapter 7. The reason for this is that, in terms of the order of *preparation* of a speech, both the introduction and the conclusion must *follow* the development of the body of the speech. After all, before we have the body of the speech in hand we do not yet know what we are introducing or concluding! Therefore, in this and in the next chapter we will deal with the *body* of the speech.

The Body of the Speech

The body of your speech will be composed of (1) the main points you use to develop your central idea, (2) the subpoints you use to develop your main points, (3) the supporting material you use to fill out your main and subpoints, and (4) the connectives you use to show the audience the progression of your ideas through the speech. In this chapter we will deal with the main and subpoints of the speech and with the connectives between the points. These parts constitute the skeleton of the speech. In the next chapter we will deal with the many types of supporting materials which flesh out the skeletal development and give it substance.

Developing Unity, Order, and Progress

We have already discussed the fact that people crave unity, order, and progress in their world. Therefore, we are working in concert with the basic tendencies of the human mind when we organize these characteristics into our speech. Conversely, if our speech lacks these qualities, we are working cross-grained to the way people think.

How can you build unity, order, and progress into your speech? You are well along the way to this goal already since you have chosen a central idea for your speech. Your next step is to develop this idea in such a way that (1) all of the parts support the whole, (2) the relationships among the parts are clear and balanced, and (3) the parts are set forth in some sequence that makes sense to the audience.

Units of Thought

When these three goals are accomplished, the speech will constitute a *unit of thought*. A unit of thought is defined as a body of discourse that is composed of an idea and its development. Every speech that is built effectively around a central idea constitutes such a unit. Furthermore, this overall unit of thought will be made up of a series of *subunits of thought*. Like the larger unit, each of these subunits will be a whole comprised of a central idea and its development. Together, the central ideas of the subunits combine to become the development of the broader unit. So a speech may be viewed in one sense as a series of units of thought which combine to make up broader units of thought, which in turn combine to make up the overall unit of thought, the speech itself. Reversing the analysis we could break the speech down into units that are so small that they consist of only a subject and complement (the necessary elements of a complete thought). These individual sentences would theoretically be the smallest units of thought in the speech.

Each of the units of thought in the speech must be related to the central idea of the speech in some way. The inclusion of each subunit is dependent upon the contribution it makes to the whole. Any unit that does not contribute to the whole should be eliminated, regardless of how interesting it may be in itself. Only

Anything whose presence or absence makes no discernible difference is no essential part of the whole. Aristotle

those subunits which somehow contribute to the goal of communicating the central idea to the audience are to be included. This stringent process of inclusion and exclusion is the factor that provides a clear sense of unity to the speech. All the pieces must point toward the same object, the central idea. Thus all of the speech hangs together; it coheres; it is a unity.

But even this coherence, important as it is, is not enough by itself. The fact that all the material of the speech is related to a central idea is the first step toward effective communication, but it must be combined with the second step of *ordering all of the pieces so that they are presented to the audience, part by part, in a sequence that is natural, clear, and balanced.*

Clear Relationships

One of the fundamental differences between humankind and the other creatures is the former's ability to see *relationships*. A cat can see two objects just as we can; perhaps it can see them better since a cat's eyesight is in some ways superior to ours. But they remain as only two objects to the cat. The animal is not able to think about them much beyond the level of what it sees, *the observables.*

But we may look at the same two objects and see far more than does the cat. What we can see and the cat cannot are the many *potential relationships* (the constructs) between the two objects. We are able to think in the abstract about things that are not directly observable. Perhaps, we might say, the first object produces the second (cause-effect relationship); or perhaps the first object is above and to the right of the second (spatial relationship); or perhaps the second object is older than the first (chronological relationship); or perhaps the first object is a copy of the second (repetitive relationship). These are only a few of the many relational possibilities which can be seen by the human mind. No other creature is able to think as we do.

There is a sense in which all learning can be viewed as (1) coming to see that something exists and then (2) seeing it in its true relationship to other things. The first step we call "discovery" and the second step we call "understanding." At the heart of things, these two steps are what all research, study, and education are about: discovering something exists and then seeing how it relates to everything else. Thus, apart from relationships, an isolated fact is an irrelevant thing. Until it can be integrated with the rest of our understanding, it is useless and meaningless.

The speaker who desires to communicate with an audience cannot afford to ignore the listeners' basic need to see relationships. If the listeners do not grasp how the parts of the speech relate to one another, if each part is not in some logical and appropriate place, then the effort to communicate will be hindered.

Furthermore, in a chronological (time-related) unity such as a speech, the audience requires that the parts be conveyed in such a way that a clear *progression* of ideas emerges. Each part must be presented at the appropriate time and in such a way that it builds upon what has gone before and feeds anticipation for what is yet to come. The listeners are never able to view the speech as a whole, nor can they juggle all the ideas until we finish and then rearrange them so that they make sense. *We must present them in order, so that they make sense in the first place!* Only then is the audience able to *feel* the movement in the speech, to sense that we are going somewhere. Audiences expect intuitively that the speech should come together in the end. A clear sense of progression through the structure of the speech (*within* the subunits of thought as well as *between* them) promotes the satisfaction of these expectations.

Not incidentally, we might add that a clear progression of ideas in a speech also serves us as speakers. If it is a difficult thing for an audience to follow a speech that does not make sense, it is no less difficult for us. When we are able to construct our speech in such a way that the natural relationships which exist between the parts of the whole are presented in a clear progression, moving one after another toward a climax, the speech virtually remembers itself. But conversely, when the speech does not flow naturally, merely remembering the points can be maddeningly difficult.

Expanding Ideas

How does one go about expanding an idea into a full speech? This is not an easy question to answer since there are so many variables at work in the process. Our ability as speakers, the idea itself, the purpose of the speech, the audience, the occasion—all of these factors and many more enter into the decision about how to shape the idea into a speech.

Some people seem to have little difficulty taking an idea, any idea, and expanding it into an appropriate speech for a particular situation. Through gift, skill, training, or experience—or in some cases, a combination of all four—the pieces just seem to fall naturally into place. But the ease with which these people cruise through the process is usually an illusion. Preparing a fully developed speech typically requires a great deal of mental effort. Conversely, a lack of such effort is usually evident in the final product.

Unfortunately, hard work by itself will seldom suffice. Handling thought effectively is as much an art as a science, and, like painting a portrait or composing music, some people do it better than others. Designing an effective speech requires a craft which can only partially be taught or spelled out on paper. As H. Grady Davis notes, "Art is skill in doing controlled by an inner sense of rightness."[2] While such skill can be honed and the inner sense can be cultivated, in the end there is still an intangible ingredient that one either has or does not have, an ingredient that is as difficult to propagate as it is to describe.

So the subject we have before us in this chapter is a difficult one. There is only so much one can say about how to think and communicate clearly about an idea. We will attempt to lay out

---

It is difficult to think. It is more difficult to think about thinking. It is most difficult to describe thinking about thinking.
Haddon W. Robinson

---

some basic approaches and some typical patterns, but beyond that the reader will have to depend upon his or her own ability and intuition as a communicator.

Actually you are much further down the line toward developing your idea into a speech than you may realize at this point. The fact that you have a central idea you wish to communicate already provides you with a narrowed focus. That is a major step forward. What is more, you have also given considerable thought to the general content of your speech as you attempted to focus the idea for your particular audience. For example, you already know where the main thrust of your speech will fall: *explanation, proof,* or *implication.* Moreover, you have also given some consideration to what emphasis, if any, must be given to the other areas. Thus the content of your message has already begun to take shape.

A Natural Expansion

The important point in what follows is to allow the speech to expand naturally. The form of the speech should not be an artificial one, but rather one that grows easily out of the expression of the idea itself. The nature of the central idea should always determine the structure of the message. Thus the form of the speech's development does not so much produce the substance of the speech as the substance of the speech leads logically to the form.

Recall that one of the characteristics of a good speech idea is that it must be broad enough to be expandable. If you have chosen your central idea well, it will not be so low on our hypothetical ladder of ideas that it cannot be expanded. Ideas that are too narrow are not expandable. Once we have expressed them, little more needs to be said. They simply lie there on the page, rebuffing all of our attempts to develop them into a meaningful speech.

A good speech idea, by contrast, is one which has far more compressed within it than can be seen on its surface. It must be expanded, probed, explored, and explained. It virtually cries out for an examination of its parts.

As Davis writes, "A good generalization can, in an instant of time, mark the full scope and contain the full meaning of the idea. Our difficulty is that a generalization cannot convey an experience of the idea to one who does not already experience it. An experience of the idea's meaning, a conviction of its truth, an apprehension of its consequences—these all rise out of particulars."[3] Thus the real trick of developing an idea into a speech is to let its natural parts, its particulars, determine the shape of the speech. Ask yourself these questions: What are the particulars of my idea? What must be explored for someone to understand or believe this idea? Take it apart into its natural parts, explore these with your audience in some logical order, and then tie them together again at the end. This is the essence of a good speech development.

Of course, it is usually not as simple as that. To be sure, at times your speech may fall together easily, and these times will occur more often as you gain experience. But what about the times when a natural development of the idea proves elusive? In other words, what happens when you are stumped?

Methods of Expansion

There are no easy or sure solutions to this problem. The difficulty may lie in the idea itself. It may be a poor speech idea, or a poorly worded speech idea, or both. In such cases the only recourse is to rework the idea until it becomes more manageable. But what if the idea is a reasonably good one, and a workable development still seems elusive, what then? Here are some approaches which may prove helpful:

The Constituent-Part Method

Break your idea down into its constituent parts. List all of the subideas that are implicit and explicit within it. When you have them listed, categorize them, and then list the categories in some progressive order. Categorizing the subideas may provide a rough outline of a development that would, when it is completed, communicate your idea in full.

This approach is based upon Noam Chomsky's concept of a transformational generative grammar.[4] According to this theory,

---

We can only produce our effect by a series of successive small impressions, dripping our meaning into the reader's mind.
Arthur Quiller-Couch

---

any complex sentence may be broken down into a series of "kernel" sentences. For example, Ephesians 2:8–9 reads: "For by grace you have been saved through faith, and this is not your own doing, it is the gift of God—not the result of works, so that no one may boast" (RSV). This is a complex sentence which can be broken down into at least seven kernel sentences: (1) God showed you grace; (2) God saved you; (3) you believed; (4) you did not save yourselves; (5) God gave you salvation; (6) you did not work for it; (7) no man should boast. With some rearranging and combining, a workable outline might emerge:

    I.   God showed you his grace by giving you the gift of salvation.

   A. It was he who saved you.
   B. He provided the salvation as a free gift.
   C. He did this purely as an act of his grace.
II. You could not save yourselves.
   A. You could not earn salvation.
   B. You can only receive God's gift through belief.
III. God did this so that no one could boast.

Taking the idea apart into its kernels, we can see all of the implicit and explicit parts of the idea which need to be included in the development. From there it is merely a matter of organizing the parts into an orderly outline. Try improving the outline by rewording and reorganizing the points.

You may be able to take your own idea apart in a similar way. You need not possess a detailed understanding of Chomsky's transformational-grammar theory to do so. All you need is to be able to think clearly and perceptively. List all of the implicit and explicit kernel sentences. Perhaps these will provide you with only the broad structure of your outline, and you will have to flesh it out more fully on your own. When your idea is more complex, the process of analysis will be more rigorous but also more fruitful. Where your idea is itself only one kernel, of course, this approach will not help you with your development at all. It may help you to see, however, that your idea as it stands is not expansive enough to carry the weight of a complete speech. This is by no means always the case with a single-kernel idea, but it may sometimes serve as a warning sign.

Here is an example of an idea and its development which was produced by looking for kernel sentences within the whole:

Main Idea: The record number of deaths on the highways last July 4 will be exceeded this year unless the American people observe the AAA's safety precautions.

  I. There was a record number of highway deaths last July 4.
 II. This record may be exceeded this year.
III. The AAA has suggested a helpful list of safety precautions.

IV.   Observing these precautions could keep Americans from setting a new record of highway deaths this July 4.

The Interrogative-and-Key-Word Method

Another method of prying a pattern of development from an idea is called the *interrogative-and-key-word approach.* When you use this approach, you begin by stating your idea. Then you raise the question posed by one (and only one) of the five interrogatives: (1) What? (2) Why? (3) How? (4) When? (5) Where? Which interrogative to use? With most ideas one or two of the interrogatives will stand out as the most appropriate, and the choice should not be too difficult.

When you use this approach, your speech will be built around multiple answers to the question being posed, answers which are represented by a plural *key word.* For example, if the interrogative is *why,* the key word might be "reasons" and the main points in the development would list those reasons. If the interrogative is *how,* the key word might be "ways" or "methods," which the main points would enumerate. If the interrogative is *where,* a key word suggesting location might be used, such as "places," "areas," or "zones." If the interrogative is *when,* a chronological key word would be appropriate, such as "times," "opportunities," or "seasons." If the interrogative is *what,* the most appropriate key words would be those which define, analyze, describe, or classify, such as "types," "attributes," or "divisions." In this way an entire outline for a speech can be coaxed out of a recalcitrant idea through the simple use of an interrogative and a key word.

Though sometimes lacking in subtlety and creativity, this approach can be a very useful one, particularly for beginning speakers. It is simple and easy to use, and will generally produce fruit. Speakers who have to generate fresh messages regularly, such as preachers, often find it a great help.[5] But be wary of using it too often with the same audience. The similarity among the speeches may become so predictable as to become boring to your listeners. For your convenience, here is a list of a few of the many key words available to you:[6]

abuses
admonitions
alternatives
answers
applications
approaches
areas
aspects
assertions
assumptions
attitudes
attributes
barriers
beliefs
benefits
blockades
categories
causes
challenges
changes
circumstances
conceptions
criticisms
dangers
declarations
degrees
differences
discoveries
divisions
doors
duties
effects
elements
examples

explanations
extremes
facets
factors
faults
fears
fields
forces
foundations
functions
generalizations
gifts
groups
guarantees
guides
handicaps
hopes
ideas
illustrations
impediments
imperatives
implications
inadequacies
irritations
issues
items
judgments
justifications
keys
kinds
laws
lessons
levels
limits

links
locations
losses
manifestations
means
measures
members
methods
misfortunes
models
motives
names
necessities
norms
objectives
obligations
observations
occasions
omissions
opponents
origins
panaceas
parallels
parts
patterns
peculiarities
perils
pictures
places
plans
points
possibilities
precautions
premises

principles
problems
processes
prohibitions
proofs
propositions
provisions
purposes
qualities
quantities
questions
ranks
reactions
reasons
recommenda-
  tions
references
regions
responses
restraints
results
rewards
scales
schools
seasons
secrets
sequences
shields
situations
solutions
sources
spheres
steps
stipulations

stresses
styles
subjects
supports
symptoms
systems
tactics
talents
tasks
tendencies
tests
theories
thoughts
times
topics
traits
trends
troubles
truths
types
uncertainties
units
uses
values
variations
views
violations
virtues
ways
weaknesses
weapons
words
worries

The Motivated-Sequence Method

Another possible approach when you are stumped is to use the Motivated Sequence discussed on pages 175–76. It is a flexible arrangement which can be effectively adapted for a speech to inform, a speech to persuade, or a speech to actuate.

Typical Speech Patterns

Regardless of what method you use to lay out the development of your idea, whether you use the above methods or strike out on your own, there are certain speech patterns which surface regularly. You will undoubtedly use several of them repeatedly even if you speak publicly only on isolated occasions. They will crop up in your subpoints as well as in your overall development of the idea. So you need to be aware of these common patterns as you prepare your speech.

Logical Patterns

Inductive Patterns

Induction, like other forms of reasoning, is a process of drawing inferences about the unknown from the known. In the case of induction, the known consists of a limited number of specifics, all of which share membership in some broader category. On the basis of what we observe about these specifics, we infer some generalization about all the members of the broader category. Obviously, the larger the number of specifics we study, the more likely it is that our induction will be valid. But keep in mind that, even at their best, conclusions drawn from inductive reasoning are probable, never certain. We can never achieve certainty about the category as a whole until each member of the category has been examined, but then at this point we are no longer depending upon inductive reasoning.

To say that inductive generalizations are never certain is not to imply that they are always unreliable. To be sure, the fact that the sun has set in the west on every occasion we have observed a sunset does not *guarantee* it will set in the west tomorrow; some cataclysmic event could prevent it from setting at all. Nevertheless, the inductive generalization, based upon all past examples, that "each time the sun sets, it will set in the west" is *probably* a reliable one. Thus, even though such tentativeness should technically accompany every inductive generalization, induction can still produce very reliable results when the inferences are founded upon a sufficient number of specific observations.

More dangerous are inductive generalizations that are based on too little experience with the members of the category. The fallacy of such reasoning is obvious: "All politicians walk in single file, at least the one I saw did." Sadly, unwarranted inductive generalizations are not always so harmless or humorous. Sometimes inappropriate generalizations can cause great harm: "All cops are crooks"; "White people in America are prejudiced against blacks"; "People on welfare really don't want to work"; "All religion is a racket." We must always ask when we use an inductive argument: (1) Are there a sufficient number of examples to draw a conclusion about the class as a whole? and (2) Are the examples typical of the members of the class?

In an *inductive speech-pattern* the reasoning is always from the specific to the general. We examine a certain number of typical examples and then draw a general inference from them. This general inference is the central idea of the speech. It is important to point out, however, that we are speaking here only of the *process of reasoning* involved, not necessarily the *order of presentation* in the speech. For example, we might present the specifics first, as the main points of the speech, and then draw the general conclusion only at the end of the speech:

I. Unlike the students at college Y, the students at college X have initiated numerous work projects to help support their athletic teams.
II. The student attendance figures for college X's games are much higher than for college Y's.
III. The pep rallies for the latest game at college X attracted twice as many students as at college Y.
   (Therefore, it is obvious that . . .)

Main Idea: Students at college X have more team spirit than do students at college Y.

Or we might begin with the general statement and then list as our main points the examples which led to this conclusion:

Main Idea: Our community is becoming a more pleasant place to live. (For example, . . .)

    I. The air and water quality are improving.
   II. The crime rate has decreased.
  III. The opportunities for employment are growing.
  IV. There are increased opportunities for recreation.

The order of presentation in these two patterns is different, but the type of reasoning involved is exactly the same. It is inductive in that it is reasoning from specifics to the general.

Because of their concentration upon specific examples, inductive speech-patterns can often score high on the scale of human interest. The kinds of circumstantial evidence, statistics, facts, examples, anecdotes, analogies, descriptions, and narratives that are typical of inductive reasoning lend themselves to the vividness and concreteness on which audience interest thrives.

Deductive Patterns

Deductive reasoning likewise follows the pattern of all reasoning: drawing conclusions about what is unknown on the basis of what is known. In deduction, however, what is known is some general observation, from which we draw hitherto unknown conclusions about specifics or particulars.

Deduction typically takes several forms. Probably the most common deductive pattern of reasoning is that in which something is known to be true of an entire category of things. On the basis of this knowledge, inferences are "deduced" about individual members of the category. Thus, if "all men are mortal" (an entire category: all men) and "Socrates is a man" (Socrates is a member of the category), then it follows inevitably that what is true (mortality) of the entire category (all men) is also true of

Socrates. Hence, we discover one of the fundamental structures of formal logic, the *categorical syllogism:*

Major premise:	All men are mortal.
Minor premise:	Socrates is a man.
Conclusion:	Socrates is mortal.

The nature of a categorical syllogism (indeed, of all syllogisms) is such that if the major and minor premises are true, then the conclusion must also be true, which is to say, *certain.* Only in deductive reasoning is it possible to make inferences about the unknown which may be considered certain, and even then only when the major and minor premises are themselves certain.

A second form of deductive reasoning is represented by the *hypothetical syllogism.* In this case the major premise establishes what will happen under certain circumstances. The minor premise then establishes that the specified circumstances do in fact pertain. Then the conclusion states the inevitable result. Here are two hypothetical syllogisms:

Major premise:	If Socrates is a man, he is mortal.
Minor premise:	Socrates is a man.
Conclusion:	Socrates is mortal.

Major premise:	Unless Socrates is other than a man, he is mortal.
Minor premise:	Socrates is not other than a man.
Conclusion:	Socrates is mortal.

A third type of deductive reasoning is the *disjunctive syllogism.* In this case an "either-or" situation is established in the major premise. Then in the minor premise one or the other of the options is denied, leaving only the remaining option for the conclusion:

Minor premise:	I must either take out a loan to buy this television set or forego its purchase altogether.
Minor premise:	I refuse to take out a loan to buy this television set.

Conclusion: I must forego the purchase of the television set altogether.

In a *deductive speech-pattern* the conclusion of the syllogism is the central idea you are attempting to establish; that is, your idea is an assertion about some particular that you will attempt to establish by deducing it from a major and minor premise your audience will accept as true.

For example, suppose yours is an evangelistic message designed to convey the idea "Jesus Christ came to salvage you from your sinful condition." The points in your outline might follow the pattern of a categorical syllogism:

      I. Christ came to salvage sinful people. (major premise)
     II. You are a sinful person. (minor premise)
Main Idea: III. Christ came to salvage you.

Or again, suppose your purpose is more apologetic and your idea is "Jesus is the Savior of humankind." In this case you might want to attempt the disjunctive syllogistic pattern:

      I. Jesus was either a liar or who he claimed to be: the Savior of humankind. (major premise)
     II. Jesus was not a liar. (minor premise)
Main Idea: III. Jesus was who he claimed to be: the Savior of humankind.

Or again, suppose you were addressing a group of Christians to encourage them to be diligent in their witness for Christ. In this case the movement through your message might take on the form of a hypothetical syllogism:

      I. In periods of social upheaval, people are more open to the gospel. (major premise)
     II. We are presently in such a period of social upheaval. (minor premise)
Main Idea: III. We have a great opportunity for witness today.

In each of these examples we have allowed the outline to follow the syllogistic sequence. It is, of course, not inherently necessary to do so. We might easily rearrange the *order of presentation* so that the conclusion of the syllogism (the main idea) is presented first:

Main Idea: I. We have a great opportunity for witness today. (The reason for this is that . . .)

          II. We are in a period of social upheaval. (Furthermore, . . .)

        III. In such periods of history, people are always more open to the gospel.

Regardless of which order of presentation one chooses, the pattern of thought in this outline is deductive, reasoning from the general (periods of social upheaval) to the specific (the *present* period of history).

We have limited our sample deductive outlines to three points, corresponding to the major premise, minor premise, and conclusion of a syllogism. This is not inherently necessary either. Some deductive speech-patterns may actually develop *only two* of the three major points, since the third can be assumed. For example, suppose one were to address a political gathering with this idea: "On the basis of candidate X's eight successful years of experience as lieutenant governor, we can be sure that he would make an excellent governor." The deductive argument behind this idea is:

Major premise: Candidate X has eight successful years of experience as lieutenant governor.

Minor premise: Experience as a lieutenant governor trains a person effectively to be an excellent governor.

Conclusion: Candidate X would make an excellent governor.

It is entirely possible that a speech developing such an idea might take for granted the audience's acceptance of the minor premise and not deal with it explicitly at all. Instead, the speech might be limited to only two main points, developing respectively the major premise and the conclusion.

Similarly, a deductive speech-pattern may also have more than the standard three points. For instance, one might want to expand the following deductive speech-pattern (which is based upon a disjunctive syllogism) into four main points:

I. There are essentially only three ways to lose weight.
   A. Burn off excess calories
   B. Reduce the intake of calories
   C. Some combination of the two
II. Attempting to burn off calories is difficult by itself.
III. Attempting to reduce caloric intake also has its drawbacks.
IV. The best way to lose weight is to combine both reduced caloric intake and calorie burn-off in a balanced program.

Divisional Patterns

Spatial Patterns

Spatial patterns of speech development depend upon the physical relationship of things or places as they exist in space. The progression through the points always represents some directional movement from near to far, front to back, outside to inside, center to periphery, left to right, top to bottom, north to south, base to the summit, this point in the circle around to that point, and so forth. Many Bible students believe that the basic pattern of organization in the Book of Acts, for example, may be found in Jesus' statement recorded in Acts 1:8: "But you shall receive power when the Holy Spirit has come upon you; and you shall be My witnesses both in Jerusalem, and in all Judea and Samaria, and even to the remotest part of the earth" (NASB). According to this view, the entire Book of Acts should be seen as the tracing of the spread of the gospel witness through concentric circles from (1) Jerusalem to (2) Judea, to (3) Samaria, and finally to (4) the remotest part of the earth. Whether this pattern was preeminent in Luke's mind as he wrote Acts we may never know, but the general fourfold spatial movement captured by the Lord's words is certainly evident in the book.

Not all subjects will lend themselves naturally to a spatial pattern of development, but some, such as geographical topics, will virtually demand a spatial treatment. For example:

1. The floor plan of Thomas Jefferson's home, Monticello
2. The missionary journeys of Paul
3. The topography of Alaska
4. The layers of a neutron star
5. The design of a space station
6. The travels of Jesus
7. The structure of a nuclear reactor
8. The geography of the Holy Land
9. The size of our solar system
10. The arrangement of buildings on a college campus
11. The best way to explore Williamsburg

In each of these examples the speech would progress through the spatial relationships inherent in the subject.

Spatial patterns tend to be graphic, concrete, and therefore more easily *visualized* by listeners than some of the other typical speech-patterns. This is a great advantage which should be enhanced by making the spatial relationships as clear and concrete as possible. Careful attention to this point will pay dividends in clarity and vividness.

Chronological Patterns

Chronological patterns depend upon some temporal relationship among the parts. Speeches which center upon "how-to-do-it" processes or procedures; historical lectures; biographical summaries and eulogies; stories, parables, and other narratives—each of these types of material will most likely be developed around a chronological pattern. The progression will trace some temporal movement wherein the parts follow one another through time, moving from latest to earliest or earliest to latest. Such subjects as these might lend themselves to a chronological pattern of development:

1. How to prepare for voting
2. The life of Abraham Lincoln
3. The process of shoe manufacturing
4. The three years of Jesus' ministry
5. The history of the computer

6. The progress of revelation about God in the Bible
7. The battle of Gettysburg
8. The biography of a single cornstalk
9. The three most important events of the Reformation
10. Christ's message in the parable of the good Samaritan

In each of these cases the development will establish some movement through time, forward or backward, and then follow that progression in a systematic way to its conclusion.

Topical Patterns

The topical pattern is probably the most widely varied of all the standard divisional patterns. In a topical arrangement the subject is divided along some natural or conventional lines inherent within itself. Since the same subject might conceivably be analyzed according to any number of principles of division, the varieties are almost unlimited. Thus the "topical pattern" is a kind of catchall term used to designate those logical divisions which do not fit in any more specific category.

A topical arrangement requires only that some orderly principle of categorization lie at the heart of the division of the overall subject into its parts and that the categories not be mixed together. For example, the subject "H_2O" might be divided according to its *elements:* (1) hydrogen and (2) oxygen. Or it might be analyzed in terms of its *forms:* (1) water, (2) vapor, and (3) ice. In both cases the principle of division (either "elements" or "forms") remains consistent. But suppose we divided the subject into these parts: (1) hydrogen, (2) ice, and (3) vapor. Such mixing of categories would be a confusing and unworkable division of the subject.

As we have noted, the topical pattern represents an attempt to trace inherent divisions of the subject which stem from an analysis of the whole. All created things—at least to the extent of our present knowledge—are susceptible to such analytical breakdown. Each time researchers have arrived at some seemingly elemental building block of nature, they have discovered that even this can be divided further still. Only God is indivisible; everything else, it seems, can be divided along some more or less natural lines, and most things can be logically divided in several different ways.

Consider a pie, for example. One might cut the pie into quarters or eighths, but this would be a division that is unnatural to the pie itself. It would be a division imposed upon the pie from

---

All created things—at least to the extent of our present knowledge—are susceptible to analytical breakdown.

---

without. A more natural analysis might produce a *spatial* division, such as (1) the exterior and (2) the interior, or a *topical* division, focusing upon the ingredients of the pie (flour, shortening, fruit, sugar, and so forth), its parts (crust, filling), or its characteristics (taste, smell, feel, sight). Each of these topical divisions would be different ways of developing the subject "pie." In the same way, all matter can be categorized variously as (1) animate or inanimate, (2) organic or inorganic, or (3) mineral, plant, or animal.

If all things are susceptible to a topical analysis, certain kinds of subjects especially lend themselves to such a treatment. For example, multiple-complement subjects almost invariably lead to a topical pattern of arrangement. Thus the multiple-complement subject "the three natural forces in the universe" would lead to this simple topical division:

1. The gravitational force
2. The electromagnetic force
3. The nuclear force

In the same way certain adverbial subjects lead to a topical arrangement. For instance, the adverbial subject "why we should vote for candidate X" would lead inevitably to a list of reasons as the major divisions. This, too, is a topical arrangement.

The parts in a topical pattern should always be presented in some progressive order. It may be an ascending order or descending order; it may be from the common to the unfamiliar; it may be from the simple to the more difficult; it may be from the least to the most important; but wherever possible there should be some clear progression in the presentation of the parts.

To illustrate, the subject "the government of the United States" might be divided naturally according to its branches: the judicial, legislative, and executive. But in what order should these be presented? One might choose the largest to the smallest, or vice versa; one might consider them in the order of their influence in our society; or one might treat them according to the degree of change each has experienced since the early days of the nation. The decision would be made on the basis of the full idea and the purpose of the speech. But in one way or another the parts should always be ordered so that there is a clear progression in their presentation.

Psychological Patterns

Cause-Effect Patterns

One of the most common kinds of relationships we observe is cause-effect relationships. Everything in our daily lives is the cause of some effect, and the effect of some cause—everything, that is, except God. He is the First Cause of all things, the Prime, Unmoved Mover. But every *created thing* is the product of some cause or causes, and in turn produces some effect or effects.

Because cause-effect relationships are so much a part of human thought processes, they also play an important role in most speeches. In fact, in many speeches the reasoning from cause to effect or effect to cause is the dominant pattern of the speech. Sometimes the speech will focus on the effect(s) and then reason to the cause(s), as in this outline:

> I. We are currently experiencing high inflation and interest rates.
> II. The primary cause of these economic problems is deficit spending in the federal budget.
> Main Idea: III. If we will balance the federal budget, we can eliminate these bloated inflation and interest rates.

In other cases the speech may focus on the cause(s) and then reason to the effect(s):

    I. The president wants to lower the federal deficit by cutting spending rather than raising taxes.

    II. But such a move will have serious negative side effects.

        A. Socially, it will bring great hardship to the poor.

        B. Economically, it will lead to recession.

        C. Politically, it will lead to defeat in the next election.

Main Idea: III. The president should raise taxes rather than cut federal spending.

In both cases, the dominant pattern of thought in the speech is based upon a cause-effect type of reasoning.

Problem-Solution Patterns

As we move through life, we are constantly confronted with problems we must solve. Inevitably, thinking about these problems and their solutions occupies a significant portion of our time. John Dewey outlined, in what he called the "reflective thinking sequence," the five phases we go through as we attempt to discover usable solutions. To solve problems we must (1) discover the problem, (2) isolate and describe the problem, (3) list possible solutions, (4) establish criteria by which we can judge the relative worth of these solutions, and (5) choose the best solution.[7]

Because this is such a familiar pattern of thought, it should not be surprising to discover that a problem-solution development is common in speeches. Conceivably, a problem-solution speech pattern might be developed along the lines of the reflective thinking sequence, having five main points corresponding to the five phases in the sequence. More likely the five phases will be telescoped into fewer main points; that is, all five of the phases of reflective thinking are included, but not in five distinct steps.

Problem-solution speech patterns in their simplest forms consist of only two major points: the first defines the problem and the second proposes and explains some solution. In more complex problem-solution patterns other main points may be inserted to propose, evaluate, and then discard alternate solutions. Or one might sense the need to address certain objections to the proposed solution. Or, where it is possible to do so, one might break the problem down into parts that are handled in sequence, demonstrating in turn how the proposed solution would solve each part of the problem. In each case, however, to be effective, a problem-solution pattern must in the end demonstrate that the remedy proposed by the speaker is both the *most workable* and the *most desirable* way to grapple with the problem.

Obviously not all ideas will lend themselves to a problem-solution pattern of development. A speech on the life of Winston Churchill, for instance, would probably have to be forced unnaturally into such an arrangement. But many social, spiritual, political, economic, and environmental subjects fit nicely into this pattern, as in this sample outline:

(The Problem)   I. There are over forty-five thousand patients in America whose kidneys have ceased to function and who must therefore have their blood artificially cleansed.

(Possible Solution discarded) II. The dialysis machine is not the best way to accomplish this artificial cleansing.
    A. It is too dangerous.
    B. It is too inconvenient.
    C. It is too expensive.

(Proposed Solution Main Idea) III. The process of continuous ambulatory peritoneal dialysis (CAPD) is the best treatment for kidney dysfunction.
    A. It is less dangerous.
    B. It is more convenient.
    C. It is less expensive.

One significant point to remember about the problem-solution arrangement: It is important for the audience not only to understand but to *feel* the existence of the problem at the outset. They must be convinced that a problem actually exists and that if no solution is implemented the problem will continue. Without this conviction the listeners may lack the motivation to adopt any solution, much less the solution you propose.

Motivated Sequence

Another well-known psychological pattern which can be used in speeches is Alan H. Monroe's Motivated Sequence.[8] The Motivated Sequence is a flexible, multistep process which can be adapted to almost any type of speech. It is, in fact, an elaboration of the problem-solution pattern of human thought.

There are five basic steps to the Motivated Sequence, one or two of which are dropped for certain types of speeches. The five steps are labeled *attention, need, satisfaction, visualization,* and *action.*

1. *Attention.* Your first task is to gain your audience's attention in such a way as to direct it favorably toward the central point of the speech. Anything which does not serve this goal, even though it might be captivating in itself, should be avoided.

2. *Need.* The problem being dealt with in the speech must be highlighted. It must be stated clearly, illustrated, and then explored to show its extent and its ramifications. It must also be made relevant to the audience by showing *how they are directly affected by it.* This raises the level of need for the speech.

3. *Satisfaction.* In the third step you present the material that will satisfy the audience's need. The nature of this material will depend upon the type of speech and upon the type of need that was pointed out in the second step. If the speech is an informative speech, you will supply the information the audience needs. If the speech is a speech to persuade or to actuate, you will attempt (a) to state and explain the attitude, belief, or action you wish to arouse in the audience; (b) to demonstrate how this attitude, belief, or action will satisfy the need that was pointed out in the previous step; and (c) to present examples of how this response worked effectively in the past to satisfy similar needs which had surfaced.

4. *Visualization.* In a speech to persuade or to actuate, having raised a problem and proposed a solution, you will now want to move your audience to accept the proposal and act upon it. The function of the fourth step is to intensify the audience's desire to respond by vividly portraying the future benefits of adopting your proposal. You can do this by showing both the positive effects of an appropriate response and the negative effects of failing to respond.

5. *Action.* In this final step, which is generally reserved for speeches to actuate, you attempt to summarize and then drive home in one final, brief, graphic way the action the audience should take.

As we have noted, the Motivated Sequence is a flexible pattern that can be adapted to many different kinds of speeches. In an *informative speech* only the first three steps occur. You attempt to (a) capture the audience's attention, (b) demonstrate that they need to know something, and (c) present the information itself. In a *persuasive speech* you will usually (a) capture attention, (b) point out a need, (c) demonstrate the attitude or belief that will satisfy the need, and then (d) visualize the beneficial results. In a *speech to actuate* you will move through all five steps: (a) capture attention, (b) demonstrate the problem, (c) describe what the audience must do to solve the problem, (d) visualize the benefits of such action, and then (e) urge specific action.

Consult figure 10 to find out how the divisions of a speech using the Motivated Sequence correlate to the traditional divisions of introduction, body, and conclusion.

Outlining

Regardless of how you choose to develop your idea—whether you use one of the common patterns we have discussed or one that is unique to your speech—you will not escape the task of outlining. Outlining is a crucial skill for a speaker, one which will serve you and your audience well if you master it, or will

Figure 10

The Relationship between the Steps of
the Motivated Sequence and the Traditional Divisions[9]

General Purpose	Introduction	Body	Conclusion
To inform	*Attention step* *Need step*	*Satisfaction step* 1. Preview 2. Discussion	*Satisfaction step* (cont.) 3. Summary
To persuade	*Attention step* *Need step*	*Satisfaction step*	*Visualization step*
To actuate	*Attention step* *Need step*	*Satisfaction step* *Visualization step*	*Action step*

undermine your entire effort if you do not. Thus you will do well to give the matter of outlining due attention.

You may sometimes be tempted to forego developing an outline altogether. After all, you may tell yourself, you have your idea and you know a lot about your subject—why not just start in writing the speech and get on with it?

Though this is an enticing option, it is also an exceedingly foolish one. Bypassing an outline is a sure prescription for producing superficial speeches which do not communicate. Any unity, order, or progress the speech might have had will likely be sacrificed by taking this costly shortcut. To put it bluntly, an unwillingness to begin work on the body of your speech by hammering out a workable outline is one of the first and most reliable steps to failure as a public speaker. Refuse to give in to the temptation!

The Nature of Outlining

The purpose of an outline is to display in an orderly way the development of some body of discourse. More specifically, an outline is designed to show (1) the main points and subpoints of the development, (2) the chronological order in which they will be treated, and (3) the logical relationships that exist among the main points and subpoints.

The primary means by which an outline accomplishes these purposes are the *symbols* attached to each point and the *system of indentation*. Each point in the outline is assigned a symbol which shows its relationships to the other points around it, delineating not only where it appears in the sequence of ideas but also with which points it is *coordinate* and to which points it is *subordinate*. The coordination and subordination of points are also indicated by indentation. Points that are coordinate with one another are indented to the same degree. A point that is subordinate to another is indented to a greater degree than is the idea to which it is subordinate. Thus, the farther to the right a point is indented, the more subordinate (and, usually, the less important) it is in the overall development of the speech. Conversely, the points which begin at the left margin of the outline are the main points and carry the greatest weight.

Rules for Effective Outlining

The nature of an outline requires that we follow a few basic rules if we desire the outline to be effective:

1. *Limit each of the points to a single idea.* This is crucial if the outline is to achieve its basic purpose: to show the sequence of and relationships among the ideas within a body of discourse. Combining two or more ideas within a single point defeats this purpose.

In this regard beware of compound sentences. While technically a compound is a single sentence, by definition a compound sentence contains more than one idea. For example, the sentence "Jesus was born in Bethlehem but he was raised in Nazareth" is a compound sentence containing two distinct ideas connected by a conjunction. Divide all compound sentences into their components and then decide how each of the components fits within the outline.

2. *Each point in the outline should be a discrete entity, distinct from its coordinates.* Overlapping meanings in coordinate points should be avoided. To illustrate, suppose these two points appeared as coordinate in an outline:

    A. The goal of outlining is to show the development of an idea.
    B. The purpose of outlining is to demonstrate relationships among subpoints in a body of discourse.

Obviously, the two points are redundant, even though one uses the term *goal* and the other uses the term *purpose*. There is no sequence or progression to these ideas; they largely repeat one another. Such overlapping should be avoided in *coordinate* points. It might be possible, of course, to make the second statement *subordinate* to the first. In this case, the second statement would serve as the beginning of the development of the first point. But in this case the arrangement in the outline would have to be changed:

> A. The goal of outlining is to show the development of an idea.
>> 1. The purpose of outlining is to demonstrate relationships among subpoints in a body of discourse.

Almost by definition, subordinate points will overlap in meaning with the superior points they are designed to develop. But between coordinate points such overlap should be avoided.

   3. *Always use a consistent set of symbols.* The standard symbols are as follows:

I.
II.
III.
    A.
    B.
    C.
       1.
       2.
       3.
          a.
          b.
          c.
             (1)
             (2)
             (3)
                (a)
                (b)
                (c)

Another symbol system, which seems to be gaining popularity, has certain advantages over the older, standard pattern. With the standard system, detailed outlines which have more than five levels of indentation become very cumbersome. They are forced to use symbols such as *aa*, or even *(bbb)*. With the newer system, however, this problem is eliminated since the system is capable of up to twenty-six levels of indentation, a number which very few outlines (not to mention *speech* outlines!) ever need. This newer system is as follows:

A1.
A2.
A3.
    B1.
    B2.
    B3.
        C1.
        C2.
        C3.
            D1.
            D2.
            D3.
                E1.
                E2.
                E3.

Whether one uses the older or newer system, it is important to use the symbols consistently. Whatever symbol is chosen for a particular level of indentation should be used exclusively for this level throughout. Using the symbols inconsistently confuses the entire outline.

4. *Be sure that the logical relationships between the points are accurately represented by their placement in the outline.* It is common to see outlines, particularly from beginners, that at first glance look perfect. On the page they appear to be balanced, clear, and easy to understand. However, upon closer examination they prove to be something quite different. The logical relationships suggested by the outline's arrangement are nonexistent. To illustrate, examine this portion of an outline:

  I. Outlining helps the speaker think through the development of her speech intelligently.
- A. The process of outlining helps the speaker clarify her own understanding of the points of the speech.
- B. The process of outlining helps the speaker think clearly about relationships between her points.
- C. The process of outlining helps the listener clearly understand the development of the speech.
- D. The process of outlining helps the speaker by calling attention to possible gaps in the speech structure.

Notice that this outline is technically correct: one idea per point; each point distinctive enough to justify a separate point; a consistent set of symbols. As it lies on the page, it appears to be a valid outline. But notice that point C does not fit. By placing point C in this position, the author is telling us, on the one hand,

---

Outlining Exercise

Organize the following statements into a balanced outline having a central idea and two main points. Check your work against the sample outline on page 183 .

1. Your experience shows that you recall well-organized talks and forget confusing ones.
2. Outlining calls our attention to gaps in logic in the structure of our speech.
3. Joe Doaks had only a hazy notion of what he wanted to say until he wrote carefully worded sentences outlining his idea.
4. A good outline helps listeners remember what is said.
5. Sometimes we quite literally do not know what we are talking about.
6. Experiments by Professor Magoo show that impressions received in a pattern are more readily understood and recalled.
7. Karen Smith did not see how little evidence she had for the main idea until she wrote an outline.
8. Outlining helps us clarify our own thoughts.
9. A good outline helps us develop ideas more intelligently.
10. All of us need help in seeing weaknesses in our speeches.

---

that its content is coordinate with points A, B, and D and, on the other hand, that it is one of the four subordinate points she is using to develop point I. However, if we look at the content of point C, we find that it does not function in this way at all. It does not develop point I, nor is it coordinate with points A, B, and D. But suppose the outline were rearranged so that the same point appeared in the outline not as point C, but as point II. In this case the outline would look like this:

I. Outlining helps the speaker think through the development of her speech intelligently.

   A. The process of outlining helps the speaker clarify her own understanding of the points of the speech.
   B. The process of outlining helps the speaker think clearly about the relationships between her points.
   C. The process of outlining helps the speaker by calling attention to possible gaps in the speech structure.

II. Outlining helps the listener clearly understand the development of the speech.

In this version, the outline is telling us (correctly) that the point in question is not directly related (in either a coordinate or subordinate way) to points A, B, and C. Instead, this new arrangement suggests that the point is actually to be viewed as coordinate with point I, perhaps as a second reason why outlining is valuable.

What these two examples demonstrate is that the arrangement of points in an outline is designed to tell us something about their *logical* relationships to one another. It is not sufficient merely to place them on the page so that they *appear to be* a coherent outline. The relationships suggested by the outline's format must accurately reflect the actual logical relationships between the points.

It would be difficult to overemphasize this point since this is such a prevalent problem in outlining. Almost any relationships we find in verbal discourse can be captured in outline form. Our task in producing an effective outline is to reflect these relationships accurately.

Sample Outline

Introduction:
1. Sue Jones decided to take a shortcut in producing her speech by skipping an outline.
2. Unfortunately, though Sue had worked hard on her speech, when she was through, few in her audience had gotten her point.
3. Sue had skipped a crucial step in producing an effective speech: the clear organization of her ideas.

Central Idea:
Good outlining improves communication in public speaking.

Body:
I. A good outline helps us develop ideas more intelligently.
    A Outlining helps us clarify our own thoughts.
        1. Sometimes we quite literally do not know what we are talking about.
        2. Joe Doaks had only a hazy notion of what he wanted to say until he wrote carefully worded sentences outlining his idea.
    B. Outlining calls our attention to gaps in logic in the structure of our speech.
        1. All of us need help in seeing weaknesses in our speeches.
        2. Karen Smith did not see how little evidence she had for the main idea until she wrote an outline.
II. A good outline helps listeners remember what is said.
    A. Experiments by Professor Magoo show that impressions received in a pattern are more easily understood and recalled.
    B. Your experience shows that you recall well-organized talks and forget confusing ones.

Conclusion:
1. Sue Jones learned the hard way that to be healthy, a speech, like the human body, must have a sound skeleton.
2. A good outline is the skeleton that makes effective communication in a speech possible.

Speech Outlines

While speech outlines function essentially as do any other outlines, they are also in some ways unique. Here are some additional rules to follow when preparing outlines for a speech:

1. *Every point in the outline should be a full sentence.* As we have noted previously, it is impossible to have a complete thought without both a subject and complement. Thus, to insure that you know precisely what you are saying at each point in your outline, you should state each thought in its complete form, a full sentence.

It is literally true that many speakers do not know what they are saying. They have settled for merely a word or phrase for each of their points in the outline and as a result have failed to state their complete thought even to themselves in their preparation. Is it any wonder that when they stand before a group their point does not come across clearly? They have not even understood it fully themselves!

Forcing yourself to state each of your points in full-sentence form will prevent this needless problem. To be sure, once you have this full-sentence outline you may want to back up and simplify it, representing each of the points with just a phrase or key word. Such simplified outlines are often more helpful in practicing your speech than is the full-sentence outline, but only provided you have first stated your exact points in full sentences.

2. *Do not use symbols for the introduction, body, and conclusion.* The symbol system should be reserved for the development *within* each of these parts. The reason for this is that the relationships between the major parts of a speech cannot be adequately represented by outline form, whereas the relationships within these parts can. Thus the best approach is simply to label the introduction, body, and conclusion separately, reserving the symbol system for the development within each part (see the sample, p. 183).

3. *Keep the design of the speech outline clear and simple.* As Davis says, "The only design useful to the listener is a design he can grasp through his ears, an audible movement of the thought."[10] An involuted or convoluted design may be accept-

able in certain kinds of writing where the reader can check back and reread portions of the text, but it will not do in a speech. The listener requires an arrangement that flows clearly and is simple enough to grasp the first time through.

In this regard you will probably be wise to limit your main points to no more than five, or perhaps six at the most. Few audiences will be able to assimilate more than five or six major points in a speech. If your initial division of your subject results in more than five or six divisions, try to reclassify these divisions into fewer but broader points so that the number of main ideas eventually falls into the range of two to five. This is an ideal range for oral discourse.

Remember, too, that all of the main points are to be directly subordinate to the central idea of the speech, as well as coordinate with each other. One should be able to examine these main points alone and at once discover the speech in a nutshell, so to speak. The overall speech pattern, the flow of ideas, the logic of the speech, the central idea itself—all of these should be immediately evident from an examination of simply the main points of the outline.

4. *Keep the wording of your outline lean and concise.* There is sometimes a tendency for speakers to allow the wording of the speech to become the wording of the outline. This can often lead to problems. In chapter 8 we will discuss the kind of wording which appeals to the ear of the listener, and we will urge you to seek such wording to communicate your speech. But an outline is not a speech manuscript. It does not have to appeal to anyone's ear. It needs only to capture your ideas clearly and accurately. Therefore it should contain wording that is as simple, concise, and straightforward as you can make it. Trim away all the fat—keep your outline lean.

5. *Put all transitions in parentheses between the points they connect.* Transitions make explicit the logical relationships between the points; they are not themselves points in the outline. Thus they should be inserted in parenthetical form. In this way they are plainly stated (in oral discourse this can be crucial!), but they do not confuse the outline form.

We began this section by noting that outlines are designed to show both *logical* and *chronological* relationships between the points in the development of some body of discourse. But there is a potential pitfall for speakers here we need to highlight.

Sometimes the arrangement of a point and its subpoints in an outline prompts a speaker to confuse the chronological and logical aspects. Because a superior point in an outline is placed above and before its subordinate points does not necessarily require the superior point to be stated first in the speech itself. The outline arrangement is basically designed to show the *logical* relationships between the superior and subordinate points, not a *chronological* relationship. Of course, the superior point *may be* stated first in the speech before going on to the subpoints, but this is not inherently necessary.

On the other hand, where a series of coordinate points is listed, a chronological relationship *is implied* in the outline. Point II will always precede point III; point D will always precede point E; point 2 will always precede point 3; and so forth. Here definite chronological relationships are built into the outline.

Inexperienced speakers often lose sight of the difference between logical and chronological aspects of an outline. They assume that the order in which the points appear in the outline is exactly the order they must take in the speech itself. To a large degree, of course, this will be the case; but *there will inevitably be exceptions.* Often with an inductive pattern, for instance, the superior point will not be stated until *after* each of the subpoints has been examined. Yet in the outline the superior point appears before and above the subpoints. The difference is due to the fact that the position of the superior point in the outline reflects a *logical* relationship in this case, but not necessarily a *chronological* relationship. By contrast, the subpoints, which are *coordinate* with each other, will all emerge in the speech in exactly the order in which they appear in the outline.

Some Final Pointers

As you attempt to grapple with the question of which speech patterns will best fit your idea and its development, keep these five pointers in mind:

1. Always attempt to arrange your points so that the speech builds to a climax at the end. To allow the speech to reach a climax before the end is to render all that follows anticlimactic. Such anticlimax is very frustrating to most people and should be avoided.

2. Remember that certain patterns fit certain kinds of subjects but not others. Be sure to let the nature of the subject matter determine how the idea is to be developed.

3. Where it is possible to do so, it is always a good practice to begin on common ground with your audience. Start with the familiar and move to the unfamiliar; explain the unknown in terms of the known. This is a basic principle of effective communication and should always be kept in mind in designing the development of a speech.

4. There is no set place where the central idea of the speech must first appear. It may appear at the beginning or be kept until the end of the speech, or it might first appear anywhere in between. The decision as to where the full statement of the central idea should first appear can be made only in the light of the type of development you have chosen. Actually, it is not particularly important where the central idea first appears; what is important is that *by the time you are through it must have been effectively communicated to your audience.* The decision as to where to allow the central idea to show itself first in its full form should be made on the basis of what will best accomplish the goal of effective communication of this central idea.

5. The typical patterns we have examined, only one of which may appear in any one speech, are not exclusive categories. Indeed, given the fact that a speech is made up of a series of units of thought (each one of which is composed of a central idea and its development), it is probable that several different patterns may occur in any one speech. Usually one of the patterns will dominate the overall development of the speech, but even here we cannot be dogmatic. You might use an inductive pattern to establish a generalization, from which you might then deduce inferences about other particulars. Or again, problem-solution types of patterns inevitably are related to cause-effect types of reasoning. Thus these two patterns might somehow

merge. Our point here is that what we have examined are merely typical patterns which are themselves susceptible to many variations, adaptations, and combinations.

Displaying Your Outline to Your Audience

It is possible to have a well-constructed outline in which each of the points is properly placed and relates to the others logically, and yet fail to *communicate* that structure clearly to the

---

The test of good writing is permanence, and the test of good speech is immediacy of apprehension and response.   H. Grady Davis

---

audience. In a speech the important thing is not what lies on the page, but what is left in the listener's mind when you are through. Thus it is not enough to *have* a clear structure; the structure *must be* communicated to the audience in such a way that they see the movement, the flow of thought, the relationships between and among the points. The audience must perceive these relationships at first hearing, for that is all they have. They must grasp through their ears how the entire structure works together to develop a central idea.

If you could distribute copies of your outline to the audience, the task might be easier. Your listeners could discern from the outline form how each of your points relates to the others. However, distributing your outline is seldom desirable, even where it is possible to do so. Instead you must create orally a structure in the listeners' minds. To accomplish this you will need to make liberal use of the four primary means of displaying structure orally: transitions, signposting, parallel wording, and time-weighting.

Transitions

Transitions are the bridges we build between the units of thought in a speech. They will sometimes be no more than a word or a phrase; at other times they will require a sentence or even an entire paragraph. Their length is determined solely by their purpose. Whatever is required to show the audience the relationships between this idea and the next one, that is how long the transition must be.

Effective transitions are crucial to any body of verbal discourse. Indeed, Wayne Booth, discussing some of the lessons in communication he learned from his own teachers, recalls how P. A. Christensen helped him understand that "my failure to use effective transitions was not simply a technical fault but a fundamental block in my effort to get him to see my meaning."[11] So it is with any audience. Transitions are the conveyors that move our audience from point to point. Without them the audience probably will not make the passage. So, even though transitions are typically brief, they play a role in communication that is all out of proportion to their size.

Transitions can take almost any form, but three major types stand out: additional, inferential, and disjunctive. *Additional transitions* are those which show one point building upon another. For example: "*In addition to* being dangerous, race-car driving can *also* be expensive"; "*Furthermore, not only* is Jesus Christ our sacrifice, he is *also* our great High Priest." *Inferential transitions* are used when some sort of logical inference is drawn from one point to another. For instance: "*Therefore,* since performing music can be such a delightful experience, every child ought to have the opportunity to learn to play an instrument"; "*So, it follows from this that* each American has the responsibility to vote"; "*Thus, because* Christ died for us, we ought to live for him." *Disjunctive transitions* are those which contrast two points or set one point apart from another: "*Yet, even though* China has made great strides in recent years, technologically it is still a very backward nation"; "*But if* the New York Stock Exchange performed poorly last year, the American Stock Exchange, *by contrast,* rose steadily"; "*On the other hand,* the fact that God knows our inner thoughts can be very threatening for sinful men and women."

Notice the *summary-and-preview* format of several of the above examples. This common and very useful format reminds the audience (sometimes using more than a single sentence) of the previous point(s) and then directs them to the next point, all the while suggesting the type of relationship which exists between the two. Another format transitions can take is the *rhetorical question*. Like the summary-and-preview format, the rhetorical-question format can be used with any of the types of transitions (additional, inferential, or disjunctive) or with all of them combined: "*But* can even these several sources of power combined satisfy America's need for energy in the decades to come? Probably not. *Thus,* America will no doubt *also* have to look to nuclear power as an important source of energy for the future."

Where should you use transitions in your outline? Generally some kind of transition should be used between the introduction and body, between the body and the conclusion, and within the body between the major points of the development. Beyond this there are no set rules. Simply remember that your goal is to take your audience with you through the flow of ideas in your speech. They must be able to distinguish between the most important, the less important, and the least important. They must grasp how the points relate to one another. They must understand the progression of your thought. Therefore you should use transitions wherever there is the possibility that your audience (1) needs a summary of what has been said before moving on, (2) needs a preview of what is coming before you can cover it, or (3) needs to see some relationship between your points which they might miss unless you make it more explicit.

Signposting

The term *signposting* refers to a number or label you attach to the points in your outline to differentiate them from one another and to inform the audience at each transition that you are moving to the next idea. The most common signposts are the numerical labels, "first," "second," "third," and so on. When these numerical signposts are attached to the main points, the audience will have little difficulty in recognizing the movement from one to the next. Variations of this basic numerical approach may also be used, such as "in the first place . . . ," "in the second place . . . ," "in the third place. . . ."

It is important to note, however, that this simple numerical signposting system can easily become very confusing to the listeners if the same numerical designations are used at several different levels of the speech's structure. Thus, if the numerical signposts are to be used for the Roman numerals in the outline (the main points), *do not* use them for the subpoints A and B, or 1 and 2. You are trying to sort out orally for your audience what is related to what. Using the same signposts for different levels of the outline confuses the order rather than makes it clear. This error should be studiously avoided.

Another common type of signposting consists of using key words as labels. This is essentially the interrogative-and-key-word approach we outlined earlier in this chapter, only in reverse. Look for some key word that will characterize the points in your outline. Perhaps your points represent "ways," "steps," "aspects," "types," or any other of a long list of plural nouns. Combine your key word with the numerical system of labeling, and you have a clear set of signposts to direct your audience's thinking: "The first way to win an election is . . ."; "The second step in the process of making paint is . . ."; "The third aspect of the problem is . . ."; "The fourth type of infectious disease is. . . ."

Again, be careful not to mix the labels in the outline. If the label for the main points is "types," use different labels for the other levels of the structure.

Parallel Wording

Another way to help your audience sort out your points and put them in proper perspective is to word coordinate points so that they are similar to each other, and dissimilar to other levels of the structure. In the outline below, notice the parallel wording of the main points, and of subpoints A and B within the first main point. Notice, too, how "outlining" has been changed to "the process of outlining" to distinguish the two levels of thought for the audience.

I.   *Outlining* helps the speaker develop his ideas intelligently.
  A.   *The process of outlining* helps the speaker clarify his own thinking.
    1.   Outlining helps us to see what we are saying.
    2.   Joe Doaks had only a vague idea of what he wanted to say until he developed a full-sentence outline of his speech.
      (Furthermore, . . .)
  B.   *The process of outlining* calls the speaker's attention to possible gaps in logic in the structure of his speech.
    1.   Bonnie Smith failed to see how little evidence she had to prove her main idea until she put her points down on paper.
    2.   Professor White has said, "Typically, the students in my classes whose speeches display the poorest thinking are those who have failed to outline their speeches first."
      (Not only does outlining help the speaker, but . . .)
II. *Outlining* helps the listener remember what is said.
  A.   Experiments conducted by Professor Magoo show that impressions perceived in a pattern are more readily understood and recalled than unpatterned stimuli.
  B.   Your own experience demonstrates that you recall well-organized talks and forget confusing ones.

Time-Weighting

The amount of time you spend developing a point is one of the most important indications to an audience of how significant that point is. This suggests at least two useful principles for speakers who wish to make their speech clear to the audience.

First, give more important points more time, less important points less time. This may seem obvious, but in practice it is quite easy to give so much time to a relatively minor point that an audience subconsciously begins to give it the weight of a major point. When this happens, confusion about the progression of thought in a speech is inevitable.

Second, continuously relate subpoints to the superior points they are designed to develop. As you move through the subpoints within one of the speech's units of thought, it is possible for the audience to lose sight of the broader point the subpoints are supposed to be serving. When this happens, the audience can become frustrated because they fail to see the relevance of the material being presented. Moreover, the listeners do not credit to the superior point the time you are spending developing the subpoints, all of which should be accruing in the listeners' minds to indicate the importance of the superior point. Thus the superior point itself is often lost in the overall structure of the speech. You can avoid this problem by designing your transitions, signposts, and parallel wording so that they regularly call to mind the superior point. This will usually be sufficient to keep the actual function of the subpoint in focus, which is to develop the superior point.

Exercises

1. Find a speech you like in the periodical *Vital Speeches*. Outline the speech and then analyze the outline to discover what principle of division was used in the speech as a whole and in its subdivisions. See if you can discover any of the common patterns we have discussed.

2. Use the interrogative-and-key-word approach to develop each of the following ideas into a speech outline: "Christians must love one another"; "Plants can liven up your living space"; and "Some of the greatest scenery in the world can be found in America's national parks." List the main points in each outline.

3. You must address a Saturday-night meeting of adults from your neighborhood on some subject relating to local politics. Come up with an appropriate idea for the speech and then develop the main points for your outline by using Monroe's Motivated Sequence.

4. In the course in public speaking you are teaching to high-school students, you must give a ten-minute lec-

ture on one of the following subjects: the role of transitions in a speech, characteristics of an effective outline, or typical speech patterns. Using the content of this chapter and any other sources you can find, develop an outline for that lecture.

Chapter **6**

How to Support
the Ideas of Your Speech

The human skeleton is not a very attractive thing to behold. Except by physicians and engineers who admire its ingenious utilitarian design, a skeleton has seldom been considered aesthetically pleasing. Few painters or sculptors, for example, have celebrated the bare human bone structure as a thing of beauty.

By contrast, the full human form, both male and female, has always been the object of artistic attention. Countless artisans have attempted to capture its beauty on canvas or chisel it into marble. The attractiveness of the human form would be inconceivable apart from a frame to give it shape, of course, but at the same time a skeleton alone is insufficient. It must be fleshed out, covered with skin, and then brought to life to be aesthetically pleasing. Anything short of this, such as the typical anatomical illustration one often finds in encyclopedias, may be informative but is seldom attractive to look at.

It is the same with a speech. We have been discussing the outline of your speech. This outline is the crucial skeleton which will give your finished product its basic form. The lack of such a skeleton would lead to a grotesque result, in a speech no less than in human form. Likewise, serious flaws in this skeleton will be impossible to camouflage in your finished product. The crippling effects of a misshapen frame will be as obvious in your speech as they are in the human body. Thus a well-constructed outline is crucial to the success of your speech.

But it is not enough in itself. As your outline now stands, it is a bare thing, utilitarian, lifeless, and probably not particularly attractive in itself (except to technicians such as teachers of public speaking!). These bones must be fleshed out with supporting material, covered with a skin of words, and then brought to life in your delivery. These, then, are our next steps in the process of developing an effective speech. In this chapter we will deal with the process of fleshing out the body of your speech with supporting materials.

Functions of Supporting Material

Supporting materials serve two primary functions in a speech. First, supporting material may be used to explain, clarify, amplify, or demonstrate the implications of your point. This is the *informative function* of supporting material. Second, supporting material may also be used to prove, verify, or provide evidence for the credibility of your point. This is the *persuasive function* of supporting material.

To be sure, the distinction between the informative and persuasive functions of a given piece of supporting material is mainly a theoretical one. In practice it is often true that the same piece of supporting material will be at once both informative and persuasive to your audience—or predominantly informative to one member of the audience and predominantly persuasive to another. Thus in any given instance it may not be easy to determine exactly which function (or combination of functions) a unit of support is fulfilling.

Nevertheless, the distinction between the informative and persuasive functions is a useful one for our purposes here since it provides us with a helpful approach to analyzing the various types of supporting material available to you as a speaker, as well as how they may serve your speech. Thus we will examine each of the various kinds of supporting material, attempting to show, where appropriate, how they may appear with both an informative thrust and a persuasive thrust.

Though the primary functions of supporting material are to inform and persuade, it is also true that such materials can serve a third, subsidiary purpose: they provide your audience with the variety and relief they need to maintain their attention.

In chapter 2 we discussed how difficult it is for people to sustain their attention upon any single stimulus for an extended length of time. Remember that you must not only win the audience's attention at the outset, but *must win it again and again throughout the speech.* Effective supporting materials tend to do just that. Since sustained attention is so difficult, each piece of support can be a new and different stimulus to grasp the audience's attention afresh. Moreover, since many types of supporting material have high "entertainment value" and are therefore easier to listen to than other parts of the speech, the audience can take a breather, so to speak, in their efforts to listen. Their attention can become "involuntary," requiring much less work from them than the "voluntary" attention required to follow some of the less entertaining parts of the speech.

First: A Sample

We want to look closely at the different types of supporting material available to you as a speaker. But before we do, let us look first at a speech that was delivered by Ernest L. Boyer before the annual convention of the Speech Communication Association. As the United States Commissioner of Education, Boyer spoke on the topic "Communication: Message Senders and Receivers."[1]

There are two reasons why we want to look at this speech. First, the speaker has some interesting things to say about the practice of communication in our society. The issues this speech raises are as pertinent as tomorrow's newspaper, even though it was delivered in 1977. What's more, with hindsight you have an added advantage. As you read this speech, think about these questions: How accurate was Boyer's analysis at the time? Are the problems Boyer described still with us? Have the electronic revolution that has taken place since 1977 and the presence today of television in our public schools improved the situation Boyer describes? In what ways have the problems Boyer addresses worsened since 1977? Has television in America become, in the words Boyer quotes from E. B. White, "a new and unbearable disturbance to the general peace" or "a saving radiance in the sky"? Because you are interested in the subject of communication in our society—or else you would not be reading this book—you should find Boyer's ideas provocative. As a Christian you may not agree with him at every point, but that will only serve to help you understand your own views more fully.

Second, and more directly related to our immediate purposes, this speech provides helpful examples of a fairly wide range of different types of supporting material. As you read this speech, make a note of all the different types of supporting material you can identify. Notice how Boyer uses them to help make his point. Try to evaluate whether the supporting material you identify is effective. Wherever possible, try to think about what *you* might have used had you had to support the same point.

When you have finished reading this speech, we will move on to examine each of the major types of supporting material you may find useful as you prepare your speech. At every opportunity, we will refer to Boyer's speech to illustrate those types of supporting material, so that you can see examples in context.

COMMUNICATION:
Message Senders and Receivers

I'm delighted to be with you at this national gathering of professionals in communication. This convocation permits me not only to meet with friends, but also to comment on a circumstance so central to our existence that we rarely take the
5   time to notice it.

It is a simple yet essential fact that, to a large extent, communication is what makes us who we are. The sending and the receiving of messages is a crucial feature that separates us from other animals whose repertoire of symbols is more meager, pro-
10   vides the social connecting tissue which binds us together, and gives us our identities and our meaning. Communication is, in short, the centerpiece of what we share in common.

And I should emphasize that the communicative process goes far beyond the need to read and write, to speak clearly
15   and connectedly, and to learn how to decode the messages of others. All of human knowledge is in fact embodied and conveyed in symbols, and even internal conversations within ourselves are mediated by the complex miracle of language. My point is simply this: "communication" is just a more specific

20 name for "consciousness." All we know, all we fear, and all we
hope is created and conveyed through symbols.

Once, in an era that differed so sharply from our own that
scholars call it "pre-history," words were traded face to face.
The sounds of the drum were mute without a listener. It was a
25 time when "you had to be there" to send or receive a message.

Then, first through art and later through the invention of
written symbols, messages could be encoded and preserved.
Meanings could be experienced vicariously by someone else,
at a later time, and in a different place. Messages became inex-
30 haustible. The same sentence could bring meaning to a thousand different ears. This was the first revolution in communication: the invention of a symbol system that endured and
could be widely understood.

The name "Gutenberg" [inventor of the first printing press
35 with movable type] has quite rightly acquired in our history a
monumental stature. The invention of movable type meant
that messages could now be transmitted to geometrically spi-
ralling numbers of people. The age of mass communications—
and the age of the "masses"—was indeed born in a fifteenth-
40 century town in Germany, and the printing press was the
midwife in attendance.

The culture of the printed page—the culture of vicarious
communication—has burgeoned since that time, especially in
recent years. In 1948, for example, the year Harry Truman
45 defeated Dewey, the *New York Times* index ran 1,211 pages;
by 1970, the total had soared to 2,291 pages. In 1960, 15,000
book titles were published; a decade later, it had more than
doubled, to over 36,000. More than 2,000 large, closely printed
pages are now required merely to list by author, title, and sub-
50 ject the paperback books currently in print.

This, then, is the era launched by Gutenberg. This is the era
in which most of us in this room were born. This is the era
upon which the purposes, the content, and the methods of
American education have been based. And this is the era
55 which, for better or worse, now confronts dramatic change.

In the summer of 1938, the great essayist and novelist E. B.
White sat in a darkened room and watched transfixed as a big
electronic box began projecting eerie, shimmering images into
the world. It was his first introduction to something called TV.
60 E. B. White, who not only wrote *Charlotte's Web* but also coau-

thored that great manual of clear communication, *The Elements of Style,* said in 1938:

> I believe television is going to be the test of the modern world, and that in this new opportunity to
> 65 see beyond the range of our vision, we shall discover either a new and unbearable disturbance to the general peace, or a saving radiance in the sky. We shall stand or fall by television—of that I am quite sure.

70 Forty years have passed and television has to a remarkable degree fulfilled both of E. B. White's predictions. It has at once become both "an unbearable disturbance" *and* "a soaring radiance in the sky." Ideas were once built and assimilated slowly, and often with great effort. Now we inhabit a
75 culture of images. Messages are sent and received instantaneously, and a premium is placed on the accessible.

Perhaps in the *print* culture, because of the effort it required, ideas were more important and enduring. Perhaps in the *video* culture, with its emphasis on speed and ease,
80 ideas have become more fleeting, and less valued. For increasingly we seem magnetically to be drawn toward those visible images which pack a bigger punch, provoke a more visceral reflex, and which capture more cunningly our mercurial attentiveness. We have in short become the age of the
85 flash and the zap, the hour-long epic, the thirty-minute encyclopedia, the five-minute explanation, the one-minute sell, the ten-second teaser, the two-second fix.

And what are we to make of all this? How do we come to terms, educationally, with a world where messages have
90 become more persistent and more varied?

First, our colleges and schools must acknowledge the expanded classroom and establish new partnerships with those who teach beyond the campuses.

When I was young less than fifty years ago there was no
95 television in our home. I was 12 years old before we purchased our first radio. We did receive a daily newspaper, and the *National Geographic,* which I eagerly devoured as soon as it arrived. Our Model A took us on short excursions from our Ohio home, rarely more than 100 miles or so.

100   As I look back on those early years, *school* was *the* central
learning place. The *teacher,* for better or for worse, was the key
source of knowledge, and the *classroom* was the intellectual
window to the world. (It was only later that I learned just how
clouded that window could sometimes be.)

105   For students coming to our schools today that world I knew
is ancient history. Today the first thing to captivate the infant
in the cradle is probably that iridescent, inexhaustible screen.
At least one study has shown that, by the age of three, children are purposeful viewers who can name their favorite pro-

110   grams. Young children 2 to 5 years old now watch television
over 4 hours every day, nearly 30 hours a week. That's more
than 1,500 hours every year. And by the time a youngster
enters the first grade he or she has had 6,000 hours of television viewing.

115   This same TV saturation continues after school begins. By
the time of high school graduation, the average child will have
spent *thirty percent more time watching television than in
school.* It's been estimated that the 1980 Olympic Games in
Moscow will be watched by 2 billion people—half the human

120   race. Small wonder that the traditional teacher is often
bypassed. A new source of information has emerged.

Several years ago our young son, who had just entered
kindergarten, said the alphabet one night when he went to
bed, rather than his prayers. At the end I complimented him

125   for having recited the alphabet without a hitch, even though
he had been in kindergarten just one week. He replied by saying: "Actually I learned the alphabet on *Sesame Street* but my
kindergarten teacher thinks *she* taught it to me." I was
delighted. My son had not only learned the alphabet; he had

130   learned the system too!

My *National Geographic,* which gave me glimpses of the outside world, has today been smothered by an avalanche of publications—some good, some bad—which open up new worlds to
students. Today, paperbacks, magazines, television, and travel

135   compete on equal footing with the classroom and the book.
Today, for better or for worse, Archie Bunker is better known
than Silas Marner, Fellini is more influential than Faulkner, and
the six o'clock news is more compelling than the history text.

It seems quite clear to me that the separate sources of

140   information which educate our children must somehow be
brought together. It *is* true of course that in recent years the

use of television as a teaching tool has expanded. *Sesame Street* and *The Electric Company* have had dramatic impact. *The Adams Chronicles, The Ascent of Man* and *Masterpiece Theatre* have been successfully linked with courses, and with special texts. And data from a recent study of television in our schools show that many teachers have instructional television in the classroom. But still, these are exceptions, I'm afraid.

Not only has education not begun to acknowledge the communications revolution in our midst, there is often open conflict between formal and informal education. For example, the Wirtz Report which looked at test score decline suggested that TV must share the blame for the drop in school performance. And on the other side of this face-off between print and video communication we have Jack Valenti, president of the Motion Picture Association of America, who tells us that watching too much television is not the easy answer for the score decline. The solution, according to Valenti, is not less television, but "discipline in the classroom, no mucking around with excellence, and a stern commitment to the basics of learning. That is the province of schools and teachers, and no amount of scolding of TV will erase the logic."

But surely this so-called stand-off between the classroom and TV reflects our narrowness rather than our vision. Surely, the various sources of information need not be in competition with each other. Surely, our job as communicators as well as educators is to recognize the world has changed, to rejoice in the marvel of expanding knowledge and to find ways to relate the classroom more closely to the networks of information beyond the classroom.

But it is insufficient for our schools and colleges to acknowledge the communications revolution in our midst—as important as the first step may be. *We also must help our students become more sophisticated themselves as message senders and receivers.*

Today in a thousand different ways, billboards, magazines, radio, the newspapers, and TV bombard our students. Through the news, TV provides them their main source of current information. Through drama, comedy, and entertainment they see images of themselves. Through the newspaper, radio and TV their stereotypes of the good life are formed. Through advertising, their wants are transformed into needs. These stimuli have themselves become a *new curriculum,* and our schools and colleges must confront this fact.

185   To educate our students wisely, we need new courses on ways to undeceive ourselves, on ways to spot a stereotype, on ways to recognize a premise, isolate a social cliché, on ways to distinguish fact from propaganda, analysis from banter, and to sort out important news from mere "coverage." In a time when the "novelization" of the show sells more briskly than

190 the novel on which the show was based, we must educate our students on how to sort out and evaluate the messages they receive.

    I have one other suggestion to propose. The time has come to emphasize not only the *receiving* of messages; we must

195 focus on the *sending* of messages as well.

    One of the unhappy characteristics of our culture is the trend toward increased passivity. We are soaking up the messages of others and becoming less effective in formulating messages of our own. All across America tonight, millions of families will be

200 transfixed by their glowing television screens. Millions of people will spend from three to five hours in those darkened rooms— watching, listening, absorbing. They will be sponges, soaking up the messages. They will be passive, not active, communicators. Instead of speaking, they will be listening. Instead of formulating

205 their own ideas, they will be the targets of thoughts hurled at them. We have, in short, become a nation of receivers, not of senders. Small wonder that signs point to a decline in our ability to express ourselves clearly and precisely.

    Every day in my own world of education, bureaucratic jar-

210 gon seems incessantly to clutter up the day. Regulations and guidelines are gnarled and contorted and warped by legalese. Buzz-words fly about with abandon. Acronyms proliferate faster than cockroaches.

    The other day I was in a meeting with some colleagues. I

215 was troubled by one sentence in a publication our Office was about to issue. I didn't understand it, and I asked for help. "Oh yes," my colleague replied, agreeing that the sentence should be clarified, "we'll have to laymanize it."

    "'Laymanize'?" I repeated in disbelief. "Do you mean,

220 'Write clearly'? Because if you do, you're an example of the disease you're trying to cure."

    Sometimes I feel as if I'm swimming in alphabet soup. One day I overheard a conversation between two associates. "Are you going to IPA him for NIE to IEL?" one asked. "Either

225 that," came the reply, "or we'll try for a 15 C in the IOC."

Other days I'm convinced the Office of Education is a kind of war zone. We have "target groups," "rifleshot policies," "thrusts," "impacts," and "zeroings": quite a way to treat small children. All too often I discover someone asks "to dialogue"
230 with me; a group wants to arrange "a productive interface"; an associate volunteers "to share" a paper with me. I cannot believe sometimes the sloppy sentences that are found in correspondence or in college compositions, and I cannot believe the unfinished, half-articulated sentences that pose as coherent speech.
235 The conclusion to all of this is clear. It's time for all of us to focus on the goal of clear and precise expression. It's time to teach children not only how to read and look but how to write and speak as well. Direct, clear, forceful expression is a reflection of clear and uncluttered thinking. I'm convinced that Amer-
240 ican education must once again focus on this essential goal.

My last suggestion is tied very closely to your convention theme. Your theme, "A Center Which Holds," is, I assume, an allusion to that great poem of W. B. Yeats, "The Second Coming." Yeats wrote:

245   Things fall apart: The center cannot hold;
         Mere anarchy is loosed upon the world. . . .
         The best lack all conviction, while the
         worst are full of passionate intensity.
         Surely some revelation is at hand.
250   Surely the second coming is at hand.

It is too much, of course, to speak of communication in apocalyptic terms, and yet, it just may be that the miracle of mass communication, which is so unsettling at times, may, in fact, help to build among us a new kind of understanding
255 in our midst, a new kind of "center" if you will.

Recently John Platt, of the University of California, observed that TV's images and waves

         represent a world larger and older than the family
         or the village night, stretching to Washington or to
260   the moon, or years into the vanished past. And
         with habit, they become more real and more
         important than the family, as the war comes nightly
         to our dinner table, and we walk on the moon
         together or attend the Kennedy funeral.

265 Not many days ago an Egyptian head of State said in an interview, almost casually it seemed, that he would like to address the Israeli Parliament. Hours later satellites beamed to every inch of the inhabited earth the news of his remark.
270 Television multiplied his comment, played and replayed it, and held him to it almost as a dare. Only days later, Barbara Walters, Walter Cronkite, and John Chancellor arrived in Cairo to accompany President Sadat on his historic trip, almost as a way of certifying it. Then, at Ben Gurion Airport hundreds of millions of viewers around the world simultane-
275 ously experienced the electric moment as an Arab plane touched down on Israeli soil.

It is not to diminish what happened last week in the Middle East to say that none of the words exchanged during that visit, none of the speeches, none of the documents, none of
280 the private meetings, none of the toasts, was as significant as the riveting of the world's attention to one single, simultaneous, breathtaking, symbolic image—the image of two former enemies as they greeted one another. Instantly 500 million people felt their connectedness. They were drawn
285 together, shared a common image, and for one fleeting moment, the center seemed to hold.

In the end, of course, it's not *how* we send our messages but what we say that truly matters, and it just may be that as we speak more thoughtfully to each other with more compassion
290 and more care, our understanding will improve and our world may for all of us become a safer and more satisfying place.

Thanks for inviting me here today.

Types of Supporting Material

Now let us examine the major types of supporting material speakers commonly use. But as we do so, keep these things in mind: First, the only real limits on the types of supporting material you can discover are the limits of your own imagination. While the types we will survey here are the most common, our list should not be viewed as exhaustive. Second, these categories are not mutually exclusive. That is, any given piece of supporting material might overlap into more than a single category. We will not quibble over categories, but will rather attempt to provide as many helpful suggestions as possible. (Note: the numbers in parentheses throughout the following paragraphs refer to the lines in Boyer's speech where you find examples of the type of supporting material under discussion.)

Examples

One of the most common types of supporting material is the *example*. According to the dictionary an example is "something selected to show the nature or character of the rest." Thus an example is always a particular specimen or instance of the more general point it is designed to illustrate.

For instance, it is not uncommon in the world of football to hear someone say that Super Bowl contenders will always be those teams with the strongest defenses. One way to respond to such an assertion would be to ask, "For example?" To which the speaker might reply, "Why, think of the 'Steel Curtain' of the Pittsburgh Steelers, or the 'Doomsday Defense' of the Dallas Cowboys, two teams who during the 1960s and 1970s were perennial Super Bowl contenders." What the speaker has done is to give examples to illustrate the general statement about the kind of teams who tend to wind up in the Super Bowl.

Examples can be long or short. A short, undetailed example which is merely cited rather than developed is often called a *specific instance* (84–87; 134–38; 142–48; 175–83; 209–13; 226–34). A longer, more detailed example is commonly termed an *illustration* (199–206; 214–21; 222–25; 265–86). The references to the Pittsburgh Steelers and the Dallas Cowboys would be considered specific instances, whereas the following example would be considered an illustration. Here William Wearly, chairman of the board of the Ingersoll-Rand Company, attempted to demonstrate to his Rotary Club audience that many of the government regulations companies must comply with today are both frivolous and costly. As part of his argument he cited this story:

> For example, a safety inspector for OSHA (Occupational Safety and Health Act) visited our Painted Post, New York, plant, one of our largest, and issued us a citation for "lack of adequate ventilation for general welding and cutting," which carried a $50

fine. He cited "Section 1910.252 (e) (2) (i)" which required 1,200 feet of ventilation per booth. This OSHA inspector refused to consider the open-ended portion of curtained welding booths as an extension of the ventilation area; and he drew an imaginary line there.

Our company contested his decision, and the case was tried right here in Syracuse before an OSHA judge. The government appeared, after lengthy pleadings, to try the case with two lawyers. The OSHA inspector's testimony on cross examination was discredited and thrown out. The judge found in our favor, but not before many days of work by both the Ingersoll-Rand and government staffs—all over a silly ruling.[2]

(Notice that much of the detail of this illustration [e.g., "Section 1910.252 (e) (2) (i)"] is intentionally included to point out the trivial aspects of the regulations. Usually you would want to exclude such detail.)

Most illustrations appear in the form of a narrative (22–41). They may be stories, anecdotes, jokes, historical or biographical allusions, or personal reminiscences (94–104; 122–30). In each case, they provide a detailed example by reciting a series of events which, when taken together, illustrate the point.

There are two things to remember when using a narrative. (1) Keep it short. Pare away *unnecessary* details so that the narrative is lean, simple, and to the point. Give emphasis to the parts of the story which carry your point and let the rest melt into the background. (2) Make it graphic. The story should come alive for the audience. Use concrete, colorful language so that the audience can actually conjure up the images of the story in their minds.

Examples need not be factual to be effective. Hypothetical examples can be very useful in developing your point. Suppose, for example (notice that I am about to provide a hypothetical example), that a speaker is attempting to argue that nuclear-power plants in our society pose a serious threat to the safety of our people. Since American power plants have to date produced no known disasters (although the Three Mile Island incident was close), each of the potential "threats" would have to be introduced as a hypothetical example: "Suppose that the cooling system were to fail. The inner core would overheat, causing a break in the retaining wall, and radioactive materials would spew out upon the surrounding population, as it did at Chernobyl in the Soviet Union. Or suppose that a band of terrorists were to steal the materials to make a crude atomic bomb. They might hold up a whole city for blackmail." Such hypothetical examples could be used to illustrate the potential threat of nuclear-power plants.

When using examples for a persuasive purpose, it is often helpful to keep them short and then compound the effect by listing a series of them quickly. Single, longer examples can also be effective if they are particularly appropriate, but the cumulative effect of a series of specific instances is usually more dramatic. Notice, for instance, how a series of examples can drive home the point that the system of measurement used in the United States is an antiquated hodgepodge and should be changed to the metric system:

> It has been estimated that every day in the United States 20 billion measurements are made, and to calculate those measurements we use a "Rube Goldberg" system that goes back to the Babylonians and Egyptians, Romans and Vikings, and some English monarchs.
>
> In early Egyptian texts there is the figure of the forearm which was the symbol used to represent the cubit. The cubit was the earliest recorded unit of measurement. It was the length of a man's arm from the elbow to the fingertip—roughly 18 inches. Noah's ark, for example, was 300 cubits long.
>
> For measuring weight in early Egypt, grains of wheat were used. The carat was used to weigh gems, and it was based upon the weight of the "tiny carob seed."
>
> The mile, on the other hand, was a measurement established by the Romans. It was 1,000 double steps taken by a Roman legionary—the equivalent of 5,000 Roman feet. Queen Bess of England added 280 feet to the mile so it would be exactly 8 "furrows long" or "furlongs." The inch was established in the tenth century by measuring the span of the knuckles on King Edgar's thumb. And Charlemagne decreed that the foot was to be the length of his own foot—12.7 inches, by present day standards.
>
> In the 16th century, the Germans had another definition of the foot. The regulation was as follows: Stand at the door of a church on Sunday. Bid 16 men to stop—tall ones and short ones—as

they happen to pass out as the service is finished. Then make them put their left feet one behind the other. The length obtained shall be a right and lawful rod, and the 16th shall be a right and lawful foot.

So much for an accurate foot. What about the acre? The acre as a unit of measurement was the amount of land plowed by a yoke of oxen in one day. And the gallon used in the U.S. today was the amount of liquid in Queen Anne's wine jug. We have, in short, a system of measurement that does not reflect order or design, but rather the accidents of history and the oddities of the anatomy.[3]

Statistics

The term *statistics* refers to any use of numerical quantification such as figures, totals, percentages, or ratios to show the extent or frequency of something. In essence, statistics represent a summary of examples in numerical form.

Statistics can be very helpful in a speech when they are used properly (44–50; 110–20). This requires that you follow one simple rule: Be sure that the statistics are communicated clearly. Since statistics are usually concise, compact, and efficient—that is, they summarize much information in a small space—it is quite easy to overload your audience's capacity to understand.

I always find that statistics are hard to swallow and impossible to digest. The only one I can ever remember is that if all the people who go to sleep in church were laid end to end, they would be a lot more comfortable. Mrs. Robert A. Taft

---

Thus you should refrain from giving too many statistics at once. Give the figures time to sink in by spreading them throughout your speech. Also, you should avoid cluttering your listeners' minds with needless details. Usually you should try to round off larger numbers. Let "4,001,273" become "approximately four million." This is much easier to assimilate than the exact figure.

Furthermore, since statistics are by definition abstract things, what you may gain in *conciseness* you give up in *vividness*. Audiences are often unable to comprehend fully the meaning of a statistic unless you help them interpret it. Always seek some way to make the statistic come to life for them so that they can appreciate its true meaning.

For example, one federal bureaucrat from the Office of Management and Budget, in an attempt to keep his employees from becoming jaded by the large amounts of money they toss about regularly, calculated that a million dollars' worth of quarters stands almost as high as Mount Everest; that the number of quarters in the current year's federal budget would reach as far as five round trips to the moon; that the number of dollar bills in the current proposed budget would weigh 531,600 tons. In each case, what might have been just a set of numbers, too immense and abstract for the audience to comprehend, is transformed into an image with a vividness that registers upon the listener.

You may not always be able to find such graphic ways to bring your statistics to life, but you must always be sure that the significance of the figures does come across. In the following example, notice how Newton Minow, in a speech about the current state of television in America, uses two brief quotations to *interpret the meaning* of his contrasting statistics:

> Studies of the 1988 campaign show that the average block of uninterrupted speech by a presidential candidate on the network newscasts was 9.8 seconds; in 1968 it was 42.3 seconds. As Walter Cronkite observed, this means that "issues can be avoided rather than confronted." And David Halberstam adds, "Once the politicians begin to talk in such brief bites, they begin to think in them."[4]

When using statistics for persuasive purposes, be especially careful that the figures you use are reliable and accurate. It is sometimes tempting to parrot figures which serve our purposes but which are based on no more than hearsay. Always be sure that your statistics are from a reliable source and then share that source with your audience. For example, "According to the *New York Times,* over eight thousand babies die in the United States every year from what doctors call, for lack of a better term, crib death." Acknowledging your sources in this way will add credibility to your figures.

Also avoid misleading figures. The old saying that statistics never lie, but liars always use statistics, is simply an acknowledgment of how easily statistics can be manipulated to create a desired impression. Notice, for example, that if the rate of inflation grows in one year from 5 to 7-1/2 percent, and then again

---

There are three sorts of lies: white lies, black lies, and statistics.
Mark Twain

---

from 7-1/2 to 10 percent in the second year, it would be technically correct to say that the *rate of growth* in inflation was down by about 17 percent in the second year, even though the inflation rate grew by 2-1/2 percent in both years. But the effect of making such a statement, even though it would be *technically* correct, could be very misleading to most audiences. Unless the audience understands thoroughly that the 17-percent figure refers to the *rate of growth* in inflation, and not the rate of inflation itself, the figures would be quite deceptive. This is only one way that figures can be manipulated. Needless to say, a Christian should always scrupulously avoid this subtle form of misleading an audience.

Explanation

Another of the most common types of supporting material available to speakers is *explanation.* When you explain something, you attempt to expand your listener's understanding of that something. Two of the most common means of explanation, the use of example and the use of comparisons and contrasts, have been or will be discussed separately. But there are other useful ways in which you can explain something to an audience:

1. *List its attributes.* For example, one way to explain to an audience what a mandolin is would be to describe it as a musical instrument with eight, ten, or twelve metal strings, usually paired, stretched over a deep, rounded sound box. Definitions of God often take this form: God is an all-knowing, all-powerful, everywhere-present, triune, spiritual being who is perfect in his holiness, righteousness, justice, goodness, and truth.

2. *Use synonyms.* Pocketbook-dictionary definitions usually rely on this explanatory device. Thus, the word *law* might be explained through the use of such synonyms as "rule," "edict," "regulation," "decree," "order," "statute," "principle," or "code."

3. *Classify it.* Describe the broader category of which the subject is a member: "To understand porpoises we must realize that they are *mammals* rather than *fish.* This means that, unlike fish, porpoises are warm-blooded, breathe with lungs rather than gills, give birth to their young instead of lay eggs, and then nurse their young on a diet of mother's milk."

4. *Describe its components or ingredients.* Another way to explain something is to describe its several parts. For example, "A pizza is a large, flat, round crust of unleavened dough, covered by a delicious concoction of cheese, tomato sauce, and a variety of spices, along with your choice of pepperoni, sausage, hamburger, onion, olives, anchovies, or almost anything you can imagine." Or again, "An idea is made up of a subject and a complement. The subject is the answer to the question, 'What am I talking about?' while the complement is the answer to the question, 'What am I saying about what I am talking about?' Only when these two ingredients are combined into a single statement does one have a full idea."

5. *Point out its source.* One way to understand more about something is to discover what produced it. This is true of most words, ideas, and objects. For example: "The word *define* comes from two Latin words: *de* ('from') and *finire* ('to set a limit to'). Thus when we define something we determine and state the limits and nature of it; we show both what it is and what it is not. So the basic idea of the word *define* is 'to place a limit around something, setting

it off from all other things.'" Or again, "The sin of stealing is no different from other sins. Like all the rest it stems from a questioning of God's goodness, and, ultimately, from a mutiny against his will. Such rebelliousness is at the heart of all sin, and every time one man steals from another the uprising spreads."

6. *Set it in various contexts.* The *Oxford English Dictionary* uses this method effectively to explain the development in the meanings of words. In many cases, especially with principles or abstract truths, explaining something contextually simply amounts to giving examples.

Seldom will any of the above means be sufficient in itself to provide your audience with a clear understanding of what you are trying to explain. Usually you will want to use these means in combination with one another.

Repetition and Restatement

The apostle Paul said, "Rejoice in the Lord always; again I will say, Rejoice!" (Phil. 4:4 RSV). Why do you suppose Paul repeated his exhortation to rejoice? Obviously it was to deepen its impact upon his audience. For the same reason you may want to utilize *repetition* and *restatement* as supporting materials in your speech.

Actually, public speakers have a greater need for repetition and restatement than did Paul in his letter to the Philippians. Paul's words were recorded and his readers could examine them at will. By contrast, the audiences a public speaker faces must rely upon their ability to listen and then recall the speaker's ideas. You can help them in this difficult task by building an *element of redundancy* into your speech through the use of repetition and restatement.

Do not fear repeating or restating important points three or four times in your speech—or even more often if need be. By nature oral discourse, in contrast to written discourse, is redundant. Audiences expect redundancy, and within reasonable limits need it and thrive on it. It is quite possible to bore your audience by becoming overly repetitious, of course, but you can usually avoid this pitfall by being aware of the potential problem and consciously guarding against it.

Two places in your speech where repetition and restatement are especially appropriate are (1) in the statement of your points and (2) in your transitions. Points that are stated in a parallel fashion always have an element of redundancy to them. In fact, it is partially for this reason that we word them similarly in the first place; that is, so that important themes in the speech are reinforced throughout. So also do we summarize, restate, and even repeat our points frequently in the transitions. Here again, redundancy serves both to clarify and give emphasis to the important ideas of your speech.

Quotations

Citing the testimony of others is another useful method of supporting the points in your outline (56–73; 154–62; 256–64). Usually quotations are used in a speech for one or both of two reasons. First, the author may have stated the point you are making particularly well. Thus, the wording of the quotation is in some way so striking, vivid, and to the point that you want to quote it verbatim. It is for this reason that wordsmiths such as Shakespeare and Longfellow are often quoted. Second, the author may possess some authority you would like to harness in support of your point. By citing the authoritative source directly, you can effectively borrow some of the author's credibility to supplement your own. It is for this reason that you might quote the surgeon general of the United States on the dangers of cigarette smoking.

Sometimes these two purposes happily coincide. The source not only states the point well, but also carries a certain authority which the audience respects. Quotations from the Bible often display this dual force. The work of those unusual few who can both think and communicate exceptionally well, such as C. S. Lewis ("God whispers to us in our pleasures; He speaks to us in our work; but He shouts to us in our pains"), Anne Morrow Lindbergh, and Alexander Solzhenitsyn, are also fruitful sources for doubly effective quotations.

Here are some pointers to keep in mind when using quotations in your speech:

1. Always identify your source when you are using the quotation to bolster your authority. Keep the identification as brief as

possible, providing only the necessary information, but do let your audience know whom you are quoting. On the other hand, when you are using the quotation because it makes the point well, citing the specific source is less important. Sometimes you may even want to avoid mentioning the source either because you do not know the author or because the information is irrelevant. In such cases, a statement such as the following would be proper: "*Someone has said that* memory is like a crazy old woman who hoards colored rags and throws away food."

2. Keep your quotations short. Long passages of quoted material can become boring to an audience. Instead of a long quotation, try to use a series of shorter passages.

3. When using a quotation to lend credibility to your point, be sure that the author is respected by your audience. Quoting Ronald Reagan to a group of liberal Democrats probably would not accomplish much. By contrast, a quotation conceding your point by a source from whom the audience would expect opposition can often be persuasive. Notice, for example, how the following quotation from Rousseau, who was no friend of Christianity, could be used to buttress a speech on a Christian view of society:

> In order to discover the rules of society thus suited to nations, a superior intelligence beholding all the passions of men without experiencing any of them would be needed. This intelligence would have to be wholly unrelated to our nature, while knowing it through and through; its happiness would have to be independent of us, and yet ready to occupy itself with ours; and lastly, it would have in the march of time, to look forward to a distant glory, and, working in one century be able to enjoy in the next. It would take God to give man laws.

4. Avoid verbal quotation marks such as "quote" and "unquote." These are stilted and usually unnecessary. Seek to let your audience know you are quoting by introducing the quotation sufficiently, pausing, and then adjusting your tone and inflection slightly.

5. Try paraphrasing the quotation wherever possible. "But according to the president, in his State of the Union address, we

will not experience a recession this year." Such brief and informal references to the testimony of others are smoother than, and can often serve your purposes as well as, more formal quotations. Advertiser Louis Hagopian used this approach when he indirectly cited David Brinkley:

> I recall the comment by David Brinkley, about the pioneer immigrants of the 19th century. When they left the shores of Europe, they expected to find the streets of America paved with gold. Instead, they quickly learned that (one) the streets weren't paved with gold, (two) the streets weren't paved at all and (three) they were the ones who were supposed to do the paving.[5]

One special kind of quotation is poetry (245–50). Because of their rhyme, rhythm, meter, and imaginative language, poems are usually more useful for amplifying or reinforcing than for persuading. But however they are used, poems can add unique elements of variety and beauty to your speech.

Sermons are often characterized as "three points and a poem."

Here are some things to watch out for when using poetry in your speech:

1. Avoid poetry of poor quality. This does not mean that you should use only serious poetry. You may find a humorous limerick which serves your point nicely—just be sure it is a good limerick. There is a large quantity of poetry around which is mediocre at best and downright shoddy at worst. You should not endorse such poetry by using it in your speech.

2. Avoid using too much poetry in your speech. If you try to find a poem to support each of your points, the speech can easily become trite and too predictable. Sermons are often characterized, for example, as "three points and a poem" because too

many preachers have fallen into a pattern in their use of verse. Do not let this happen to your speeches.

3. Avoid the use of long poems. Keep any poetry short and to the point. When there is a portion of a poem which serves your purpose, you need not quote the entire piece. Use only that part which supports your point.

4. Avoid reading the poem if possible. Try to recite the poem from memory. This will add to its usefulness considerably.

Comparisons

One way to clarify and strengthen an idea is to place it beside another which is clearly understood by the audience, and then show the similarities between the two. Sometimes such comparisons are brief and passing. The most common of these are called similes and metaphors.

A *simile* is an explicit comparison using the term *like* or *as*. Notice how the simile in the last sentence of the following paragraph clarifies the author's point:

> There are talkers who have what may be called jerky minds. They say bright things on all possible subjects, but their zigzags rack you to death; their thoughts do not run in a natural sequence. After a jolting half-hour with one of these jerky companions, talking to a dull friend is a great relief. It is like taking a cat in your lap after holding a squirrel.[6]

A *metaphor* is an implied comparison. Examples: "the sword of the Spirit"; "All the world's a stage"; or these lines of Wordsworth about Sir Isaac Newton, a man of profound intellect who had thoughts no one had ever had before—one could see "the index of his mind, voyaging strange seas of thought, alone." Similes and metaphors peppered throughout your speech can add measurably to the clarity and impact of your ideas.

Of greater interest here are the more detailed comparisons wherein several points of similarity are explored. Such comparisons may be literal or figurative. In *literal* comparisons, what is unknown is placed side by side with an essentially similar object that is more familiar, and their likenesses are explored. For example, an unfamiliar college might be compared with a familiar one to point out their similarities.

Figurative comparisons, by contrast, relate two basically different items which are alike only in certain essentials. Thus James compares the human tongue to a ship's rudder when he says, "Take ships as an example. Although they are so large and are driven by strong winds, they are steered by a very small rudder wherever the pilot wants to go. Likewise the tongue is a small part of the body, but it makes great boasts" (James 3:4–5 NIV). Or again, Robert Jastrow, director of NASA's Goddard Institute for Space Studies, used the analogy of mountain climbing in his analysis of modern man's scientific pursuit of the origin of the universe: "For the scientist who has lived by his faith in the power of reason, the story ends like a bad dream. He has scaled the mountains of ignorance; he is about to conquer the highest peak; as he pulls himself over the final rock, he is greeted by a band of theologians who have been sitting there for centuries."[7]

Analogies such as this can be especially useful in clarifying difficult ideas. By choosing an analogy that is (1) appropriate for your audience and (2) parallel to the idea you are attempting to explain *at just the right points*, you can accomplish more than with almost any other type of support. We began this chapter with an analogy between a speech and the human body. Hopefully, this comparison helped to clarify the roles of both the outline and the supporting material in the preparation of a speech. Notice in the following example how the difficult idea of true freedom is clarified by analogy:

> Many people believe that freedom is the license to do whatever they desire. But true freedom is the ability to do what you ought to do. Thus, true freedom requires obedience and self-restraint. For instance, when I sit down at the piano, I am free to play any keys that I desire. But I am not free to play great music. I can only make noise. It is only after years of practice and obedience to the principles of music that I can be free to play my choice of music at the piano. Thus it always is with true freedom.

As may be seen in this example, analogical material is especially effective in communicating moral truth. Jesus used this approach constantly in his teaching. His messages were filled with extended analogies such as parables, allegories, and fables, each of which was designed to drive home some spiritual truth (see Luke 8:4–15; 10:29–37; 15:3–32; John 15:1–8 for some famous examples). Modern speakers will do well to follow this pattern. Notice how pointedly the following indirect, figurative comparison manages to demonstrate the truth that we learn to know the counterfeit in life through familiarity with the genuine:

> A young Chinese boy who wanted to learn about jade went to study with a famous old teacher. This elderly gentleman put a piece of the jade into the boy's hand and told him to hold it tight. Then he began to talk of philosophy, men, women, the sun, and almost everything under it. After an hour, he took back the stone and sent the boy home. The procedure was repeated for weeks. The boy became frustrated—when would he be told about jade?—but he was too polite to interrupt his venerable teacher. Then one day when the old man put an ordinary stone into the boy's hands, the boy cried out instantly, "That's not jade!"

Contrasts

As comparisons clarify an idea by showing its similarity to something your audience already knows, *contrasts* clarify by showing differences between two things (73–76; 77–80; 94–121; 202–6). For example, suppose you wanted to give a speech on the *effectiveness* of the American economic system. One way to support your point might be to contrast the American system with the other major economic systems in the world. In each instance the differences you bring up would tend to support your point. On the other hand, if you were attempting to demonstrate the *unfairness* of America's economic system, you might try to contrast the plight of underprivileged Americans with the lives of those who prosper in our society simply because of their positions of privilege. You would have to buttress both of these contrasts with other arguments and evidence, of course, since neither issue is unclouded; yet in both cases one of your most effective types of support might be the use of contrast. In the following example, notice how John McKelvey uses both comparison and contrast together to explain one important use of solar energy in the United States:

How many of you were Boy Scouts? Do you remember starting a campfire by focusing sunlight through a magnifying glass? Remember how hot that sunlight got when you focused it down to a tiny point? You were using solar energy in a concentrated form at that moment. And that's what we're trying to do with another relatively new technology called solar thermal electric generation.

The biggest difference is that solar thermal systems use mirrors—usually movable mirrors called heliostats—to reflect sunlight and focus it onto a receiver. Temperatures in the thousands of degrees can be achieved that way.

The receiver—called a power tower—uses the heat to produce steam or heat some gas, which is then used to drive a turbine generator. In effect, the concentrated sunlight has simply replaced natural gas or coal in a conventional power plant.[8]

Visual Aids

Why bother to use visual aids? Such a question is usually the product of apathy rather than antipathy. Many speakers simply do not feel the need to make their ideas visual. After all, they ask, are not words enough?

The answer is, often they are not. We need to make our ideas visual as well as verbalize them, thus acknowledging the wisdom of Proverbs 20:12: "The hearing ear and the seeing eye, the LORD has made both of them" (NASB).

The Biblical Example

Actually, there are many places in the Bible where visualization is used and recommended as a means of communication. Even a brief study of the history of revelation shows that much of what is known about God has been communicated through the sense of sight. Many examples could be offered, but the mention of only a few will be sufficient. In the Old Testament, Psalm 19:1 declares the entire creation to be a visual example of the power and glory of God: "The heavens declare the glory of God; and the firmament shows his handiwork." The rainbow was specifically used to teach Noah and his children in a visual way the lesson that God would never again destroy the world with a flood (Gen. 9:12–17). God used the stars in the heavens to make clear to Abraham the extent to which he would bless him (Gen. 15:5). The tabernacle was designed as a visual demonstration to the Israelites of the way of approach to God. Exodus 12:26 explains that the Passover was a teaching device to be used "when your children will say to you, 'What does this rite mean to you?'" (NASB).

Much of what is known about God has been communicated through the sense of sight.

In the New Testament, Christ used, at different times, birds (Matt. 6:26), a coin (Matt. 22:15–22), a child (Mark 9:36–37), bread (John 6), and numerous other visual helps to teach various lessons. In John 15 he depicted the relationship between himself and the believer by using the image of the vine and its branches. Even the two ordinances, baptism and the Lord's Supper, are visualizations of great spiritual truths.

Not only did God himself teach with visuals, but those who spoke for God used this method as well. Inasmuch as God himself employed the "eyegate" in communication, it was natural that his messengers should do the same.

Some of the clearest examples of visualization in the Bible are found in those sections of the Old Testament which tell of the prophets. The prophets had a powerful message in a time of serious need, and they used the most effective means possible to communicate it. For example, in 1 Kings 11:29–31 is the account of how

Ahijah the Prophet found Jeroboam, the son of Nebat, outside of Jerusalem and prophesied that he would be king over ten tribes in a divided kingdom. He symbolized his promise by tearing his own new robe into twelve pieces and giving ten of them to Jeroboam, the ten pieces symbolizing the northern ten tribes.[9]

Or again, in Ezekiel 4:1–3 we read that

the prophet Ezekiel, in order to depict to the Jews already exiled in Babylon the imminent destruction of Jerusalem at the hands of the Babylonian invaders, constructed a "working model" of the city with its besiegement. He took a large tile, and on it he engraved a representation of the city. Then he constructed around it some of the equipment that the enemy would use in the siege: forts, a mound, camps, and battering rams.[10]

Ezekiel then placed an iron pan between himself and the model, exhibiting "the attitude of Jehovah Himself, cut off from His people by the iron wall of an inexorable purpose which no prayer could penetrate."[11]

As Gene Getz puts it, both the "theory and philosophy of visual education are rooted and grounded in the Word of God."[12] The Bible, by an abundance of examples far greater than those cited here, shows the use and value of visualization in attempting to communicate with an audience.

Audiovisual Research

Since visual communication is strongly endorsed by the Bible, it should not be surprising to see secular researchers come to the same conclusion. It is not our purpose here to delve deeply into the theoretical aspects of visualization, but some of the more important research findings relating specifically to the use of visual aids in public-speaking situations do merit our consideration.

Researchers have found that when audiovisuals are used properly, learning can be increased as much as 300 percent, with a reduction of more than 13 percent in the time it takes to communicate the material. Dramatic improvements in recall can be achieved by combining showing and telling (see table 1).

The significant improvement in results may be explained, at least in part, by the "principle of redundancy." When a message is communicated both orally and visually, it is being delivered through two channels to the listener. Thus the listener has a bet-

Table 1
Method of Communication and Recall

Methods	Recall 3 hours later (%)	Recall 3 days later (%)
Telling alone	70	10
Showing alone	72	22
A blend of telling and showing	85	65

Source: Francis M. Dwyer, *Strategies for Improving Visual Learning: A Handbook for the Effective Selection, Design, and Use of Visualized Materials* (State College, Penn.: Learning Services, 1978).

ter chance of correctly receiving and retaining the message than if she merely heard it.

Research also seems to indicate that there are at least two other ways in which the use of visuals in communication helps the listener. First, visualization can benefit those who find it difficult to learn by merely listening. The evidence suggests that below-average listeners are able to understand visualized material better than that which is simply verbal. Interpreting the results of this research, George L. Gropper explains: "Below-average students can respond to visual examples because, it is suggested, along with their brighter counterparts, they have had considerable prior experience in responding to the concrete attributes of many physical objects and events."[13] Thus, visualized material better meets the needs of more listeners than does verbal material alone.

Second, visualization reduces the difficulty level of complex material. The research of Gropper and Robert M. Gagne supports what has been postulated for some time. Information, and especially that which is somewhat complex, becomes easier to grasp when it is presented visually. "To the extent that visual techniques can be imagined, formulated, and implemented for such purposes," concludes Gropper, "they might be recommended as a means of reducing the difficulty level of what would otherwise be complex and not easily acquired concepts or principles."[14]

Types of Visuals

There are several common types of visuals you might consider:

1. *Objects.* Whenever you are speaking about something that you can also show your audience, bring the object with you and use it as part of your speech. Object lessons, in which you use some seemingly unrelated object in a visual analogy, can also add a very helpful dimension to your speech.

2. *Charts and graphs.* The purpose of charts (for example, organizational, flow, or tree) and graphs (circle, column, bar, or line) is usually to portray statistical information. These kinds of visual aids help in attracting and holding attention. They also enable you to communicate more information more quickly. Information which is by its very nature abstract, complex, or invisible—and therefore difficult to understand—can be communicated more effectively if you use graphs or charts.

To achieve peak effectiveness, graphs and charts must be kept simple. This may be accomplished by (a) designing each graph or chart to convey only one major idea and (b) using any wording judiciously. The pictorial elements should be allowed to make the point of the visual, while the function of legends and titles should be limited to identification. Abbreviate the wording whenever possible.

3. *Diagrams.* Diagrams are another means of representing difficult material visually. They are especially helpful in showing processes or the relationship of parts to the whole. Thus diagrams might be useful in representing biblical material, places, concepts, and grammatical relationships. Like charts and graphs, diagrams should be kept simple to achieve maximum effect.

4. *Maps.* Maps are especially helpful in speaking on biblical topics. Since the biblical lands are foreign to the average listener, he or she needs to be shown the territories visually. Moreover, in

order for many passages of Scripture to be understood fully, a knowledge of the land is necessary. For these reasons, maps are often invaluable tools to the speaker who desires to speak on biblically related topics.

5. *Illustrations.* As we have noted, an illustration makes clear or explains some concept. A visual illustration might take the form of a picture, a cartoon, or a comparison. Whatever the illustration may be, its function is to explain or make clear some particular point. You should be certain that the visual serves this function and is not being used merely to entertain.

6. *Simple lettering.* Some visuals may include no pictorial representation at all. Although they should be used sparingly, such visuals can sometimes be useful in public speaking. For example, you might decide to present the major points of your outline on a poster. In such cases, be sure to mask the points, uncovering each of them only as you are ready to deal with it in turn.

We cannot here provide detailed information on how to design and use effective visuals. For that you will need to consult a good manual, such as Gene Getz's *Audiovisual Media in Christian Education.*[15] Nevertheless, here are a few basic pointers you might keep in mind.

1. Keep your visual aids neat and simple.
2. Limit each of your visuals to a single idea (except where you may be listing your outline, of course). For a second diagram, chart, picture, or illustration, use a second visual.
3. Be sure your visual aids are large enough for your audience to see. Visuals that are too small defeat your purpose and frustrate the audience.
4. Do not hesitate to use overhead or slide projectors wherever possible. These can often be even more effective than posters, pictures, or other hand-held materials.

Where to Find Supporting Material[16]

The big-game hunter stalking his prey, the white-coated researcher peering through a microscope, the archaeologist digging through dusty ruins, the deep-sea fisherman scanning the waves, the speaker moving through the day with a trawling eye—all have this in common: they are hunters. And to the speaker who is eager for the hunt, all of life can yield a rich catch of supporting material.

Where can you find the supporting materials you need? Some speakers move immediately to encyclopedias of quotable quotes, anecdotes, and illustrations. Others reject this approach, responding with the scorn an expert angler would feel for a "sportsman" who goes to the supermarket to buy a fish to show his friends. To be sure, there is validity to the argument that "canned" supporting materials are usually dated, lacking the freshness and appropriateness for a given audience which characterize materials drawn from more creative sources. But the ones who so argue often speak from the comfortable position of those who have personal files filled with illustrative wealth. For the neophyte speaker who needs help in getting started, there is a place for an honest use of such aids.[17] But the following restrictions should be kept in mind when you turn to published collections of supporting material:

1. Materials from such books should be used only as prompters to spark your imagination toward finding or inventing your own illustrations.
2. The background and factual basis of such illustrative material should be carefully checked, to keep you from the embarrassment of quoting incorrect sources.
3. Such books should be used sparingly so that you do not become dependent upon them, thereby failing to develop your own ability to find fresh material which will usually be more effective with your audience.

So, encyclopedias of supporting material may have some limited usefulness to help you get started, but they are at best interim aids. For the most part you should look to other sources to find the supporting material which can put muscle and flesh on the skeleton of your speech outline.

All of life is fair game to the hunter of supporting material, since all of life is full of pictures waiting to be caught and used by the imaginative speaker. The following list is only partial and should spark your thinking to find additional sources:

The Bible

Perhaps the richest treasury of illustrations about people is the Bible. Scripture is marvelously graphic in its portrayal of every conceivable type of personality, situation, and experience. Furthermore, while in the past many listeners were likely to know the ending as soon as a speaker began to tell a Bible story, thus spoiling any element of surprise, today's widespread ignorance of the Bible generally relieves that risk, making scriptural illustrations all the more potent. Consider the wealth of illustrative material in Scripture awaiting the speaker willing to seek it out: the vivid Old Testament stories of such characters as Abraham, Joseph, Ruth, and Jonah; the prophetic images of Jeremiah, who envisioned baskets of figs, and of Ezekiel, who envisioned burning wheels and a valley of dry bones; the pointed parables and analogies of the Gospels; the fascinating historical episodes of the Book of Acts; the graphic figures in the Epistles; the brilliant imagery of the Book of Revelation. All these and more make the Bible a peerless, God-given source of supporting material. It should perhaps be your first recourse when you need supporting material relating to the mental, emotional, moral, or spiritual dimensions of people.

To find usable supporting material in the Bible, try looking in any good topical index or in such works as Charles E. Little's *10,000 Illustrations from the Bible.*[18]

Current Events and History

A good newspaper is a sheet of history in the making. If you read with a pencil in your hand, you can mark a wealth of human-interest stories, statistics on social problems (divorce, housing, etc.), and other likely items for use as support. If Jesus saw the educational value of passing events (as was evidenced by his public reference to the fall of the tower of Siloam [Luke 13:4] and to the fate of the Galileans whose blood Pilate had mingled with that of their sacrifices [v. 1], we too can make use of current events for illustrative purposes. Magazines can also yield numerous types of supporting material. For example, *U.S. News and World Report, Time,* and *Newsweek* can be a continual source of information. *Reader's Digest* contains a wealth of human-interest stories and "quotable quotes" (its "Towards More Picturesque Speech" section will also usually contain some useful figures of speech).

In the same way, the events of the past provide illustrations as readily as do current events, if not more so. You can often scan both secular and church history to seek out suitable supporting material.

The life stories of great people are particularly rich in usable illustrative material. People love to hear about other people.

People love to hear about other people.

For example, the biographies of Martin Luther or Helen Keller or C. S. Lewis's autobiography, *Surprised by Joy,* might be fruitful sources of certain kinds of supporting material.

Personal Experience

You can often glean useful illustrations as you move through the daily round of life—going places, meeting people, observing children. The school, the supermarket, the highway, the lawyer's office, the surgeon's operating room, the restaurant, the home— all can offer their own special illustrations.

Personal experiences from your past can also be one of your most profitable sources of supporting material. Because they are yours, they often have a special freshness to them. Moreover, by using such materials you are revealing a bit of yourself to the audience, and that is something they will usually appreciate. But be careful not to overdo it. We have all heard those speakers who suffer from an "I" problem. Be sure the illustrations serve the point you are making and not simply your own ego.

Nature and Science

There is a boundless store of supporting material in the world of plants, animals, and natural forces. Your own observation can be supplemented by reading books on plants and animals and magazines such as *National Geographic* and *Natural History*.

The world of scientific investigation opens up realms of materials far beyond the reach of our unaided powers of observation: galaxies invisible to the naked eye appear to the astronomer through his powerful telescope, and minute organisms swim into view beneath the microscope. The entire universe, with all its telescopic and microscopic splendor, is available to you through the intermediary of science. Try reading, for example, books like Isaac Asimov's *Collapsing Universe: The Story of Black Holes*, Paul Davies' *God and the New Physics*, David Landes' *Revolution in Time: Clocks and the Making of the Modern World*, or Barry Lopez's *Arctic Dreams: Imagination and Desire in a Northern Landscape*. Or try checking out some video documentaries from your local library.

Audiences today are especially attuned to supporting material drawn from scientific sources because we live in the age of nuclear power, space travel, computer technology, and the deification of science by the secular world. You can use this confidence in science to lend credibility to your own ideas. But be careful not to make your illustrations too involved or technical. Furthermore, always be doubly certain that your scientific information is sound. Many so-called facts that are passed off as scientific are in truth little more than someone's opinion or educated guess.

The Arts

Fictional literature can also be a useful source of supporting ideas. While fiction by definition is not historical, great fiction is true to life. Thus novels and short stories offer a wide range of supporting materials for the speaker.

Drama can likewise provide illustrative material. Though much in the worlds of film, television, and theater is unworthy of your time, still you can profit from a judicious exposure to good drama, culling insights into human nature from the perceptive pictures drawn by skilled dramatists.

The realms of painting, sculpture, and music can also be an excellent source of certain kinds of supporting material. For example, Francis Schaeffer, the well-known Christian thinker, used art extensively to illustrate the idea of his message.

Many an otherwise good speech has died for the lack of good supporting material. The structure may have been sound, but the audience rejected or, perhaps worse, *ignored* the speech because the speaker failed to discover or use effectively the many types of material available to him or her.

Discovering the support for your ideas will seldom be easy. It usually requires hard work and can be time-consuming. It can also be frustrating; many are the times when the experienced speaker would give a twenty-dollar bill for just the right illustration—quite literally. But effort expended here will pay rich dividends in the end. Your speech, if it is well supported by a variety of interesting and pertinent material, will be a delight to your audience. They will give you their attention willingly, and your message will be much more likely to have its intended effect.

One bit of counsel we have saved to the last because it is extremely important. We have surveyed a wide range of types of support. *Try to use, in any given speech, as many of these different types as possible. Do not settle for only one or two of the types, but seek to use them all if possible! Such an array of material will add weight and texture and interest to your speech in a way that nothing else can.*

Exercises

1. Suppose you must deliver a speech on the pros and cons of nuclear power in America. Find four samples of effective supporting material for both sides of the issue. Analyze what type of support each sample is and evaluate which of the four might be most effective for use

with some group of which you are a part. List the reasons for your evaluation.

2. Examine the speeches in a single issue of *Vital Speeches of the Day*. Seek out three samples of each of the major types of supporting material we have discussed in this chapter. Which of the three samples will members of the audience find most effective? least effective?

3. Sample a range of the literature on both sides of the abortion issue in contemporary society. Analyze which types of supporting materials both sides use. Compare and contrast the use of supporting materials you discover, evaluating which side makes the more responsible presentation of the evidence.

4. In the public-speaking course you are teaching to high-school students you must give a ten-minute lecture on one of these subjects: the role of supporting material in a speech, using audiovisuals effectively, or how to collect illustrations. Using the content of this chapter and any other help you can find, design a complete outline for your lecture.

Chapter **7**

How to Introduce
and Conclude Your Speech

Every speech must have a beginning and an end. Since no speech is eternal—though we have all heard some which have *seemed* so—every speech must begin in one moment of time and end in another. The only real questions you must answer are *how* your speech is to begin and *how* it will end.

These two questions are far more important than you might think. The first and the last things you say will often overshadow most of what falls in between. Thus a well-organized and well-supported structure throughout the body of the speech can suffer irreparable harm from a poor introduction and weak conclusion. Even though your introduction and conclusion together will occupy perhaps only 20 to 25 percent of your speaking time, these two divisions in many ways will determine your success (or lack of it) as a public speaker.

Rationale for the Speech Divisions

It would be quite possible, of course, to begin your speech without an introduction and end it without a conclusion. It would be possible, but also foolish. The reason this would be foolish reaches to the heart of why introductions and conclusions exist as major divisions of a speech at all. Like most of the rest of the principles we have discussed in this book, the reason springs from the very nature of your listeners, from the way they think.

You want your audience to receive and assimilate the ideas of your speech. However, almost invariably they will not at the outset be *ready*, mentally or emotionally, to do so. You must begin where they are and then prepare them (or, perhaps more accurately, help them prepare themselves) to be able to receive your ideas with maximum effectiveness. This is your first and most important task as you step up to the lectern.

In the same way, your audience usually needs your help at the end of the speech. You have developed a more or less complex structure of thought in the body of your speech. Ideally, it has been clearly organized and well presented. You have taken the whole apart and presented it to your listeners piece by piece. Now their need is to see how the parts fit together again, one last time. Whereas in the body of your speech you have *analyzed* (dictionary definition: "to separate or break up [any whole] into its parts so as to find out their nature, proportion, function, relationship") your idea, now you need to *synthesize* ("to bring together into a whole; to form by bringing together separate parts") the idea one final time so that your audience can see how all of the many parts fit together. This is the primary task of the conclusion.

Plainly, then, the divisions of introduction, body, and conclusion are not arbitrary distinctions that ornery teachers of public speaking enjoy foisting upon their students. Rather, these divisions (which have been recognized for three thousand years) represent attempts on the part of the speaker to meet the various needs of the audience at different, distinct points in the speech. The audience's needs at the beginning of the speech are quite different from their needs at the end of the speech. Likewise, their requirements in the middle of the speech differ significantly from the requirements at both the beginning and the end. Thus, the tasks you must face as a speaker differ during the various phases of the speech. Recognition of this should prompt you to divide your speech into an introduction, body, and conclusion.

The verbs *introduce* and *conclude* are both transitive; that is, they are incomplete in themselves (except in those cases in which "conclude" means simply "to come to an end"). They require a direct object. You introduce *something* or conclude *something*. In the case of a public speech, of course, it is the central idea and its development in the body of the speech that you are introducing and concluding. Thus the introduction and conclusion must be developed *after* the body of the speech has been prepared. Though the introduction will be the first thing you present in your speech, you cannot design the introduction until you have first finished preparing the body of the speech, for *it is only then that you know what it is that you want to introduce!* The same is true of a conclusion. So, having discussed the body of your speech, let us now look at the other two major divisions in turn.

Purposes of an Introduction

We have said that there are unique tasks you will typically face at the beginning of your speech. These tasks can be classified into four categories. These categories may not, however, be as distinct as they seem at first glance, since it is quite common that several of them will be accomplished simultaneously in your introduction. Nevertheless, for our purposes the four may be considered separately. The four tasks that an introduction should attempt to accomplish are:

1. Capturing the attention of the audience
2. Building rapport with the audience
3. Showing the audience why they should listen to the speech
4. Orienting the audience to the subject matter of the speech

Capturing the Attention of the Audience

Capturing the attention of your audience is perhaps the least difficult task you will face in the introduction. In most cases your audience will at the outset give you their attention willingly. It was for this reason that even in ancient times Aristotle counseled his budding orators to appeal directly for the audience's attention *elsewhere* in the speech perhaps, but not in the introduction. The beginning of the speech, said he, "is just where there is least slackness of interest; it is therefore ridiculous [to ask for your audience's attention] at the beginning, when everyone is listening with the most attention."[1] Listeners in our relatively polite society will usually give you their attention at the outset; the more difficult part is to hold that attention and then do something with it.

Despite this, however, we probably ought not *assume* that we have everyone's attention even at the outset. The safer course is to assume the opposite and proceed accordingly. Why? Because every audience is made up of a variety of people. Each of these people lives in his or her own world. Each has a unique

---

The introduction is the beginning of the speech, corresponding to the prologue in poetry and the prelude in flute-music; they are all beginnings, paving the way, as it were, for what is to follow. **Aristotle**

---

set of concerns and interests, and each will probably be thinking of something different prior to your speech. So at the moment you begin you will probably have to corral these many minds and direct them to the subject of your speech.

Depending on what has gone before, this may or may not be difficult to do. As we have said, you may find your audience prepared, quiet, attentive, and expectant. But it is also possible that you will find them far less interested and far more indifferent or distracted than you had expected. Thus you will probably be wise to plan on some method of drawing their attention and focusing it upon your idea.

The first three or four sentences of your speech will be especially important if you are a stranger to your audience. All you need to do to realize just how important these first sentences can be is to think about all of the first impressions of a speaker you construct when he or she begins speaking. The sound of the voice, the articulation of the words, the rate and vigor of expression, the command of the situation (or lack of it), the words chosen—all of these factors and many more combine to give an immediate first impression which we later change only reluctantly. Remember that in the first seconds of your speech your audience will be drawing these same sorts of conclusions about you!

If you are known to the audience, of course, their impressions of you are already formed, and these first three or four sentences carry less weight. Yet the early moments of your introduction are extremely important nonetheless. Even if the audience grant you their immediate attention, you will need to use that attention to suggest to them that the rest of the speech will be interesting, fresh, and worthwhile. One of the best ways to do that is to work on making the very early moments of your speech as captivating as you can.

How can you captivate your audience in these early moments? How can you draw their attention from whatever it may be focused upon to you and your subject? As a basis for answering these questions, let us review for a moment the characteristics which attract involuntary attention (p. 47). You will recall that a person's attention is commonly drawn to those things which are characterized by (a) novelty, (b) movement or activity, (c) proximity, (d) concreteness, (e) familiarity, (f) conflict, (g) suspense, (h) intensity, (i) humor, and (j) life-relatedness.

These characteristics can help us understand better our task of capturing the attention of the audience. In one way or another some combination of them ought to be utilized in the material you place in the opening moments of your speech. If you can do this, there will be a good chance that the attention of the audience will be drawn to your message and focused upon what you are saying. What's more, if the audience finds these early movements of your speech arresting, they will be likely to assume that the remainder will be interesting too. As a result you will have set the stage for your audience to remain attentive throughout.

Here are some examples of the kinds of devices you might use at the outset of your speech to capture the attention of your audience:

a. *Novelty:* a startling statement or statistic; a new discovery; a prophecy or prediction; a familiar idea in a novel setting or vice versa

b. *Movement or activity:* active, vivid wording, conjuring up images of movement; changes in your style of delivery

c. *Proximity:* a problem closely related to the audience; a news item from the local newspaper; a commendation of the audience; a reference to a previous experience of the audience or a previous speaker

d. *Concreteness:* a well-told narrative, hypothetical or actual; any concrete or specific wording

e. *Familiarity:* a comment on a homely or familiar matter; a common experience, vividly told; an epigram; a proverb; an apt quotation with an unusual way of putting something; a comparison or analogy

f. *Conflict:* a disagreement; an argument, fight, or struggle; any "cognitive inconsistency"

g. *Suspense:* a challenging rhetorical question or series of questions; a problem raised for a solution; a conundrum or riddle

h. *Intensity:* use of particularly colorful wording, delivered with strength; a forceful quotation

i. *Humor:* a joke; a humorous incident; a witty remark

j. *Life-relatedness:* a discussion of needs; a vivid story of human interest with which the audience can identify

In using any of these devices, keep the following pointers in mind:

1. When you use any of these devices, be sure that you use it in such a way that it accomplishes its goal. These devices will not *automatically* produce results. They must be shaped so as to capture attention. For example, we have suggested that you might begin your speech by using a rhetorical question (or series of questions) to raise an element of suspense. But many rhetorical questions do no such thing. They are trite and do not require the audience to think at all. Take this question, for instance: "Have you ever had a headache?" Such a question would hardly be an attention-grabber. But a question which is intriguing and forces the

audience to think a bit would be much more likely to corral the thoughts of the audience. For example, "How many children do you suppose will die at the hands of their own parents this year?"

2. Keep whatever you use—a story, a statistic, a joke, a quotation, a question—lean and concise. Nothing can as quickly sap the strength of material designed to capture attention as can wordiness. Keep it brief, succinct, to the point.

You never get a second chance to make a good first impression.

3. Avoid sensationalism and gimmickry. Anyone can *merely* capture attention by making a fool of himself, but this is hardly your goal. Wayne Booth tells a story of one of his former students:

> In my first year of teaching, I had a student who started his first two essays with a swear word. When I suggested that perhaps the third paper ought to start with something else, he protested that his high school teacher had taught him always to catch the reader's attention. Now the teacher was right, but the application of even such a firm principle requires reserves of tact that were somewhat beyond my freshman.[2]

The student seems to have had the right idea but was going about it all wrong. Cheap sensationalism may indeed capture attention, but it will not in the long run serve the purpose of your speech. Avoid all such gimmicks entirely.

4. Avoid material which does not actually relate to your idea. Irrelevance is one of the most common faults of speech introductions. The speaker discovers some interesting, humorous, or otherwise captivating piece of material and so decides to shoehorn it into his speech, even though it has little or nothing to do with the subject. We have noted that this tendency is to be avoided in choosing supporting material, and the point is no less important here. H. Grady Davis explains why:

The people want to get the point at once, no hedging or foolishness about it; the [speaker] may not, but the people do. If he plays a game with their interests, if, for example, he gives them a story that is interesting but irrelevant, they will be as trusting as he is dishonest. They will take what he gives them as being to the point whether it is or not. They will be waiting for him to go on with the subject he has introduced.

If later he wants their attention to something else than the thing he started with, he will have two jobs on his hands: First, he will have to win them back from the interest he has misdirected toward the wrong thing, then win a brand new interest in the right thing. The misdirected interest, far from being a gain, becomes a heavy liability. Many a [speech] never recovers from a story told in the introduction. The more interesting the story, the more disruptive it may be.[3]

Regardless of how strong the temptation, avoid using anything that does not directly accomplish your purpose.

Building Rapport with the Audience

Public speaking is one of the three major kinds of interpersonal relationships. Unlike one-to-one settings or small-group settings where each participant may speak in turn, public address is distinguished by the presence of a primary speaker and an audience whose main task is to listen. Nevertheless, the encounter is still an *interpersonal* one. Speaker and listener meet face to face and engage in an interpersonal relationship; a social bond or agreement exists between the parties as to how the session is to be conducted; each participant is related in some way to every other participant, and to the speaker. It is a social occasion.

If this is true, then the question must be asked, What *kind* of relationship exists between the speaker and the audience? A healthy relationship will greatly aid the speech; conversely, an unhealthy relationship can sometimes present such a huge obstacle that it is impossible to hurdle. Thus the matter of rapport with the audience can be crucial for a public speaker.

Your initial relationship with your audience will be shaped largely by two things: (a) their attitude toward you and (b) their attitude toward your subject. These attitudes, which can range all the way from very favorable to very unfavorable, can be plot-

---

Establishing Rapport

Secretary of State William Maxwell Evarts (1818–1901) was a popular after-dinner speaker. At an important Thanksgiving function he rose and said, "You have been giving your attention to a turkey stuffed with sage; you are now about to consider a sage stuffed with turkey."

Clifton Fadiman

---

ted on two scales. When the two scales are combined, they form a graphic such as figure 11.

This graph can help you analyze just how easy or how difficult your task of establishing rapport will be. Once more, the audience analysis you have done will be useful. Think back over all that you know of your audience. Then give a numerical value to your estimate of the audience's attitude toward your subject, with 1 representing a very favorable attitude and 7 representing a very unfavorable attitude. Next, do the same for your estimate of their attitude toward you as a speaker. Mark these numerical values on both scales of the graph. Now plot your results by drawing two straight lines until they intersect on the graph: first, a vertical line through the number you selected on the "Attitude toward You" (horizontal) scale and, second, a horizontal line through the number you selected on the "Attitude toward Your Subject" (vertical) scale. The point where these two lines intersect defines the task you have before you. Note the quadrant in which this point of intersection falls and then check the appropriate passage below for a discussion of your task. If the point of intersection falls within the center circle, see the section on the center circle (pp. 246–47).

Quadrant A

Your audience is favorably disposed toward both you and your subject. This will vary in degree, of course, depending upon

Figure 11
Estimating Audience Attitudes

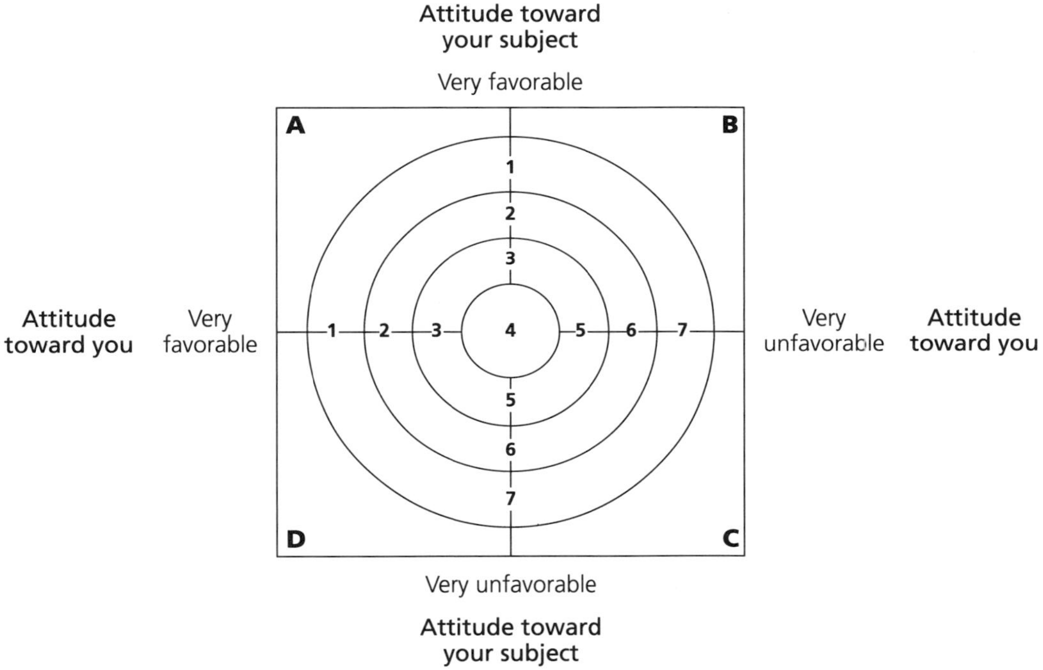

Attitude toward
your subject

Very favorable

Very unfavorable

Attitude toward
your subject

where the point of intersection falls, but the most important factor is that you will not have to placate a hostile audience. You have a built-in rapport with your audience, and the closer to the outside corner of the quadrant the intersecting point falls, the stronger that rapport will be.

`You may want to reinforce the positive disposition of the audience by explicitly alluding early in your introduction to some of the favorable aspects of your subject or of your relationship to the audience. The apostle Paul often practiced this in writing his epistles. This way the audience is reminded quite consciously of their own reasons for being favorably disposed to the speech. (If the point of intersection falls close to the center circle, you may want to consult the section on the center circle [pp. 246–47].)

Quadrant B

Your audience is favorably disposed toward your subject, but unfavorably disposed toward you as a speaker. This will not happen often, but when it does, the task is a considerable one. Inevitably, what your audience thinks of you will to some extent shape their response to the entire speech.

The reasons your audience is unfavorably disposed to you may be many. We cannot deal with all of them here. So we will have to limit ourselves to several broad observations.

You may want to try to offset in your introduction the audience's negative predisposition toward you. One possible way to do this is to acknowledge to the audience, straightforwardly and candidly, that you are aware of their negative view and that you understand why it exists. A bit of honest humor at your own expense might lighten the atmosphere. You might even try explaining to the audience any extenuating circumstances or appealing to their sense of fair play.

All of this can backfire, of course, especially if you have underestimated or misestimated the audience's disposition in any important way. Thus you may want instead to avoid mentioning yourself at all and simply plunge as quickly as possible into the subject matter of your speech. Their favorable disposition toward the subject gives you a common ground with them, and it may be that you can minimize or eliminate negative feelings toward you by simply handling your subject well. Begin as concretely, as creatively, and as interestingly as you can, and it may be that their negative disposition toward the source of the words will dissipate as they get caught up in the content of the words. (If the point of intersection falls close to the center circle, you may want to consult the section on the center circle [pp. 246–47].)

Quadrant C

Your audience is unfavorably disposed both toward you and toward your subject. You face the most difficult obstacle a speaker may confront: a hostile audience.

If the point of intersection falls near the outside corner of the quadrant, the obstacles to your speech may be insurmountable. The closer to the center circle the point falls, the less hostile your audience and the less difficult your task will be. You face one of the few situations in which the indifference represented by the center circle is to be considered preferable.

There are no easy answers to the kind of problem you confront. Much depends on the nature and degree of the audience's hostility toward you and your speech. But perhaps we can summarize generally a workable strategy for building rapport with a hostile audience.

First, try to establish some common ground with regard to both your personal relationship to the audience and your treatment of the subject. Try to show that you may not be quite what they expected. For example, if you are a conservative Republican addressing a group of liberal Democrats (or vice versa), try to conciliate their fears by conceding whatever you can (honestly) to their position. Show where you agree with them and deemphasize the areas of difference. By demonstrating that you are a reasonable person, you may be able at least to win a hearing.

Second, build upon this common ground slowly, unemotionally, and indirectly. With a thoroughly hostile audience you will usually want to avoid a frontal assault in favor of a more delicate and tactful approach, building gradually from the acceptable to the less acceptable. In this way you may be able to establish a case for your ideas without sacrificing your audience's willingness to listen. There may be times when confrontation will be a more workable approach, but these will be exceptions.

If this indirect approach seems less than honest, the appearance is misleading. There is nothing dishonest about facing up to potential hostility in your audience and adapting your approach accordingly wherever possible. Examine Paul's speech to a hostile audience recorded in Acts 17. There you will discover the apostle practicing both of the above suggestions. (If the point of intersection falls close to the center circle, you may want to consult the section on the center circle [pp. 246–47].)

Quadrant D

Your audience is favorably disposed toward you as the speaker, but unfavorably disposed toward your subject. They may like the source of the speech, but they will probably be inclined to resist its content.

Audiences usually appreciate a straightforward manner. Thus you may want to acknowledge quite candidly their negative disposition to your subject. Try to show you understand why this negative disposition exists and give due credit to any valid reasons for it. Then try to suggest reasons why you think they should revise their negative views.

On some occasions you may not want or be able to acknowledge outright their negative disposition toward your subject. In such cases you will probably be wise to begin with material the audience finds familiar and acceptable, and then build to the less favorable ideas from this positive base. Perhaps in this way they will be able to see the subject in a fresh light.

You may also be able to use the favorable disposition of the audience toward you to serve your message. As a way of reinforcing this favorable attitude, you could perhaps remind them somehow of their reasons for being positively disposed toward you. Through the use of appropriate phrases ("It seems to me that . . ."; "I have found that . . ."), you could then emphasize that *you* have seen the wisdom of accepting the ideas of the speech.

Such attempts to identify yourself with your ideas may have the opposite effect of lowering the audience's estimation of you, of course. This is something you need to keep in mind. The audience will struggle to retain their "cognitive consistency," to bring their feelings toward speaker and speech into harmony with one another. Thus it is probably safe to predict that as a result of the speech your listeners will think (a) more highly of the subject or (b) less highly of you or (c) some combination of the two. Your goal, of course, is to improve their attitude toward your ideas, but you will not always be able to achieve such an outcome. Thus you should perhaps be prepared to accept the possibility of some negative reaction toward you as a result of the speech. (If the point of intersection falls near the center circle, you may want to consult the following section.)

Center Circle

If the point of intersection falls within or close to the center circle, your audience is at best in a position of neutrality, and at worst in a position of active indifference. Your audience is neither positively nor negatively disposed to either you or your subject. As yet they probably do not care one way or the other.

Your major task with such an audience is to overcome the inertia of their indifference and bring them to a point where they do care. This you can do in your introduction by capturing their attention at the outset and then demonstrating that the speech is to be interesting and relevant to them. Make a special effort to arouse their interest by using concrete, vivid language and by exploring fully their need for your ideas.

Try to inject energy into the way you deliver your opening paragraphs. Show your audience that you are a person with something to say, that you care about the ideas of the speech and are willing to expend yourself for them. Lay out your opening ideas forcefully and dynamically. People are usually intrigued by a speaker who demonstrates a strong desire to communicate.

Try also to show your audience somehow that you are interested in them as people. Do not hesitate to include a personal note in your opening remarks, or perhaps some allusion to the occasion, setting, previous speakers, or the special interests of the audience. Your listeners will be striving to establish their ideas of what you are like as a person and to determine what their attitude toward you should be. Allowing them a personal glimpse can help them in this attempt. Avoid, however, any self-serving references that could be construed as name-dropping or bragging. You may want to begin by complimenting your audience, if you can do so honestly and sincerely, but avoid all forms of flattery.

Humor can often be a helpful bridge-builder with an indifferent audience. People enjoy humor and they generally like those who can present it well. But the humor should be concise, appropriate to the occasion, in good taste, and to the point. Long-winded, lamely told, irrelevant, or distasteful jokes will usually do far more harm than good. They leave people uncomfortable, embarrassed, and generally unimpressed by the speaker.

Showing the Audience Why They Should Listen to the Speech

As an important part of your speech preparation, you have grappled with the need your audience has for your idea, and you have focused the development of the body of your speech to meet that need. Thus you are well prepared to think about why your audience should pay attention to your message.

You will recall from our discussion of audience commonalities that people—all people, your audience included—are *need-fulfillers*. They have all sorts of needs, and much of their time and energy is devoted to fulfilling them. People are not consciously aware of all of their needs at once, of course. Many needs lie dormant until they become urgent or until something triggers their rise to a conscious level. But at the core of things people are interested in what they perceive as related to their own needs.

So, one of the most important objectives of a good introduction is to demonstrate to your listeners how the ideas of the speech will meet their needs. If you can accomplish this, you will provide your listeners with the motivation they need to stay tuned throughout the speech.

Creating Anticipation

Look at the body of your speech as the answer. Here before you is the *answer*—what is the *question?* What is the problem or dilemma this material solves? What interests do these ideas satisfy? Why should your audience pay attention to this speech? What need does it fulfill for them? Perhaps the need will involve no more than a question of curiosity, or perhaps it will involve some aspect of their deepest spiritual longings, or anything in between. But if the speech is not totally irrelevant to the audience—if it is, why bother to give it?—then there will always be some need you can bring to the surface in the introduction. If by the end of your introduction your audience can *see* this need—indeed, if they can *feel* it—then the stage will be well set for them to remain tuned to your speech throughout.

Notice that we are not speaking here about "creating" a need. Advertisers create needs, often by manipulating people into wanting what they do not at all need. By contrast, you are seeking to find the point of contact between your ideas and this audience, the point of relevance, and then to bring it to the surface of your audience's conscious mind. Though when you begin, your listeners may not have been thinking about their need for these ideas—in fact, they may never have been aware of their need at all—by the time you have finished your introduction, they should see clearly, and even, where appropriate, *feel* their need for the speech. They should ideally possess a sense of anticipation, a sitting-on-the-edge-of-the-seat attitude toward your speech.

He [the listener] will be ready to attend to anything that touches himself and to anything that is important, surprising, or agreeable. . . . Aristotle

Exploring the Need

Achieving such a sense of anticipation will usually require more than merely announcing your subject or stating that it is somehow a relevant topic. Simply *asserting* its relevance will seldom suffice to develop a sense of "felt need" in the listener. Rather you will usually have to explore the area of relevance a bit, so as to demonstrate to your listeners that the message will be relevant to them. You will have to be sure they understand not only the nature of the topic, but its pertinence to their lives as well.

Raising the Subject

Since the thrust of your idea is usually embedded in the complement rather than the subject, one standard way of exploring the audience's need is to state the subject and then raise the question which the complement is designed to answer. Suppose, for example, that your idea is "The chief cause of inflation in our economy is deficit spending by the federal government." This idea breaks down into subject and complement as follows:

Subject: The chief cause of inflation in our economy
Complement: is deficit spending by the federal government

With this idea you might want to raise, in some interesting way, the subject of inflation in our society and then pose the question, What is its primary cause? This is the question the body of your message is designed to answer.

But even so you would not want merely to state the question and then proceed into the body of your speech. Rather you would probably need to pause with it and savor it a bit. Explore it so as to allow it to register upon your listeners. Why do they need to have this question answered? Why is the question relevant to them at all? What difference will the answer make? These questions explore the audience's need for the speech. If you can do this well, and perceptively, by the time you are finished with your introduction, your listeners will be quite willing to hear you out.

Raising the Idea

But suppose that you decide to state the entire idea in the introduction, both subject and complement. Is there some way in which you can still hold the audience's attention throughout the rest of the speech? The answer lies in three *functional questions* which correspond to the three things (recall our discussion of the three purposes which a speech may have) you can do with an idea: (a) you can explain it, (b) you can prove it, or (c) you can show the implications of it. Thus the three functional questions are:

a. What does this mean? (explanation)
b. Is this true? (proof)
c. What difference does it make? (implication)

Whenever you offer your entire idea in the introduction, try to raise one or more of the three functional questions. If you do not, the remainder of the speech will likely be anticlimactic. After all, you have already given the audience your idea. Why should they now listen to the rest of what you have to say? The answer is that you want to explain, prove, or explore the implications of the idea in some way that will be useful to them. The best way they can see this is for you, having stated your idea, then to raise the appropriate functional question(s).

For instance, suppose yours is an informative speech with this idea: "The key to getting optimal gas mileage is a properly tuned engine." Having stated the idea early on, you would want then to pause and ask whether we fully understand what this means. What is a properly tuned engine and how does such tuning affect gas mileage? Here you are posing the first functional question in such a way as to encourage your audience to stay with you even though they already know your full idea.

Or suppose that yours is a persuasive speech designed to communicate this idea: "The easiest way for most people to lose weight is by watching their diet rather than increasing their exercise." After stating this idea, you would want to raise the second functional question, perhaps by saying, in effect, "You may not believe this—let me see if I can prove it to you." Once more, even though the audience knows your full idea, raising the second functional question encourages them to hear you out.

Or again, consider an idea such as this: "God has blessed us with all spiritual blessings in Christ Jesus." Suppose you were attempting to use this idea to mobilize an audience that already had grasped its basic theological content. In this case, having stated the idea in your introduction, you would probably want to raise the third functional question by asking, in effect, what difference this truth will make in our lives (see Eph. 4:1–6).

As we have suggested, sometimes you will raise more than one of the functional questions. It will depend entirely upon the actual content of your speech. For instance, in the last example above, suppose that your audience understood little of the theological content of their "spiritual blessings in Christ Jesus." You might have to use the first half of the speech (or more) to explain the idea; its implications, then, would be demonstrated only in the second half. In this case, having stated your full idea early on, you would want to raise two functional questions: What does this mean? and What difference should it make in our lives?

Whether you provide your listeners with the entire idea or only the subject in the introduction, be sure that by the time you are through with your introduction they have seen clearly why they should stay with you throughout the speech. Be sure, too, not to mislead them. To point out a need which you promise to meet and then not to meet it is misleading, disheartening, and frustrating to an audience. They will not be appreciative of your speech—nor should they be. Be very careful that you understand clearly what need of your audience your speech is designed to meet and then work to bring precisely this need to their attention.

Orienting the Audience to the Subject Matter of the Speech

Orienting the audience to the subject matter is the central purpose of an introduction. Your goal is "to introduce" something, and that something is the subject matter of your speech. By the time you are through with your introduction the audience should have a clear picture of exactly what you are going to talk about, if not what you are going to say about it.

As we have noted above, sometimes you will raise only your *subject* in the introduction and then develop the *complement* in the body of the speech; on other occasions you will want to focus your audience's attention upon the entire idea. Be sure you are aware of which of these options you have chosen so that you know precisely what it is you want your audience to understand by the end of the introduction.

At times you may be able simply to announce your subject to your listeners: "My subject for today is the influence of materialism on the evangelical church." This will be an especially workable approach if your audience is already favorably disposed both to you and to the ideas of the speech. But under less ideal conditions you will probably have to raise the subject in a less direct fashion, utilizing a much more delicate and roundabout approach.

If orienting the audience to the subject were the only task to be accomplished in your introduction, all you would need to do to get started would be to state your subject in a clear voice. Unfortunately this will seldom do, at least if your goal is to communicate effectively with your audience. Instead you will have to *balance* the goal of introducing your topic with the other three goals we have discussed above: (a) capturing attention, (b) establishing rapport, and (c) pointing out a need. Again, if your audience is already strongly favorable toward you and your subject—that is, they are already highly motivated to hear you out—then these latter three goals can possibly be assumed or taken for granted and you can get on with the speech. But with a less motivated audience—and, frankly, this includes most of the groups you will address—such an assumption would be a very dangerous one. With most audiences you will have to strive to achieve *all four purposes at once.* You will have to raise your subject before the audience in such a way that you also capture attention, establish rapport, and arouse a need—simultaneously. As we have noted, this is quite a delicate and difficult balancing act to perform. But when it is done well, the resulting introduction will be very effective.

It is difficult to say much more than this about orienting the audience to your ideas. Because of the interplay of attention, rapport, need, and the content of the speech, it is hardly possible to discuss orienting the audience to the subject matter apart from these other topics. Remember: the attention you are after is attention focused, ultimately, on the subject matter; the rapport you seek is, finally, a rapport with your ideas; the need you are attempting to point out is, in the last analysis, a need for the content of the speech. Thus in the previous sections dealing with attention, rapport, and need, we were already discussing how to orient the audience to your subject. If the attention of the listeners is properly focused, if the appropriate bridges of rapport are built, if the right needs are pointed out, the audience will automatically be ready to interact with the ideas of the speech.

One word of caution, though. Be sure that the subject you raise in your introduction is *exactly* the subject you will explore in your speech. Any shifting between the introduction and the body of the speech is very confusing to an audience. For example, it is not uncommon to see a speaker focus the audience's attention upon a subject such as "the *causes* of water pollution," only to shift in the body of the speech to deal with "the *effects* of water pollution." Like a magician the speaker has drawn the audience's attention *away from* what he is really doing to a related but different subject. But the goals of a magician and a public speaker are diametrically opposed. A public speaker ought not use a magician for a model! If you want to explore the *effects* of water pollution in your speech, be sure it is precisely *this* that you raise as your subject in the introduction.

Conclusions

Aristotle said that a good conclusion "merely reminds us of what has been said already."[4] That is as good a definition as any of the purpose a conclusion serves in a speech. You have introduced your ideas and then displayed them to your audience one by one. Now your goal is to show one final time how they all fit together to support your central idea. You need to remind the audience of what you have already said so that they are left with the entire picture.

A strong conclusion can often compensate for previous weaknesses in the speech. Perhaps your introduction was less interesting than it might have been; or perhaps your structure was cloudy, your transitions weak, or your supporting material too vague. But if your audience is still listening to you at the end of the speech, you can partially overcome these shortcomings with a strong conclusion. If you can draw together the threads of your idea so that it becomes clear at last with impact upon the listener, the conclusion may be what he or she will remember most.

There should always be a sense of completeness or finality to your conclusion. There should be a clear awareness that you have *finished;* you have come full circle; you have arrived where you set out to go. This is what the speech has been all about, and if it has not been entirely clear as of yet, it finally becomes clear here. Now, says the audience, I see it all plainly.

Note how Solomon closes the Book of Ecclesiastes: "The conclusion, when all has been heard, is: fear God and keep His commandments" (12:13 NASB). Here is the message of Ecclesiastes in a nutshell. We have no doubt of it. If we were not aware of it before, we realize now that this is where Solomon has been going all along. This is the thought that ties all of the book together. So does a good conclusion function in a speech. The entire message is rounded out in the conclusion in such a way that the sense of completion is plain. The message is hereby *concluded*.

Too often, inexperienced speakers simply quit. They do not finish, they just stop—and there is a difference. A good speaker will avoid this error. Davis makes the point well:

> The conclusion is the moment in which listeners can come nearest to seeing the idea whole and all at one time. It is the moment in which the issue can be seen at its clearest, felt at its sharpest, and carried back into life where, if anywhere, it must be resolved. The conclusion is the last chance to accomplish the [speech's] purpose, whatever that may be.
>
> Consequently, this moment is perhaps the most important single moment in the entire continuity. A [speech] should conclude, not just stop; it should finish, not just dribble off.[5]

When it is constructed properly, a good conclusion will unify the speech. It will not be merely a perfunctory ending, something arbitrarily tacked on as a sort of rhetorical caboose. Rather it will grow logically out of the body of the speech and correspond to it. It will be organically related to what has gone before. If the body of the speech is complex, the conclusion will probably be complex as well. If the body is simply constructed, the conclusion will probably be simple, too. Thus there are no formulas for designing an effective conclusion. Each conclusion must be custom-tailored to meet the needs of the individual speech.

Nevertheless, there are some general principles concerning conclusions you may want to keep in mind.

1. Do not include new material in your conclusion. You may want to state your points in a new and fresh way in the conclusion; in fact, you should probably strive to do so. But do not include *new ideas*. Any new ideas should be placed in the body of the speech where they can be appropriately developed. Keep the conclusion for merely reminding the audience of what you have said already.

2. Try to make your conclusion especially vivid. Look for fresh ways of driving home your points. Avoid trite expressions. Perhaps you can find some story, illustration, analogy, or other concrete way

of capturing your ideas in just the right light. In fact, do not hesitate to hold some of your best illustrative material for the conclusion. It may be more useful here than anywhere else in the speech.

3. Work on clarity and conciseness. Your speech's central thrust must be clearer in the conclusion than anywhere else in the speech. Indeed, a failure of clarity here can unravel much of what you have worked hard to accomplish in the body.

To insure clarity you will usually want to include some sort of recapitulation or summary of the speech's content. It will often be direct, straightforward, and overt, but it might also at times be indirect and roundabout, such as in a concluding story, quotation, or anecdote. But some sort of summary is almost always useful, and often mandatory.

4. Return your audience to the introduction and to the need you pointed out there. By reminding them of this early material and then showing how the speech has answered the questions raised, you come full circle. Few things in your speech will do more to provide your audience with a sense of unity and of completion than this feeling of the circle's having been completed.

5. Do not use the words, "In conclusion . . . ," to alert your audience that you are finishing your speech. They should know you have come to your conclusion without your having to tell them so. Also, do not say, "Thank you," when you are finished unless you have genuine reasons for gratitude. Usually this is just an ineffective way of saying, "I'm through." Try to find a more creative way to end your speech.

6. Seek to make your conclusion long enough to accomplish its purpose, but not so long as to drag the speech out unnecessarily. As a general rule your conclusion should require no less than 5 percent and no more than 15 percent of the entire time you have for the speech. So try to avoid overly abrupt or extended conclusions.

7. Be careful of false conclusions. Some inept speakers seem to be concluding at several different points in their speech, only to disappoint their audience each time by continuing. Be careful to avoid giving the impression that you are concluding when in fact you are still within the body of the speech.

Sample Introductions and Conclusions

The rest of this chapter consists of six examples of introductions and conclusions. They are provided here, not because they are exemplary in every way, but because they provide some concrete samples for your examination and evaluation. In each case, try to think about the strengths and weaknesses you see.

Example One

Waldo Braden, a professor of speech at Louisiana State University, delivered a message entitled "In the Heads of the Listeners: Principles of Communication" to the Louisiana Trial Lawyers Association. The following is the introduction to that speech.[6]

1   When I looked over your program I felt very much alone. Among your speakers are the mayor of New Orleans, a former governor of Arkansas, a dean of a law school, the speaker of the Louisiana House of Representatives, a law professor and a psychiatrist. I noted that the other speakers are speaking upon highly technical subjects connected with the practice of the law. What is a speech professor doing in this company?

2   As I studied the program I was reminded of a story that Sol M. Linowitz, a prominent lawyer, told about William Howard Taft's great-granddaughter.

3   When she was asked to write her autobiography in the third grade, the young lady responded: "My great-grandfather was President of the United States, my grandfather was a United States senator, my father is an ambassador, and I am a brownie."

4   On this morning at this elegant hotel here in the French Quarter in this distinguished company, I feel like a brownie.

5   Perhaps the explanation for my presence here is similar to why I was invited to serve on my church board. It was a real surprise to me when the minister invited me to join the board. I could not help but ask myself, "Why have they chosen me out of all the available members of the congregation?" At my first meeting I studied my colleagues carefully. Represented there were pillars of the congregation. They were the big givers or they could be. Many taught Sunday School classes. Some were among the volunteers that helped repair the roof, cut the grass, and take up the collection. Besides, the most pious and faithful members of the flock were included. It was evident to me that I just did not

Paragraphs 1–5 serve the primary purposes of capturing attention and establishing rapport. Humor, at the expense of the speaker, accomplishes these purposes well.

match up to those good people. Then I remembered that "the Lord works in mysterious ways," and I surmised that the minister wanted me for another reason. He wanted represented on the board one good practicing, profane sinner. He knew that my lonely voice could not shake the faith. He had selected me as a dramatic example of the wayward professor who was so much on the minds of the church goers.

In paragraph 6 the speaker begins the transition to his subject. Paragraphs 7–9 explore the subject in such a way as to point out the audience's need for the speech. By the time the speaker finishes the intro-duction, the audience is no doubt ready to listen to the rest of the speech. Notice the specificity in paragraph 9.

6   I assume that this morning I am here for similar reasons. At this gathering I seem to be the only civilian present. I am cer-tainly not here to talk about the law or the courts. I am here to represent those who deal with lawyers and who employ them when the need arises. I am here to discuss how to communicate with the average citizen: the ordinary people who have no under-standing of the law.

7   I shall not discuss how to improve your communicating with other lawyers, judicial administrators or judges, for you are already well trained and have had much practice in give and take among your colleagues. As a group, you are among the well edu-cated, the studious, the most vocal of our society.

8   To put briefly my assignment, I am to discuss with you the problems of making your words count with persons like myself who do not understand legal terminology—which to the unin-formed may be no more than jargon. How can you reach house-wives, mechanics, farmers, policemen, the unemployed, the dropouts, and even criminals?

9   What are the elements of successful communication? By the word successful, I mean how can you put over your message in such a way to gain understanding, get your own way, win the votes, sway the city council, settle a conflict between neighbors, and convince the members of the PTA that Johnny should be spanked?

Here is the conclusion of Braden's speech:

Notice the clear summary and restatement of the idea in paragraphs 10 and 12. What do you suppose was the purpose of para-graph 11? How might this conclusion have been made more creative and interesting?

10   To summarize—meaning is in the head of the listener. You cannot stir up what is not already there. You communicate through all the senses. Often the where and the when may influ-ence those that listen to you. If you can't put your message in the language of your listener, you are likely to fail.

11   The eager young executive or the fledgling salesman wants to know, "What are the tricks of going over big?" They seek the answer to this question in a single lecture or a how-to-do-it man-

ual. I am sorry that I can't recommend any sure-fire tricks of communication. I only know that influencing others is complex, that no two persons are the same, that no two audiences react alike, and that what may work today, may fail tomorrow.

12   Effective communication comes through constant awareness and study of how listeners respond. Regardless how naive or difficult, the beholder must supply meaning to what you offer. Let me close by paraphrasing a well-known quotation: "Meaning is altogether in the mind of the beholder."

Example Two

On May 9, 1961, Newton Minow, then chairman of the Federal Communication Commission, delivered a stinging address to the National Association of Broadcasters in which he labeled the television fare of the day a "vast wasteland." The label stuck and Minow's speech became famous, being cited countless times since. On May 9, 1991, thirty years later to the day, Minow was asked to update his assessment of television to a group of media experts gathered at Columbia University in New York. Here is the introduction to that address.[7]

1   After finishing that speech to the National Association of Broadcasters (NAB) thirty years ago today, I remained near the podium talking with LeRoy Collins, a former governor of Florida who was serving as NAB president. A man from the audience approached us and said to me, "I didn't particularly like your speech." A few moments later the same man returned with, "The more I thought about it, your speech was really awful." A few minutes later he was back a third time to say, "Mr. Minow, that was the worst speech I ever heard in my whole life!" Governor Collins gently put his arm around me and said, "Don't let him upset you, Newt. That man has no mind of his own. He just repeats everything he hears."

> The speaker begins, in what is sometimes called a *cold open*, by referring immediately to "that speech." Given the occasion, his audience knew just which speech he meant. The self-deprecating humor is designed to establish rapport with his listeners and put them at ease.

2   Thirty years later I still hear about that speech. My daughters threaten to engrave on my tombstone "On to a Vaster Wasteland."

3   My old law partner, Adlai E. Stevenson, loved to tell a favorite story about the relationship between a fan and a fan dancer: There is really no intent to cover the subject—only to call attention to it. Like a fan dancer, it is not my intent today to cover every part of that speech, but rather to use its anniversary to

> In paragraph 3 the speaker relies on humor again—this time to deftly establish the exact subject and purpose of his speech. The reference to Adlai Stevenson,

a respected statesman from the past, helps to establish the speaker's own credibility.

Paragraph 4 serves as a transition from the introduction to the first major movement of the speech. Was the introduction too brief, or simply appropriate to the occasion given the expectations of the audience?

The body of the speech began with a lengthy reminiscence about President Kennedy and broadcasting in the sixties, and then went on to assess the contrast with today. In paragraph 5 the speaker returns to that former era to sum up his ideas and borrow some of the idealism of the earlier period.

To summarize both his concerns and the challenge he wants to leave with his audience, in paragraph 6 the speaker quotes (as we saw Ernest Boyer doing earlier in this book) the prophetic words of E. B. White. Does the speaker's central idea come through clearly in this conclusion?

examine, with thirty years' perspective, what television has been doing to our society and what television can do for our society.

4   Thirty years cannot be covered fully in thirty minutes, but let us begin by reminding ourselves of the times, circumstances and optimistic spirit of the Kennedy administration in the early '60s. What was broadcasting like at that stage of development?

Minow concluded his speech as follows:

5   The '60s started with high hopes, but confronted tragedy and ended in disillusion. Tragically, our leaders—President John F. Kennedy, Reverend Martin Luther King Jr. and Pope John XXIII, left too soon. We cannot go back in history, but the new generation can draw upon the great creative energy of that era, on its sense of national kinship and purpose, and on its passion and compassion. These qualities have not left us—we have left them, and it is time to return.

6   As we return, I commend some extraordinary words to the new generation. E. B. White sat in a darkened room in 1938 to see the beginning of television, an experimental electronic box that projected images into the room. Once he saw it, Mr. White wrote:

> "We shall stand or fall by television, of that I am sure. I believe television is going to be the test of the modern world, and that in this new opportunity to see beyond the range of our vision, we shall discover either a new and unbearable disturbance to the general peace, or a saving radiance in the sky."

7   That radiance falls unevenly today. It is still a dim light in education. It has not fulfilled its potential for children. It has neglected the needs of public television. And in the electoral process it has cast a dark shadow.

8   This year, television enabled us to see Patriot missiles destroy Scud missiles above the Persian Gulf. Will television in the next thirty years be a Scud or a Patriot? A new generation now has the chance to put the vision back into television, to travel from the wasteland to the promised land, and to make television a saving radiance in the sky.

Example Three

Kenneth Mason, president of the Quaker Oats Company, delivered a speech to a meeting of the American Association of Advertising Agencies in Chicago. Here is Mason's introduction.[8]

1   The subject I want to talk to you about today is one that is of great interest to me and should be of great interest to you. That subject is the way this country uses television to entertain, educate and advertise to young children.

2   One of the reasons this subject is of such great interest to so many people, in my opinion, is that it is a microcosm of three of the most important issues of our times:

3   One, the increasing intrusion of government into our personal and business lives. In this case, the Federal Trade Commission deciding for parents what their children should be allowed to see advertised on the air.

4   Two, the increasing incidence of situations where legitimate economic interests of business conflict with legitimate social concerns of society. It is a perfectly legitimate activity for a cereal company to want to advertise its pre-sweetened cereal on television. But at the same time, it is also a perfectly legitimate activity for parents to express concern if the television programs their children watch the most appear to overemphasize the role of sugared products in the diet.

5   Three, the increasing awareness on the part of persons in all walks of life of the pervasive influence of television on our society. We used to broadcast the World Series on the days they played it. Now we play the World Series on the days they can telecast it.

6   It has been said that the most powerful social forces of the last 100 years in America were the automobile, the motion picture and now television. As far as young children are concerned, the evidence suggests that television has been the most important of all. Very few children in pre-television days spent four to six hours a day in an automobile, or at the movies. But today the average preschool child in the United States spends four to six hours a day watching television. By college age, this child will have spent more time in front of a television set than in school, in church or in conversation or play with his or her parents.

The speaker seems to take for granted his rapport with the audience. Thus, in paragraph 1 he plunges immediately into a statement of his general subject. The straightforward assertion of relevance is designed to capture attention.

The entire section from paragraph 2 to paragraph 13 represents a detailed attempt to explore the problem the speech is designed to solve for the audience. This exploration serves to point out the need for the speech within the audience. Do you suppose this much detail was necessary?

7   These statistics have to be of enormous concern to all of us, and I think that from the point of view of society they raise two basic questions:

8   One, are the television programming and the television advertising that young children are watching four to six hours a day the kind of programming and advertising we would want them to watch if we had our druthers? And secondly, do we, in America, have our druthers?

9   A surprisingly large number of people believe that the answer to the first question is "Yes." I have received many letters and phone calls from individual parents and citizen organizations urging The Quaker Oats Company to resist the efforts of the Federal Trade Commission to interfere with the free choice of parents to make their own decisions on what their children should or should not watch on television. These parents and citizen groups say they think children's television is OK. Executives of television networks and major advertisers have also indicated in recent speeches their belief that there is nothing wrong with children's television in this country.

10   And there is no doubt that the medium has improved noticeably in recent years. But when you think of the assets available to us—the size of the budgets for these programs, the superb talent being employed—writers, directors, artists, actors—when you think of the opportunity that's there to do something really wonderful for children, then I submit that there is just no way a person interested in the future of this country can sit in front of his television set on a typical Saturday morning from 9:00 a.m. to 12:00 noon and not be visually and mentally very disappointed by the lack of intellectual content in most of the scripts, the lack of realism in most of the characters, the lifeless and mechanical animation employed in most of the programs, and the frequency, the blatancy, and often the sheer idiocy of so many of the commercials.

11   Clearly the vast majority of these television programs are not what most of us would put on the air if we had our druthers. Which leads us to the question: Do we have our druthers? And the answer to that question is a resounding "No" from everyone who has addressed it.

12   The reasons for this negative response are familiar. Better programming would cost too much money and draw smaller audiences. That would raise advertisers' costs and reduce their reach. Advertisers would then reduce their advertising investment in

children's television, the networks would lose revenue, and the result would be fewer programs for children produced on lower budgets. Aside from which, and even more important, there is the American principle of letting the marketplace make the decision. The very success of children's television in drawing large audiences would seem to prove that it is satisfactorily performing a needed public service.

13   Facing this formidable array of arguments in favor of the status quo in children's television, is it realistic to expect the system can be dramatically changed? No, it is not realistic. So what should be done? One answer is to let public broadcasting provide the kind of children's television the nation thinks it needs—and leave commercial broadcasting alone. That is essentially what The Quaker Oats Company proposed at the FTC hearings on this subject a year ago. Just 10 days ago, Charles Ferris, Chairman of the FCC, echoed this approach in a speech stating that public broadcasting can provide the enrichment and competition which will make possible reduced government regulation of commercial broadcasting.

14   The trouble with this solution to the problem, effective though it might be, is the implication it makes that only the non-profit institutions in our society can serve the public interest. That's an implication I don't think business should accept, and that is why I want to propose something quite different, something that I believe everyone in commercial television today—the networks, the advertisers, the agencies—can join and benefit from its success.

Here is the conclusion to Mason's speech:

15   The proposal I am asking you to support is not a perfect one by any means. I'm sure valid objections to it will be raised. For one thing, it addresses only Saturday morning, not all the weekday afternoon periods where viewing by youngsters is even heavier than on Saturday morning. But it could be a beginning. And it could do two important things. One, it could turn Saturday morning on American television into a stunning creative and artistic showcase for the most brilliant writers, actors and producers in the country. And secondly, it could be an important step forward, not just in improving the quality of television programming for children, but also as a model to the nation on how the interests of business, the interests of government and the interests of citizens

At last in paragraph 14 the speaker holds out the hope that the speech will solve the proposed problem. Is it too late in the speech to do so? In other words, do you suppose his audience was still paying attention by this time?

The speaker does not attempt to summarize his proposal but does summarize the reasons suggested for adopting it. What could the speaker have done to strengthen this conclusion? Is it long enough to accomplish its tasks?

can, at least on occasion, work together instead of at odds with each other in addressing issues, like this one, which affect not only our own lives, but the lives of generations that will follow us.

Example Four

Here is an introduction to a speech by William H. Webster, the director of the FBI, to the Abraham Lincoln Association of Springfield, Illinois. The speech was entitled "The Lincoln Assassination: Its Investigation."[9]

The speaker seems to take for granted that his audience will be favorably disposed toward him and especially toward his subject. This assumption is no doubt a sound one, given the nature of his audience. Thus the varied, almost rambling, comments about Lincoln in paragraphs 1–5 probably serve the speaker well in capturing attention and establishing rapport with the audience. They also raise the general subject of presidential assassinations, and of Lincoln's assassination in particular.

1   It would be very tempting for me to build my remarks on the spirit of Abraham Lincoln, the vitality of his special place in our hearts. His life continues to be the epitome of the American dream and his death the American tragedy. Here in Springfield, especially at this time of year, the spirit of Abraham Lincoln is pervasive.

2   In Washington, where he served the Nation and where he died, the monument erected in his memory stands as perhaps the noblest building in the Capital. For years I have tried to find time on my visits there to slip away and spend a few moments at the Memorial, especially at night. Now that I make my home in Washington, I like to take visitors from this country and from abroad to share this experience with me. Recently I took the Attorney General of Switzerland to visit the Memorial. Afterward, he wrote to me of the sense of the American spirit present within those walls. Often I find that our visitors can recite from memory some of the great lines from the Gettysburg Address and the Second Inaugural. The hush at night is awesome—truly the words inscribed on the wall behind the famous statue of Lincoln speak for all of us:

> "In this Temple, as in the hearts of the people for whom he saved the Union, the memory of Abraham Lincoln is enshrined forever."

3   There is another building, just one block from FBI Headquarters, which is a reminder of an American tragedy—Ford's Theatre. When Lord Scarman, an ardent student of American history, visited the United States, I took him to see both the Memorial and the Theatre. Ford's Theatre is a part of our history. It is also a

part of our history that Abraham Lincoln was the first President, but not the last, to be assassinated in office.

4   Only recently a committee of the Congress completed its investigation into the 1963 assassination of President Kennedy. But the inquiry will not end there.

5   This isn't too surprising. Various aspects of the Lincoln assassination are still the subject of inquiry and speculation. As recently as 1977 we received a request from the National Park Service (which has responsibility for Ford's Theatre and the Petersen House) asking that the diary of John Wilkes Booth be examined by our Laboratory. It was desired that the writing in the diary be authenticated as Booth's and a determination made of the possibility that secret writing existed. Letters written by Booth were borrowed from the National Archives as known handwriting specimens for the comparisons. Our Laboratory Document Section conducted the examinations, using all possible nondestructive tests. Forty-three pages were missing. No secret writing was found. One page thought to bear secret or obliterated writing was determined instead to bear a transfer of the text and lead residue from an adjacent page. The Laboratory experts found that the diary was written by Booth.

6   In December, when I began to consider what kind of a paper I might present that would be within my sphere of competence, I was preparing information for a Congressional Committee concerning Presidential assassinations. I was being asked by that Committee what the FBI response to such a calamity would be today. I naturally drifted into thinking about the investigation of President Lincoln's assassination. How had it been conducted? By whom? With what results? What protective and preventive measures guard the modern President, and what would be the response if those defenses were penetrated? How do they differ from those of 1865?

In paragraphs 6–7 the speaker suggests the relevance of the topic for today. This, along with the natural curiosity of a group of Lincoln buffs, represents the audience's need.

7   The assassination of a President invariably produces a distraction of enormous proportions. That is serious enough. It can be far more serious. As Carl Sandburg has observed:

"The single event of an assassination swept away a thousand foundations carefully laid and protected by the living Lincoln."

8   My purpose this evening is not to retell in every detail the investigative story following Lincoln's assassination. That story

In paragraph 8 the speaker finally states his subject. Is it clear *why* he wants to discuss this subject?

has been fully and ably chronicled by historians and Lincoln scholars. I want to concentrate instead upon progress 114 years later in dealing with assassination.

Here is Webster's conclusion:

Is the focus of the speech clear from the conclusion? From the above introduction and this conclusion, could you discover the speaker's central idea? Do you think he had one? Would you consider this a strong or weak conclusion?

9   In our recent history we have seen again the uncertainty that lingers even after the most searching investigation and Congressional review. The restoration of certainty can best be achieved by the highest level of professionalism during the tense and anguished period which follows any assassination of a President. The legitimate limitations placed on investigative procedures to protect the constitutional rights of citizens should be viewed only as a challenge to increase the level of professionalism. The FBI accepts that challenge.

10   I wish this evening my final words were wholly optimistic and could assure you that the possibility of political assassinations is remote. To do so I would have to be unmindful that nine Presidents, nearly one in four, have been targets of assassins' bullets and four of them died from those attacks. Nevertheless, we have the will to deal with it with all the tools made available to us in a free society.

11   But on this day as we pause to think once more of our fallen Captain, we rejoice that the indomitable spirit of Abraham Lincoln has survived his assassination to vindicate the American dream, and we pledge anew that government of the people, by the people, and for the people shall not perish from the Earth.

Example Five

This is the introduction to a speech delivered by Samuel L. Becker to the Central States Communication Association. The speech was entitled "Tolerance Is Not Enough."[10]

In paragraph 1 the speaker conjures up a strong visual image—opposing sides screaming at each other through bullhorns—to orient the audience to his subject. Then, the application of the image to society in paragraphs 2–3 sets up

1   Have you ever thought about the communication symbol or image that might best characterize our age—the closing years of the 20th century? One which seems to me particularly apt is the bullhorn—or, even better, two bullhorns, one on either side of a wide, deep chasm, directing loud and often obscene arguments at the other side, and never pausing long enough to hear any of the arguments from the other side. Of course, there is an even worse image. In Northern Ireland and many spots around the

world, they have advanced—if I can call it that—to the next stage of confrontation; the bullhorns have been forsaken in favor of pipe bombs.

the need of the audience for the speech.

2   That image of the bullhorns, though, clearly fits the discourse in this country throughout the last few decades, the discourse on every issue about which we have deep disagreements: Operation Desert Storm, the appropriate locus of control for abortions, equal opportunities for ethnic minorities and women. It even fits the talk in many of our academic departments.

3   Now one could argue that there is no great harm done by those who use those bullhorns, except when they drown out others who wish to be heard. On the other hand, there is no great good done by them, either; I know of no people who have ever been persuaded by someone else wreaking havoc on their eardrums with more decibels than they can stand. What is harmful in all of this is the assumption that those amplified screams have anything to do with persuasion, with communication, or with sharing understandings. What is harmful is the loss of our ability—and even apparently of our desire—to work out our disagreements in a thoughtful way, in a way that seeks understanding, a way that brings others in rather than locking them out, a way that *builds* community instead of destroying it.

In paragraph 3 the speaker anticipates an objection some in his audience may be voicing to themselves and addresses it directly.

4   Thus, the theme of this convention, "Discourse, Dialogue, and Social Power," is fitting for our communication association, for our field, and for our times. Those terms—"discourse, dialogue, and social power"—serve to remind us of what we who study and teach communication are about and what our responsibilities are. I hope they also motivate us to examine our activities and our society to assess the degree to which we have been successful at fulfilling those responsibilities. Everyone in our field, I assume, knows well what we mean by "discourse" and "dialogue." I sense some disagreement, though, about the concept of "social power." It may be helpful to think about two definitions of the term "social." One refers to "the welfare of human beings as members of society." The other, which I believe is more useful for our field, is "the formation of cooperative and interdependent relationships." Thus "social power" is that power that comes from such relationships; it is the power of community; it is power from within, rather than power over. And it is the achievement of that power, through discourse and through dialogue, that I want to talk about today.

Paragraph 4 is designed to relate the speech to the broader occasion and pinpoint the purpose. Do you find your interest slipping away as the ideas become more abstract in this paragraph? Presumably, the original audience would not have, but for most people abstraction does tend to sap interest.

Example Six

Here is a conclusion very different from the others. The idea of the speech, a Christmas-banquet message, was this: "The only way to enjoy Christmas is to keep our attention firmly focused on the birth of Christ." Here is how the speaker concluded his speech:

Notice how the idea of the speech is summarized by this story. This is done indirectly, but that simply makes the point all the more powerful. The body of the speech has developed each of the ideas implicitly included here. The conclusion simply ties them together and drives them home one last time.

1   All I have said tonight can best be captured, I think, in this parable from our own times: There was once a family by the name of Hathaway. They were an extremely poor family. They lived in terrible poverty and hardship. They were very hard workers, industrious in every way, but it had never gotten them anywhere, for they had nothing.

2   One day a wealthy man by the name of Wilson learned of the plight of the Hathaways and decided to do something about it. He arranged to give the Hathaway family a tax-free gift of $1 million.

3   When the Hathaways were presented with the gift, they could hardly believe their eyes and ears. Why would anyone want to give them such an incredible present? What had they done to deserve such a thing? As they began asking questions they learned that they had done nothing to deserve the gift, but rather it was simply a product of Mr. Wilson's goodness and generosity. The Hathaways were astonished that anyone could care so much about them and determined themselves to be eternally grateful for Mr. Wilson's gift.

4   The Hathaways used Mr. Wilson's gift wisely and at the end of the first year they had made a good profit on their holdings. Out of gratitude, on the first anniversary of the gift they decided to have a celebration to commemorate the generosity of Mr. Wilson. They made it a festive occasion with feasts and decorations and the exchange of gifts, all of which were designed to remind them of the wonderful gift Mr. Wilson had given them. The whole occasion was a very meaningful one for them, and they decided to so commemorate the giving of the gift every year.

5   Thus, at the end of the second, third, and fourth years the Hathaways celebrated the giving of the gift, adding a little more tradition each year and enjoying the celebration more each time. But with the passage of time a strange thing began to occur. Each year the celebration became bigger and more elaborate and more costly, but each year one also heard less and less about Mr. Wil-

son and his gift. The family greatly looked forward to the yearly celebration, each one thinking about how much fun they had had the years before, but fewer and fewer were the references to the generosity of the original gift and its giver. Lip service was paid to Mr. Wilson as the originator of the celebration, but more and more the occasions became celebrations of past celebrations, rather than responses from grateful hearts to a generous gift-giver.

6   The Hathaways never ceased to celebrate yearly the giving of the gift. In fact, they celebrate yet. But with the passage of time and the proliferation of all the trappings, the whole thing has become almost a chore. Each year they gamely try to recapture the lost spirit of celebrations past, celebrations which had grown out of grateful hearts in response to the wonderful gift of Mr. Wilson. Each year they exhort each other to try to work up the feelings of joy and wonder and love for one another they had felt at previous celebrations, but it has become a futile effort. In losing the true meaning of the occasion, they seem to have forfeited the occasion itself.

Exercises

1. Listen to a speaker addressing an audience. Evaluate the speaker's introduction. First, did the speaker have an identifiable introduction? How long was it? What proportion of the speaking time did it occupy? How well did it capture attention, build rapport, point out a need, and orient the audience to the speaker's content? What might the speaker have done to improve the introduction?

2. Find a speech in *Vital Speeches of the Day* which in your estimation appears to have a weak conclusion. Analyze *why* the conclusion is weak. After studying the content of the speech, design and write your own version of a conclusion for the speech. Then identify the ways your version is an improvement over the speaker's version.

3. Suppose you must give a speech to present clearly the gospel of Jesus Christ. Now imagine four different audiences: (a) favorable toward both you and your subject, (b) favorable toward you but unfavorable to your subject, (c) unfavorable toward both you and your subject,

and (d) unfavorable toward you but favorable to your subject. Analyze how you might attempt to begin your speech with each of these four audiences.

4. As the teacher of a pubic-speaking course to a group of high-school students, design the outline of a ten-minute lecture on one of these topics: why speeches have introductions, bodies, and conclusions; the purposes of an effective introduction; or how to design a good conclusion. Use as resource material the content of this chapter and any other help you can find.

Chapter **8**

How to Word Your Speech

Have you ever heard the story about the boy who watched an artist sculpt an elephant from a block of marble? Later the child was asked how the sculptor had created such a beautiful work of art. Said the boy, "He just chipped away everything that didn't look like an elephant."

That is one way to produce a sculpture—but not the only way. Some sculptors start with nothing at all. They draw their materials—wood, stone, metal, plastic, or whatever—from many different sources, bring them together, and then organize them artfully into a unified whole.

Constructing a speech is much more akin to this latter process. Beginning with nothing, you sift your materials from various sources, bring them together, and then organize them artfully into a unified whole. The difference, of course, is that the medium in which you are working is not wood, metal, or stone; your work of art is to be sculpted of *words*.

As we shall see in the next chapter, there are many important *nonverbal* aspects to public speaking. But all of these nonverbal aspects should be shaped so as to serve and reinforce the *words* of the speech. In the end, the essence of the speech must show itself in the words you use to express your ideas. That is, after all, why we call a speech, a *speech*.

Ideas may exist in our heads in some vague, unworded form, but to be examined or communicated they must be pinned down in words. Shakespeare put it this way:

> And, as imagination bodies forth
> The forms of things unknown, the poet's pen
> Turns them to shapes, and gives to airy nothing
> A local habitation and a name.[1]

To share your ideas you must give them a "local habitation and a name." You must give them verbal form. You must state the ideas in words. The purpose of this chapter is to show you how you can give your ideas the finest habitation and the most attractive name possible.

Style and Content

We have used in a previous chapter the analogy of a body: your outline is the skeleton, your supporting material the flesh, and the words you use to express your message the skin. This is a helpful picture as far as it goes, but it can also be misleading. Why? Because the words with which you express your ideas are not *merely* the external covering, the skin, of your speech. Rather, they *are* your speech. Your word choice (also known as your *style*) and your content are *one*. In the final analysis style and content, or form and substance, cannot be distinguished.

Consider this example: Suppose that after the Battle of Britain, during which England's Air Force saved the country through heroic efforts, Winston Churchill had said, "We ought to be grateful to the Air Force." His statement would have died upon his lips and been soon forgotten. But what Churchill actually said was this: "Never in the field of human conflict was so much owed by so many to so few." As long as Western history is kept, Churchill's statement will be remembered and quoted.

What is the difference between the two sentences? Do not both convey the same idea? In one sense they do. But on a deeper level we must also grant that there is a profound difference between them. The one has an impact; the other leaves not even a fingerprint. The one is memorable, the other boring and eminently forgettable—in fact, it fairly cries out to be forgotten. So the end product, the ultimate result, the final communicative impact of the two sentences, is dramatically different. The lesson? When we change the form of a message, we also change the *content* of what is said, along with the impact that content will have upon our audience, for better or for worse.

The question of good style versus bad style, then, is one of substance as well as form. Hence when we speak of style we are not speaking of the mere decoration of ideas, like putting tinsel and bright lights on a Christmas tree. Similarly, working to improve our word choice is not a matter of adding superimposed beautification, as if an otherwise homely child were to paint herself up with her mother's rouge, lipstick, and eye shadow and then deck herself out in gaudy jewelry and adult clothing. Rather, when we speak of good word choice versus poor we are speaking of *good-quality communication versus poor.* It is not a question of doing with or without the baubles; it is instead the difference between a feeble pawing at our audience and a powerful punch, a matter of *substance as well as form.*

Someone has said that ideas are like Jell-O—they tend to take the shape of the mold into which they are poured. In this light, the way a thought is expressed becomes as important as the thought itself—indeed, it *becomes* the thought itself. We can choose to word our ideas in language that merely sits there, like soggy cornflakes in a bowl of warm skim milk. Or we can choose words that snap, crackle, and pop; words which rise up and demand attention; words which pierce the shell of indifference behind which so many listeners hide. Whichever you choose,

---

Just Words?

There are bright words as brilliant as a tropic sunrise, and there are drab words as unattractive as an anemic woman. There are hard words which punch like a prize fighter, and weak words as insipid as tea made with one dunk of the teabag. There are pillow words that comfort people and cold steel words that threaten them. Some words transplant a listener, at least for an instant, close to the courts of God, and other words send him to the gutter. We live by words, love by words, pray with words, die for words.

Haddon Robinson

---

remember this: the *content* of your speech is always as much at stake in your word choice as is the form of the speech.

Composing for the Ear

To be effective, a speech must be composed for the ear, not the eye. Perhaps this is why so many speeches sound "canned"—they were written with a reader in mind, not a *listener*. You can avoid this canned sound by composing your speech to be received through the ear rather than the eye.

Oral discourse (i.e., speech) is in some ways quite different from written discourse, so much so that good writers of books, articles, and papers do not always make good speech writers. Likewise, good speakers often compose poorly written literature. Aristotle long ago explained how this can happen:

> Compared with those of others, the speeches of professional writers sound thin in actual contests. Those of the orators, on the other hand, are good to hear spoken, but look amateurish enough when they pass into the hands of a reader. This is just because they are so well suited for an actual tussle, and therefore contain many dramatic touches, which, being robbed of all dramatic rendering, fail to do their own proper work, and consequently look silly. Thus strings of unconnected words, and constant repetitions of words and phrases, are very properly condemned in written speeches: but not in spoken speeches—speakers use them freely, for they have a dramatic effect.[2]

What are some of the differences between oral and written discourse? First, oral discourse tends to be more *direct* than written discourse. When we communicate orally, we are usually addressing some particular individual or group, and our efforts are therefore focused and specific to their situation. Written discourse, on the other hand, usually addresses a much larger, less defined group of receivers. An exception, of course, would be a personal letter, but most written documents aim for a broader readership. As a result oral discourse tends to lean more on direct address. There is a stronger sense of "you-ness" to it. Written discourse is not usually addressed to a specific audience and is therefore less frontal in its approach.

Second, speech tends to be more *repetitive*, even redundant, than written discourse. We can go back and rework what we write, paring away all the fat. Not so with oral discourse, which is usually quite spontaneous.

In some ways it is just as well that we are unable to take a scalpel to what we communicate orally. The listener seldom takes in all that we say at its first mention; we need to say it

---

True beauty and usefulness always go hand in hand.   Quintilian

---

repeatedly. Also, the listener cannot think about anything we have already said except by rummaging through his or her own memory. Redundancy helps the listener remember. Thus the repetitious element in oral discourse actually helps the listener receive and retain our message. Perhaps it is for this reason that listeners are often more forgiving of repeated words, phrases, and sentences than are readers.

Third, oral discourse tends to be more *fragmentary*. Partial sentences, contractions, ellipses, ungrammatical constructions, interjections—all of these are used somewhat in written discourse. But they are much more prevalent in oral discourse due to both its greater spontaneity and the addition of such factors as vocal inflection and facial expression as aids in communication. It is a good thing that listeners are again much more forgiving of grammatical and verbal shortcomings than are readers.

Fourth, oral discourse tends to be more *personal*. Written discourse lives on a page. Once it is composed, it can in a sense exist quite apart from the writer. Oral discourse, on the other hand, lives only momentarily in a personal transaction between speaker and listener. Thus it tends to be a more immediate extension of the speaker and therefore, correspondingly, more personal. It will usually include more personal pronouns. It will also contain fewer unusual words drawn from the speaker's broader reading vocabulary, in favor of the more familiar words the speaker is comfortable saying aloud.

Thus, when you compose your speech, be sure you are designing it to be heard, not read. Be sure you are wording it for the ear, not the eye. Be sure it is *oral* discourse, even though it may be written down on paper. It is not as important that it *look* right as that it *sound* right. For example, you might choose to use a sentence which would appear on paper to be far too long (and even ungrammatical), but which communicates very nicely to the ear. And, as H. Grady Davis explains, your choice could be a perfectly acceptable one:

> Effective speech is not heard as sentences, separate sentences, at all. Speech is heard as larger and more complex units of thought. If it cannot be fitted together into larger units, it cannot be taken in. And we not only hear in larger units, we speak in larger units when we talk naturally.
>
> It is nothing unusual for a man to utter what must be six or eight written sentences in one sustained flow of speech, even in tempo and volume and with no breaks other than oratorical pauses, so that when transcribing I cannot tell whether to punctuate the passage as a number of sentences or as one extremely long one. Many a sequence of short sentences will be taken in by the listener as a single unit of thought, consisting of several parts that cohere, and he would hear it just the same if it were written as one long sentence. The short sentences are more help to the eye in rapid reading than to the ear in listening.[3]

Elements of an Effective Style

But even designing your speech to be heard rather than read is no guarantee that it will communicate effectively. Your speech may be both direct and personal, with all the fragmentary and repetitive characteristics of oral discourse, and still be poorly worded. Why? Because an effective style requires more: It requires that your word choice be *appropriate* and *interesting*.

Appropriate Language

An effective style always requires a choice and arrangement of words that are *appropriate*. To what? Appropriate to the audience (taking into consideration both the subject and the occasion) and appropriate to you as the speaker.

Appropriate to the Audience

As we have noted so often throughout this book, your audience is a crucial factor in shaping what you do as a speaker, and nowhere is this more true than in the words you choose to communicate your ideas.

It would be foolish to give a speech in English to an audience that speaks only Chinese. The words used to convey the ideas

---

Eschew obfuscation!

---

would be completely inappropriate. The audience would not be able to understand them, and no communication could take place. This is an extreme example of what happens when a speaker chooses words that are wrong for a particular audience. But even though speaker and audience may speak the same language, if the words chosen are inappropriate, communication will still be inhibited and the audience will fail to understand.

There are several guidelines to help you choose *appropriate* words for your speech, words your audience will be able to understand.

USE CLEAR WORDS. Your audience will soon lose interest in your speech if the meaning of your language is not clear. Their eyes glaze over, a fog clouds their minds, and they give up. As we shall see, there are numerous important features of an effective style—but none is more important than *clarity*. If your language is obscure, nothing else really matters. As Aristotle so simply put it, "Style to be good must be clear."[4]

I recently received a letter that was designed as an annual report. It was written by a dedicated, hardworking staff member of a national Christian organization. Here are two excerpts from that letter. The names have been changed to protect the guilty, but otherwise the words are verbatim. Let us suppose the letter is from the Midwest regional director of the Society of Christian Plumbers (SCP), which is made up of both student and graduate plumbers who meet together in local chapters. The letter begins:

> To aspire to quantify the activity of the Midwestern Region amidst the proscription of God to David for such endeavors (II Samuel 24:2ff.) creates a tension which resolves itself in the postulate that stewards prove themselves accountable *without* equating either the pace of activity or the results of the activity with success. Each item, because of His presence within that entity, has intrinsic ultimate value apart from linking those items into an annual evaluation. But I do enumerate the past year as part of this report, and I offer to elucidate, upon request, any issue.

The third paragraph reads as follows:

> If the student work provides a "paean of mien" the graduate rubric, with notable exceptions, might read, "atrophy amidst entropy." While a Regional Director considers SCP to be fulcral, a graduate lifestyle understandably ascribes SCP importance *locally* to a secondary or tertiary role personally for involvement and envisages success in what the Regional Director "produces," not to mention (but here I do!) the Central Office. The vestigial archetype of SCP as members determining the Society which *they* comprise (and not the staff) while assisted by the staff (Field and Central) will be resurrected (or memorialized) as national economic and spiritual attrition enervates the scope and abilities of the staff.

Did you read both excerpts completely? Why not? How many people do you suppose read the original letter through? Here was an attempt to communicate which almost certainly failed because of the author's word choice. The letter is lacking in almost everything that characterizes effective communication, but most importantly, it lacks *clarity*! We must struggle to find the author's meaning, a wrestling match most people in our busy time and complex culture will prefer to skip.

Speeches are no different than letters in this respect: People will not struggle to understand you—they will simply tune you out. Unless you are *clear!*

USE FAMILIAR WORDS. To be clear, your words must be familiar to your audience. "Clearness is secured by using the words (nouns and verbs alike) that are current and ordinary," said Aristotle.[5] The listener must be able to identify (and identify *with*) them at once. Esoteric jargon, unusual words, foreign phrases, technical terms—all must be avoided unless you are willing to define them as you go. Said the great English preacher Charles Haddon Spurgeon to his student preachers, "The marketplace

---

He who knows himself to be profound endeavors to be clear; he who would like to appear profound to the crowd endeavors to be obscure. **Friedrich Nietzsche**

---

cannot learn the language of the college. Let the college learn the language of the marketplace."

When you have studied a subject thoroughly, it is not difficult to lose sight of your audience. You can easily come to assume too much knowledge on their part. After all, *you* understand the words, and you do not consider yourself to be superior to the audience. But on this occasion you probably are superior, at least insofar as the use of certain terms is concerned. Be careful that you do not assume a familiarity on the audience's part which does not exist.

To be sure, sometimes the context alone can provide enough information for your listeners to understand an unfamiliar word—but do not count on it. Numerous studies have shown that context alone is seldom sufficient for most people to grasp the full meaning of words. For example, in one study subjects were given a series of sentences in which the word *sorrow* had been removed. In its place they supplied *anger, hatred, loneliness, confusion, destruction, horror, grief, fear, pain, anxiety,* and *doom.* In a group of sentences where the word *red* was removed, the subjects inserted such words as *pale, bright, hot, green, large,* and *brown.* Context alone was not sufficient to supply the full meaning.

Sometimes it is tempting to use unfamiliar words because their very unfamiliarity is impressive. After all, it proves that we know something our listeners do not. But such gamesmanship is hardly worthy of a Christian, especially a Christian who desires to communicate. As the German philosopher Nietzsche observed, "He who knows himself to be profound endeavors to be clear; he who would like to appear profound to the crowd endeavors to be obscure."[6] Seek out the language that is familiar to your audience if you want to be clear.

USE SHORT WORDS. Remember that familiar words tend to be short. The more frequently a word is used, the shorter it becomes: *laboratory* becomes *lab, telephone* becomes *phone, gasoline* becomes *gas,* and so on. We like short words because they are easy and efficient to use. Your audience is no different.

"Never use a fifty-cent word when a ten-cent word will do,"[7] counsels Sue Spencer, and this is wise advice to follow. Always choose the shorter word if you can do so without sacrificing meaning. Say *face* instead of *visage; try* instead of *endeavor; read* instead of *peruse; hopes* instead of *aspirations; calm* instead of *imperturbable; begin* instead of *inaugurate; buy* instead of *purchase; drink* instead of *imbibe; gifts* instead of *donations.* Use as few syllables as possible. Keep your wording as lean and simple as you can make it without sacrificing your meaning.

Again, it is sometimes tempting to try to sound sophisticated or erudite by using big words. We become "inebriated by the exuberance of our own verbosity." But few will be impressed by such wordiness. As humorist Josh Billings once told a budding speaker, "Young man, when you search Webster's Dictionary to find words big enough to convey your meaning, you can make up your mind that you don't mean much."

Effective communicators know better than to fall into the big-word trap. They seek out the shorter, more familiar words that

---

On Writing . . . and Speaking

Sherwood Wirt, interviewing C. S. Lewis:

Wirt:
How would you suggest a young Christian writer go about developing a style?

Lewis:
The way for a person to develop a style is (a) to know exactly what he wants to say, and (b) to be sure he is saying exactly that. The reader, we must remember, does not start by knowing what we mean. If our words are ambiguous, our meaning will escape him. I sometimes think that writing is like driving sheep down a road. If there is any gate open to the left or the right the readers will most certainly go into it.

God in the Dock

---

will reach their audience. According to George Williams in his book *Creative Writing for Advanced College Classes,* 70 to 78 percent of the words used in the writing of five of the most famous writers of English prose (Katherine Mansfield, John Galsworthy, Sinclair Lewis, Robert Louis Stevenson, Charles Dickens) were words of only one syllable.[8]

USE ACCURATE WORDS. Clarity also requires accurate words, words which say exactly what you want to say and no more. You want words which conjure up in the listeners' minds just the image you desire. This usually requires that you work hard to find concrete language to communicate your ideas.

The more abstract your language is, the more ambiguous and vague will be the images in the listeners' minds, and therefore the more likely it is that they will misunderstand your thought. Suppose, for example, you wanted to discuss your dog Fido. Examine the abstraction ladder below. Notice how the terms become progressively more abstract and general as you move up the ladder.

living thing
animal
dog
cocker spaniel
Fido

You *could* describe Fido as a "living thing" (that is, your state-ment would be *true*), but this term is so ambiguous that it would be almost impossible for your listeners to see in their heads what you see in yours. They could see an elephant or a rosebush as easily as Fido. As you move down the ladder toward the increas-ingly concrete terms, however, the ambiguity diminishes (though it can never be eliminated) and the likelihood of effective com-munication about Fido increases. Finally, when you have descended far enough, describing Fido not in broad ambiguous categories but as a six-month-old tan cocker spaniel with four white paws and a wagging tail, your audience will begin to gain a relatively accurate picture of what you mean. So it is that spe-cific, concrete language will always promote clear communica-tion by being less ambiguous, more explicit.

Ambiguity does not always stem from using language that is too abstract, of course. Sometimes it arises from using relative words without establishing a standard. How big, for instance, is a *large* house? How wealthy is a *rich* man? How far is a *short* journey? How high is a *big* mountain? At what point does a restaurant become *expensive*, or a college course become *diffi-cult?*

There is an old joke about a fellow who was asked, "How's your wife?" He replied, "Compared to what?" This should be our reply to each of the above terms—large, rich, short, big, expen-sive, difficult: Compared to what? All relative terms rely upon some standard for their meaning, and until the standard is clearly understood, only ambiguity can result.

I once saw a prescription which stated on the label, "A great deal of water should be taken with this medicine." How much is "a great deal"? A large swallow? Two glasses? A quart? The use of a relative term without a clearly defined standard results in ambiguity and probably inaccurate communication.

But ambiguity is not the only culprit. Sometimes emotions get in the way of accurate communication. There are certain terms which may be "red-flag" words to your audience. Once you use them they tend to warp the audience's ability to see or hear clearly. The terms *liberal, fundamentalist, communist, redneck, evolution,* and *literal interpretation of the Bible* are red-flag words for many. They arouse such a strong automatic reaction that all else becomes distorted.

Try to avoid using red-flag words in a way that inflames the emotions of your audience and inhibits their ability to think with you about your subject. In some coldly objective sense these terms may accurately capture your idea, but audiences are sel-

---

Ugly people try to make themselves pretty; uneducated people try to speak literary language.   Vietnamese proverb

---

dom made up of people who are coldly objective. So red-flag words may convey more than you intend, making their actual impact far different from what you desire. When this happens, of course, the clarity you are working toward is quickly sacrificed.

USE FITTING WORDS. To be accurate your words must "correspond to your subject." Said Aristotle, "'Correspondence to subject' means that we must neither speak casually about weighty matters, nor solemnly about trivial ones."[9] A speech on the death of Christ, for example, would require a very different tone than would a humorous travelog. Similarly, you would not use highly poetic language to describe an exhaust manifold, but you might use such language to describe a deeply moving experience you have had. Choose words that are apt, that is, appropriate to your subject.

You will also have to fit your wording to the occasion. On formal occasions the audience will expect a more formal choice of words. Slang, colloquialisms, and puns, for example, will probably be out of place. On informal occasions, however, such language might be entirely appropriate. For every occasion there is a proper level of formality; your task will be to find the right balance. As Aristotle observed, your style "must be appropriate, avoiding both meanness and undue elevation."[10]

USE MODERN WORDS. Have you ever read a speech or sermon from the 1800s? Did it sound strange to your ear? Could it be delivered today with a straight face? If your answers are yes, yes, and no, you already have some conception of what it means to use modern words.

During the nineteenth century people had few of the diversions available to modern Americans. Television, radio, and film were unknown. Instead, plays, pageants, and public speeches were prime attractions. People flocked to hear speakers who pulled out all the stops with their florid, high-blown oratorical style. The people loved it. It was a different time and a different world.

Today, if a speaker tried to speak like those giant nineteenth-century orators, he would be laughed off the rostrum. Why? Because people have changed, or been changed. As Sue Nichols says in her advice to those who want to communicate the gospel today, the modern American is sophisticated, free, and pressured:

> He is sophisticated. If he is not city- or suburban-bred, he is on his way to being so. Statistics indicate a depopulation of our farmlands. The country yokel is joining the smart set. He is the fruit of a several-generation-public-school-system, and his comprehension and tastes manifest it. . . .
>
> He is also free. Free to tune the communicator in or out at will. Free to pore over or to wastebasket our leaflets and tracts. Free to drive to the country or take to the golf links on Sunday morning.
>
> And even when he shows up at church he is still free. He has not necessarily come to worship or be instructed. Some are there to impress the boss, some to pursue a romance, some to show off a new fur coat. A quiet congregation is not per se a listening congregation; everybody may simply be off gathering his own wool.
>
> For Americans are a busy, distracted lot. A myriad of activities and worries vie for their attention. . . .

Americans are sophisticated, free, and pressured. If we hope to reach them with the good news of Christ, we must communicate in a strictly twentieth-century manner.[11]

These are the people to whom we must speak. As Ernest Boyer noted, they live in "the age of the flash and the zap, the hour-long epic, the thirty-minute encyclopedia, the five-minute explanation, the one-minute sell, the ten-second teaser, the two-second fix."[12] The grand style of the past will not reach them. It is too bloated and verbose. You will have to speak more pointedly, with lean and compact wording. Use active rather than

---

In first-rate writing there is a reason not only for every word, but for the position of every word.   **Samuel Taylor Coleridge**

---

passive verbs: "The man hit the ball," not "the ball was hit by the man." Pare away all unnecessary adjectives and adverbs. Use the present tense wherever possible. Eliminate old-fashioned terms. Only such a tight-fisted style befits today's listener.

USE PROPERLY ARRANGED WORDS. Clarity also depends, of course, on how you arrange your words. Try to keep your sentences straightforward, uncluttered, and tight. As we have noted, sentences in oral discourse can be longer and more involved than those in written discourse. You can get away with this because you have nonverbal aids such as vocal inflection, gestures, and facial expressions to help the audience perceive your meaning. But do not allow your sentences to become *too* long. Try to vary the length of your sentences, with some short and simple, others longer and more complex. Perhaps an average sentence length of fifteen to twenty words is about right.

Above all, avoid convoluted sentence structure. Keep pronouns as close as possible to their antecedents and all descriptive clauses and phrases as close as possible to what they are describing. Use dependent clauses sparingly, and be sure when you do use them that their relationship to the independent clause is clear. And avoid expressions such as "It is true that . . ." and "There is reason to suppose that. . . ."[13]

Appropriate to the Speaker

The words you choose for your speech must fit the audience, the occasion, and the subject. They must also fit *you, the speaker.*

We all have at least two vocabularies: a speaking vocabulary and a reading vocabulary. Our speaking vocabulary consists of all those words we use regularly in our daily speech. Our reading vocabulary includes a much larger body of words we recognize and understand but do not usually use in our speech. Figure 12 is a depiction of this phenomenon. The inner circle is represented by a broken line because there is really no clear-cut demarcation between the two vocabularies. Instead, our speaking vocabulary merges into our reading vocabulary through a gray area consisting of those words we use only occasionally in our speech. In any case, we can let the center of the circles represent the words we use most commonly in speech, and the outer edge of the larger circle represent the words we recognize in our reading but never use in speech.

The words which are most appropriate to you as a speaker are those which fall into the inner circle. They are the words you are comfortable saying aloud in ordinary conversation. Words from the outer circle may occur to you as you think about how to communicate your ideas, but if you use them, they are likely to be foreign to your tongue. They will seem strange and unnatural to you, and, what is more, they will sound canned and artificial to your audience. And the further you fish toward the outer limits of the diagram, the greater the problem will be.

This is no argument for settling for a limited speaking vocabulary. The larger the repertoire of words you have to choose from, the better your wording is likely to be. As one who desires to communicate publicly to an audience, you should be striving constantly to enrich your word power.

But this enrichment process is something you should be doing regularly as part of your daily life; it is not something you

Figure 12
Speakers' Vocabularies

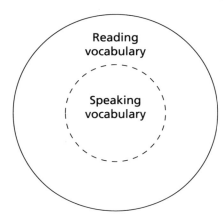

should attempt in your speech preparation. Try out new words often, and once they become comfortable, then include them in your speeches. But until then avoid words that still sound false—to your own ear—coming out of your mouth. Stick with language which is easy and natural, so that you do not have to concentrate upon it as you speak and so that you do not put your audience off. As Aristotle noted, "Naturalness is persuasive, artificiality is the contrary."[14]

Interesting Language

Your words must also be *interesting*. If they are not, your audience will not stay tuned despite the weightiness of your arguments. People lose patience with boring words very quickly. They will turn their attention to something more interesting unless you constantly work to hold their attention.

We discussed the matter of attention in chapter 2. There we pointed out that a speaker must not only win the audience's attention at the outset, but must win it again and again throughout the speech. Here we may say categorically that there is nothing you can do that will contribute more to winning and hold-

---

The Style of C. S. Lewis

Lewis had a superbly unaffected delivery—a deep voice that went well with his cheerful and bucolic appearance (all pictures of him that I know are good ones). It was a voice that really did vindicate the saying that the medium is the message. No rhetorical tricks; he read every word. Yet the way he used words as precision tools, the effortless rhythm of the sentences, the scholarship made friendly, the sternness made beautiful—these things all made it impossible for the listener to notice the passing of time. I call this passage a "vintage" example of his style. . . .

"At present we are on the outside of the world, the wrong side of the door. We discern the freshness and purity of morning, but they do not make us fresh and pure. We cannot mingle with the splendours we see. But all the leaves of the New Testament are rustling with the rumour that it will not always be so. Some day, God willing, we shall get in."

I would counsel any preacher, or any public speaker, to study every letter of that short passage; to notice how many of its words are of one syllable; and what contrasting effect the two-syllable words have. Who else would have spoken of the leaves of the New Testament "rustling"? That's poetry in the service of the Gospel. Well—imagine what it was like to hear that.

Erik Routley
in *C. S. Lewis at the Breakfast Table*

---

ing attention than choosing *interesting words.* Consider this: Take a good, well-constructed, well-illustrated speech and word it in a boring, mediocre way. Past experience indicates that it will accomplish very little. The audience will sit politely, trying to hide their boredom. They will be restless and discontented, covering their yawns with lifted hands.

But now take that same speech and bring it to life with fresh, creative, interesting words. The picture will be transformed: the audience's attention rapt, their boredom gone, their restlessness and discontent evaporated. And they will be sorry when you are through. The words make all the difference.

Your ideas, if they are worth communicating at all, deserve the best wording you can give them. People seldom even hear what is said poorly, but what is said well leaves a long-lasting imprint. As someone once remarked, the important thing about a speech is not what people can remember, but what they can never forget. Interesting words leave tracks which, in the last analysis, people can never forget.

How can you word your speech so that it will be unforgettable? What kinds of words are *interesting* words?

An idea is his who best expresses it.   Francis Bacon

Use Sensory Words

Sensory words are those which tap into our past experience, prompting us to conjure up fleeting, subconscious memories of our past. Here is how this works.

Experience is composed of all the data we have accumulated during our lifetime, primarily through the five senses: sight, hearing, touch, smell, and taste. Usually the trustworthiness of experience is unquestioned. Hence the old adages, "Seeing is believing" and "I'm from Missouri—show me." Unless we know better than to believe our senses (such as when we see a magician pull something out of thin air), our experience provides us with a deep sense of reality. "I have experienced it, so I *know* it's true," people say, or so they think. Experience automatically inspires belief, and what people experience leaves the deepest of all impressions upon them.

Curiously, we can utilize this great pool of experience in our listeners to lend to our ideas some of the striking qualities of firsthand experience. We can do this because of the relationship between the *word* and the *event*. Though an event may not be as realistic when we reconstruct it in words, still, we can by the skillful use of sensory language gain a response from the listeners that approximates direct experience. Why? Because people tend to respond to the word in much the same way they respond to the thing the word stands for. Paint the gory details of an accident and people become queasy; give a graphic description of sex and people become aroused (as pornographers well know); recount a suspenseful story and people become frightened. The sensory words conjure up within us memories of similar experiences so that we in some subtle way respond to the words in the same way we responded to the actual events. This explains the impact of sensory words. When we hear them, a fleeting subconscious image flashes across our minds. A memory—however small—is jogged, an impact registered, an interest aroused.

Sensory words, then, are concrete appeals to the senses. We can see this clearly by contrasting them with words which make no such appeal. Try this test: What happens when you think of each of these phrases?

    a. a lonely foghorn in the night
    b. the aroma of coffee perking
    c. sour as a lemon slice
    d. father's sandpaper beard
    e. glistening black stallion

In each case there is a momentary image in your mind which arouses interest and leaves a mark. You can *identify with* each of these sensory reminders. Now read these phrases:

    a. a definite motive
    b. concentrated industrial presence
    c. the allowable consideration
    d. certified rejuvenation
    e. epitome of revolutionary omnipotence

What happened inside your head this time? Without looking back, how many of the first five can you remember? How many of the second five? If you are like most people, the first five phrases made an impact on your mind and were therefore more memorable. The second five made no impact at all. They conjured up virtually nothing in your mind and so were less interesting and less memorable.

Information's pretty thin stuff unless mixed with experience.   Clarence Day

There is a lesson here for every public speaker. If we want to communicate in words that arouse interest and leave an imprint, we should use concrete, sensory words whenever possible.

Use Specific Words

Abstraction is the process of leaving out details. When we abstract, we select the most relevant information and leave out the rest. For example, a map is an abstraction of the terrain it represents. The map does not try to show all the details of the terrain, but only those which are relevant to the purpose of the map.

The ability to abstract is of great benefit to us. It is one of those gifts of God which separate us from the other creatures. It is that part of the image of God in humans which allows us to think in categories. Thus we do not have to name each individual detail we encounter. We can group the details into categories. For instance, we do not usually name the individual pieces of furniture upon which we sit. We think of them simply as sofas or chairs. The ability to use such abstract categories as *sofas, chairs, cars, animals,* and *people,* so taken for granted by us in our everyday life, contributes greatly to the preservation of our sanity in a complicated world.

But as we have already seen, the more abstract a word is, the more ambiguous it is and the more likely it will be misunderstood. We may add to these principles another one: The more abstract a word is, the less interesting and memorable it is. Abstract words tend to be bland because of their generality. They arouse no images in the listener's mind. But conversely, as language becomes less abstract, it grows more concrete, more specific—and the more concrete and specific it is, the more likely it is to strike flint in the memory of your hearer.

Should we, then, avoid abstract language altogether? We could not do so if we tried. But we can work to avoid *unnecessary* abstraction. We can work to make our language as specific as possible. For instance, suppose you decided to say, "The man went down the road." The word "went," the past tense of *go*, is much more abstract than "stumbled," "meandered," "darted," "trotted," "pranced," "lurched," "skipped," "shuffled," or "slinked." Which of these specific verbs might more exactly capture your thought? Any one of them, or others like them, would be more concrete and therefore more interesting and memorable. In the same way you might want to replace "she said" with "she shouted," "she blurted," "she cried," "she whispered," "she lisped," or "she mumbled." Nouns as well as verbs can be made more specific. Instead of saying, "There were several things wrong with the way he fulfilled his office," you could put it this way: "Three abuses of power sank his administration." Here are some other examples:

Instead of saying:	*Try this:*
few men	five astronauts
a long time ago	in December of 1876
many foreign cars	52 percent of all Hondas and Toyotas
in the near future	two weeks from tomorrow
some vegetables	corn, peas, and carrots
a weapon	a heavy lead pipe
reference books	dictionaries and atlases
a lot of flowers	five hundred yellow roses

Such specific language adds zest and interest to your speech. You cannot remain on a concrete level throughout, nor would you want to, but by the same token you must resist the greater temptation of remaining on an abstract level. Ideally you should range up and down the ladder of abstraction, moving from the abstract to the concrete, then back again. This is the mark of an effective communicator.

Use Active Words

Another way to make your language more interesting is to enliven it with action words which make the sentences *move*. You can do this by (a) emphasizing the active voice over the passive and (b) minimizing your use of linking verbs.

When you use the passive voice, the emphasis falls upon the recipient of the action. When you use the active voice, the emphasis falls upon the one who initiates the action, and upon the action itself. So passive constructions tend to be just that—*passive*. They are often limp and without punch. But active verbs bring your ideas alive. They scoot across the page: actor-action-goal. The principle is, somebody *does* something. The verb prompts the listener to see some action in his mind, and the impact is correspondingly stronger. Thus, "Abe Lincoln *freed* the slaves" is stronger than "The slaves *were delivered* by Abe Lincoln"; "Water *wears* away stones" (Job 14:19) is stronger than "Stones *are eroded* by water"; "I *watched* the game with great excitement" is stronger than, "The game *was observed* by me with great excitement."

Of course, when the recipient of the action is more important than the doer, you may want to use the passive voice: "The bullet *was buried* six inches into the wood." Do not try to eliminate the passive voice altogether. But whenever possible, and especially when you want the emphasis to fall on the doer, use the active voice.

Linking verbs also sap your language of strength. Again, they cannot be entirely avoided, but you should use them sparingly.

A linking verb (copula) is one which carries little meaning of its own. It is used chiefly to connect a subject with a modifier. The verb *to be* in all its forms (am, was, are, were, will be, have been, had been, will have been) is the most widely used linking verb, but there are as many as sixty others in current usage:

The tank *is* empty.
She *used to be* a cheerleader.

The evening *turned* chilly.

He *became* angry.

The climb *seemed* dangerous.

Linking verbs are inherently weaker than action verbs. They are essentially statements about some state of being and signify no movement at all. Thus they have less interest appeal than the "man bites dog" type of sentence. So try to avoid using linking verbs when a more active construction is available. Instead of "Going to Jerusalem *was* dangerous, but Paul was determined to go there," try to make the sentence more lively: "Jerusalem spelled trouble in bold letters, but Paul set his course for there anyway."

Use Imaginative Language

When you cannot find concrete, sensory language to express your ideas, with a little imagination you can sometimes borrow the benefits of concrete language by using figures of speech which compare your idea to something else. The most common such figures are *metaphors* and *similes*.

Metaphors are implied comparisons. They tend to be short and compact: "the bread of life"; "footprints stitched across the snow"; "buses elbowing their way through the traffic."

Similes are explicit comparisons, using the words *like* or *as*, wherein otherwise dissimilar items are shown to be alike in some way: Spurgeon spoke of a time when "the great universe lay in the mind of God *like* unborn forests in the acorn's cup"; "Sincerity is *like* a spice: too much repels you but too little leaves you wanting."

Personification is another figure of speech which implies a comparison. Some impersonal thing (such as an object, quality, ideal, or animal) is given the attributes of a human being: "Love treated him gently"; "The gaze of history was upon me"; "the eyelids of the morning" (Job 41:18 NASB).

Such comparisons allow you to borrow the high interest value of concrete expressions. They add color, texture, and interest to your wording. But remember these three pointers: (a) Metaphorical language can be overdone. Avoid making your language too flowery. (b) The comparison must be clear. "Like a modern-day Uzzah he decided to do it himself"—but does the audience know who Uzzah was and what he did? If the comparison is too obscure ("a Pyrrhic victory") for your listeners, it will hinder rather than help your style. (c) Metaphors should not be mixed. "He burned with anger, and a cascade of hot words flooded out of his mouth"; "When God opens the door, it lasts forever; if you open the door, it has a built-in fizzle." Such competing images (hot versus cold; opening doors and fizzling) jangle in the listener's mind. Keep the imagery unified.

Use Fresh Words

The freshness of language is related to its predictability. Trite, hackneyed, cliché-ridden language is boring precisely because it is so predictable. We have heard it all before. Once the expression begins, we can finish it without the speaker. It requires nothing from us, so we grant it what it asks: nothing.

Fresh language is unpredictable. It is in some sense novel and creative. We have not heard it put quite like *that* before—and our interest is piqued. We must hear it out, and interact with it, in order to grasp it. Creative language thus requires something of us, and we willingly grant it. Why? Because its unpredictability renders it interesting to us.

Language becomes predictable through overuse. What was once fresh and creative becomes trite and overworked through repetition. At one time a phrase may have prompted some colorful picture in our minds, but no longer. The image-producing qualities of the words have, so to speak, died. For example, the first time a speaker (or writer) described something that quickly passed without much effect as a "flash in the pan," the image (probably of a turn-of-the-century photographer's "flash" powder going off suddenly in his upheld "pan" or of gunpowder "flashing" in a musket's "pan" instead of exploding) was undoubtedly a vivid one. But do these words any longer conjure up this—or any other—concrete image? Probably not. We know what the speaker means, of course, but this is no longer a fresh or interesting way of expressing the thought. Here is a sample of other expressions which, though fairly clear, are also entirely predictable and therefore uninteresting.

a method in my madness	opened a can of worms
playing second fiddle	an irony of fate
right from the horse's mouth	have your cake and eat it too
passing the buck	burning the midnight oil
had the time of my life	apple of his eye
beating around the bush	let the cat out of the bag
die a thousand deaths	dead as a doornail
better late than never	pretty as a picture
put the cart before the horse	fly in the ointment
last but not least	flat as a pancake

Avoid such overworked expressions in favor of fresher, more creative language. Use your imagination. Ask yourself, what can I do to render my word choice less predictable and, therefore, more interesting? Here are some expressions which are notable for their freshness. Notice in each case that it is the unexpected that makes them interesting:

Some people would rather brush with regular toothpaste and have 21 percent fewer commercials.

Fools look for happiness in the distance, but the wise grow it under their feet.

People can be divided into two types—those who still possess the fierce hunting instinct and those who pay to park their cars.

Ask not what your country can do for you—ask what you can do for your country.

I was jostled by two children tugboating their mother to the toy counter.

Use Human-Interest Words

People are interested in other people. *Time* magazine conducted a survey and discovered that one of the most popular parts of the magazine was the human-interest section entitled "People," which contains each week a series of brief, gossipy items about famous individuals. The editors felt that they had made a notable discovery, so they launched a new magazine, *People*, which in its entirety takes the same approach. The success of *People*, in turn, has spawned several other human-interest magazines. Readers are interested in learning about other people.

Actually the writers at *Time* have always known that stories told in terms of people communicate better. That's why they often put people on the cover, regardless of the lead story. Even abstract subjects are presented by describing the experiences of people. Why? Because the editors know that readers are inter-

---

Time [magazine] didn't start this emphasis on stories about peo-
ple; the Bible did. Henry Luce

---

ested in human experience. When ideas are kept close to life, people can identify with them. They sit up and listen.

Why do people sit up and listen? The reason, of course, is rooted again in the difference between the abstract and concrete. People are naturally drawn to the concrete. As Sue Nichols explains:

> Celery at its best is served raw. So is modern [communication]. It is as concrete, specific, and close to life as possible. Recall the two reports of work camp experiences:

> | We lived in close quarters with young people from other lands. We had to learn to understand their points of view. We had to adjust to their forms of courtesy and accept them even when they seemed strangest. We had to. . . . | I met Ingrid in our bunkroom and took an instant dislike to her. She wore her hems one inch below the fashion line and criticized me for chewing gum. |

> The account on the left has been plucked, boiled until flavorless, then canned for consumption. The account on the right

arrives plucked but unprocessed. It retains all the pulp and juices of the original experience.[15]

It is worthwhile to remember that God did not reveal his truth to us in the form of systematic theology—that is, a series of integrated abstract propositions. Rather, God's Word has come to us largely in the form of human drama, stories about people living real lives: victories and defeats, a shortened ministry, a disgrace averted, a sad death or a happy birth, a ministry fulfilled. Even the Epistles come to us in the very human form of letters from a concerned spiritual father to needy spiritual children. The entire Bible appears in a form that is very close to life.

Try to follow this pattern. Look for the human side of your subject. Try somehow to touch the subjective elements of experience. Think about the interests, fears, hopes, and dreams of real people who are or might be affected by your subject, and then help your audience to see the issues through their eyes. Give your ideas flesh and blood. Incarnate them for your listeners in words which breathe and bleed and sing. Follow Jesus' example, who when he was pressed to answer the abstract question, "Who is my neighbor?" responded with the story of the good Samaritan: "A man was going down from Jerusalem to Jericho, when he fell into the hands of robbers. They stripped him of his clothes, beat him and went away, leaving him half dead. . . ." (Luke 10:30 NIV).

Use Euphonious Words

Remember that you are writing for the ear rather than the eye. Thus you want words that sound attractive and interesting when used together. They should be, to use the technical term, *euphonious*.

One typical kind of euphony in speech is called *alliteration*: repetition of the same sound at the beginning of words or of stressed syllables used close together. Examples: "Fourscore and seven years ago our fathers brought forth . . ."; "our poor power"; "winter's blustery blow"; "the crowded columns of men crept forward."

Parallel wording often provides a pleasant sound as well. Read Lincoln's Gettysburg Address and look for the parallel constructions.

Fourscore and seven years ago our fathers brought forth on this continent a new nation, conceived in liberty and dedicated to the proposition that all men are created equal. Now we are engaged in a great civil war, testing whether that nation, or any nation so conceived and so dedicated, can long endure. We are met on a great battlefield of that war. We have come to dedicate a portion of that field as a final resting place for those who here gave their lives that that nation might live. It is altogether fitting and proper that we should do this. But in a larger sense, we cannot dedicate, we cannot consecrate, we cannot hallow this ground. The brave men, living and dead, who struggled here, have consecrated it far above our poor power to add or detract. The world will little note nor long remember what we say here, but it can never forget what

Euphony: the quality of having a pleasant sound; pleasant effect of a combination of agreeable sounds, as in speech or music.

they did here. It is for us the living rather to be dedicated here to the unfinished work which they who fought here have thus far so nobly advanced. It is rather for us to be here dedicated to the great task remaining before us—that from these honored dead we take increased devotion to that cause for which they gave the last full measure of devotion; that we here highly resolve that these dead shall not have died in vain; that this nation, under God, shall have a new birth of freedom, and that government of the people, by the people, for the people, shall not perish from the earth.

Did you notice these?

we cannot dedicate
we cannot consecrate
we cannot hallow

it is for us the living rather to be dedicated here
it is rather for us to be here dedicated

that . . . we take
that we . . . resolve
that this nation . . . shall have
that government . . . shall not perish

of the people
by the people
for the people

Verbal antithesis can also produce euphony. Observe Lincoln's, "The world *will little note nor long remember what we say here,* but it *can never forget what they did here."* Or, note John F. Kennedy's words in his inaugural address:

We observe today not a victory of party but a celebration of freedom.

not as a call to bear arms, though arms we need

not a call to battle, though embattled we are

Ask not what your country can do for you—ask what you can do for your country.

Ask not what America will do for you, but what together we can do for the freedom of man.

Rhythm is another contributor to euphony in speech, but it is very difficult to discuss briefly. Rhythm in speech is dependent upon the regular recurrence of sounds or patterns of sounds so that a meter or beat is produced. The beat is much less metrical in speech than in poetry or music, of course, but snatches of it in the wording of a speech can be very attractive. Lincoln's Gettysburg Address is graced with a beautiful set of rhythms. Reread the speech aloud, listening for the cadences of the words.

Use Concise Words

Prune away every unnecessary word. Say exactly what you mean and say it concisely. Trim away all the deadwood.

Supposedly in ancient Rome unscrupulous sculptors filled the cracks in their marble statues with wax and then sold them as flawless. Only later, when the wax dried and flaked out of the cracks, did the buyer realize that he had been taken. Hence reputable sculptors began to certify their statues as *sine cera*, meaning that they were without wax (compare the English word *sincere*). Perhaps honest speakers should certify their speeches in a similar way as being "without word wax"; that is, without flaws covered over with verbal filler. Some examples of word wax:

Redundant expressions are word wax. Such phrases as "converge together," "each and every," "brown in color," "repeat again," "return back," "habitual custom," "large in size," "refer back," and "the same identical" are unnecessarily repetitive. They should be trimmed away.

Unnecessary overstatements are word wax. "This is absolutely and positively essential" would be better as, simply, "This is essential." "Completely unique" would be better as, simply, "unique."

Groping expressions are word wax. Vocalized pauses such as "ah," "um," and "er" are groping expressions designed to fill in the cracks of your speech. So also are phrases used to stall for time, such as "What I mean is . . ."; ". . . you know?"; "What I'm trying to say is. . . ." Prune them away.

"Et cetera" expressions are word wax. Someone has said that *et cetera* simply means, "I cannot think of any more examples"— and that is more often the case than most of us would want to admit. Eliminate phrases such as "et cetera" and "and so forth" from your speech.

Unnecessary qualifiers are word wax. Avoid phrases such as "more or less"; "Of course it's only my opinion but . . ."; "or something like that"; "If you'll permit me, I'd like to say . . ."; "I've told this story before but it bears repeating." They add nothing to your speech but detract a great deal. Perhaps the worst of all is "I've not had much time to prepare for this speech, but I'll give you what I've got." If you are unprepared, your audience will know it soon enough; you do not need to announce it. Trim away all unnecessary qualifiers from your speech.

Word wax chokes your meaning, clutters your sentences, and undermines the conciseness which appeals to listeners. In other words, it makes your language less interesting. Instead of filling in the cracks with word wax, try to construct your speech so that such verbal filler is unnecessary.

Developing Your Style

Style is inevitable. It is always present when we speak. We can ignore the process of word choice, but we cannot avoid choosing words. We can avoid studying style or attempting to improve our style, but we cannot avoid the impact our style will have on our audience—for better or worse.

Thus you already have a style. It is the product of your choice and management of words. The only questions are, How effective is it? And can you improve it and, if so, how? Here are three steps to improving your word choice:

Become a Student of Effective Language

You now know some of the prime characteristics of an effective style. Begin observing how writers and speakers use language. Look for both effective and ineffective ways of expressing a thought. Seek examples of fresh wording such as you might find in books of poetry or in the *Reader's Digest* under "Quotable Quotes" or "Toward More Picturesque Speech." Consider what makes these examples work. You might also try reading some books on how to increase your word power. Your local bookstore will likely carry a number of highly readable little paperbacks designed for just this purpose.[16]

You must come to appreciate language and how it functions. Spend time regularly with a dictionary or thesaurus evaluating the color, weight, and texture of the words you find there. Read great speeches and literature, looking for examples of effective wording. When you discover a well-turned phrase, stop and mull it over: Why is it effective? On the other hand, when you discover a poorly expressed idea, try to discover why it is poor and how you might reword it in language that communicates more effectively.

Learning to handle language well is like learning any other art. As Davis says, "Art is skill in doing, controlled by an inner sense of rightness."[17] Thus you must not only learn how to speak well;

Eloquence will come more readily through reading and hearing the eloquent, than through pursuing the rules of eloquence. **Saint Augustine**

you must also develop that taste which allows you to discern the good from the bad, both in your own language and that of others. Exposure to effective wording in your reading and listening will hone that "inner sense of rightness" and provide the discernment you need.

Write Out Your Speech

Quintilian, the great Roman teacher of public speaking, wrote, "As regards those [aids] which we must supply for ourselves, it is the pen which brings at once the most labor and the most profit. Cicero is fully justified in describing it as the best producer of eloquence."[18]

Both Quintilian and Cicero were right. There is nothing you can do that will contribute more to improving your speaking style than writing out your entire speech, word for word as you intend to say it. Unfortunately, Quintilian was also correct when he said that writing requires a great deal of labor. Combine this with the facts that writing out a manuscript is one of the last steps in the process of preparation and that the speaking date always seems to approach with accelerating speed—and it is not difficult to see why some speakers never bother with a manuscript. But then these are often the same speakers who produce speeches with which their listeners need not bother either.

If you want to improve your style, you cannot afford to skip this important step, particularly in your beginning years as a speaker. As Quintilian says, "It is an ordinance of nature that nothing great can be achieved in a moment, and that all the fairest tasks are attended with difficulty."[19] You will need to take the time and make the effort to write out your text in full, for it is only when you have captured your ideas in words that you can best work to improve your style. Until then the wording of your thought remains elusive and changing, and very difficult to evaluate or revise. Once you pin your wording down, however, you can work it over mercilessly, paring away the trite, cumbersome, or boring words in favor of language that is fresher, more pointed, more lively.

Thankfully, the word processor has transformed the task of writing and rewriting. A pencil, pen, or typewriter used to be the best possible tools. The problem with these common instruments, however, was that they inevitably collapsed writing and editing into one process—when you recorded a word, by defini-

---

The art of writing is the art of applying the seat of the pants to the seat of the chair. Collin Brooks

---

tion you also "printed" it. If you wanted to edit your work, you either had to start over or else erase, cross out, or scribble around what you had already written.

But the word processor has changed the task. This machine enables you to write and edit your work electronically on a screen without printing. Only when you have a finished product do you need to print the result. The separation of printing from editing, which is the genius of the word processor, makes the process of editing wonderfully easy and fast. In turn, you are able to create and revise numerous drafts of your work, in a fraction of the time. For a public speaker who desires to concentrate on his or her word choice, this is no small advantage.

If you have access to a word processor, the process will be much easier. But even if you do not have a word processor (and many do not), you still need to work at the business of writing and rewriting. Without it, your style will never measure up to what it might possibly be.

If you are not able to use a word processor, legal-size pads of lined yellow paper are ideal for writing out your speech. Be sure to allow plenty of room between the lines and in the margins for corrections, for as Quintilian says:

> Erasure is quite as important a function of the pen as actual writing. Correction takes the form of addition, excision and alteration. But it is a comparatively simple and easy task to decide what is to be added or excised. On the other hand, to prune what is turgid, to elevate what is mean, to repress exuberance, arrange what is disorderly, introduce rhythm where it is lacking, and modify it where it is too emphatic, involves a twofold labor. For we have to condemn what had previously satisfied us and discover what had escaped our notice.[20]

Whether you are using a word processor or a pen, you should probably count on producing several drafts of your speech—as many, in fact, as the time for preparation will allow. Each draft of the speech should be more polished than the last, each one closer to the most effective wording of which you are capable.

Try to allow an interval of time between working on the various drafts. Says Quintilian, "There can be no doubt that the best method of correction is to put aside what we have written for a certain time, so that when we return to it after an interval it will have the air of novelty and of being another's handiwork; for thus we may prevent ourselves from regarding our writings with all the affection that we lavish on a newborn child."[21] The process is laborious and time-consuming, but it will pay great dividends, both in the effectiveness of your wording and in your control over the content of the speech. The more time you spend grappling with your wording here, the better you will know your own ideas, and the less time you will need to invest later in committing to memory the flow of ideas in the speech.

This is not to say, of course, that you should try to commit your entire manuscript to memory the way an actor memorizes a script. In fact, to do so is to court disaster. There is nothing quite so terrifying as standing before an audience and, halfway through your speech, finding your mind a complete blank. This is just what tends to happen when one tries to memorize a speech, word upon word, phrase upon phrase, line upon line. Lose one word, phrase, or line, and the entire speech comes tumbling down like a house of cards. This will happen to you only once before you decide never to try memorizing a speech again.

What's more, even if you could get through the entire speech without missing a word, the chances are that it would sound artificial and memorized. The ideal tone for a speech is much more spontaneous.

But how can a speech which has been written out sound spontaneous? This is not difficult, provided you allow the manuscript to fulfill its proper role. *It* is designed to serve *you*, not the reverse. You must not let "the tail wag the dog." Keep the manuscript in its proper place, and it will prove to be of great help to you.

What is the proper place of a manuscript? Once you have completed your writing and revising, you are ready to rehearse your speech for delivery. You have been working hard on your manuscript, so it will be tempting to give it a prominent place in your rehearsal. But it is just now that you must set the manuscript aside and revert to your outline.

Here, then, is an important rule: Never rehearse your speech from the manuscript. Always rehearse from an abbreviated version of the outline. Be sure that you have the entire flow of ideas completely memorized, so that you can move through the speech's structure quickly and without hesitation. Practice this repeatedly until you are sure you have it totally under control.

After the flow of ideas (both main ideas and subideas) has become second nature to you, then—and only then—should you attempt to think about the language you have built into your manuscript. Even now you do not memorize the manuscript, however. The work you have done on the manuscript will pay off, for the words you use to express your ideas will tend to be those you have used in the manuscript. You may go back to check (and even revise) your manuscript, of course, but do not memorize the words by rote. Better to sacrifice a well-turned phrase and keep your train of thought, than to reach for the phrase and lose the lively spontaneity that is such an important part of your delivery.

Speak Often

Take every opportunity you can find to stand up and speak to an audience. Refuse nothing. Look for opportunities at church, in the classroom, at work, or in the community. If five people want you to deliver a speech at a backyard barbecue, do it. And use each of these occasions as an opportunity to work on your word choice.

Developing fully an effective style takes time and experience. Each occasion provides you with an opportunity to put into practice the principles we have outlined in this chapter. Each time you do so, the process will become easier and more natural to you.

Seek out especially those occasions when you can use the same speech twice. As we have emphasized strongly in this book, no two audiences or speaking occasions are identical. So you should never use the same speech a second time without thoroughly reworking it to fit your new audience. But it is also true that in such situations you do not have to start your preparation from scratch. Much of your work will already be done. The ideas and the basic structure of the speech will be largely familiar to you. Thus you can use the time you save to polish the wording of the speech. Such situations provide excellent opportunities to develop your style.

Exercises

1. Select two speeches from the periodical *Vital Speeches of the Day,* one which shows excellent word choices and one in which the word choice is much less impressive. Compare and contrast the two styles by citing examples of how the one is strong and the other is weak. Seek examples which illustrate as many aspects of effective and ineffective wording as possible.

2. How many of these clichés can you complete?
   > sly as . . .
   > don't count your . . .
   > now the shoe is . . .
   > like shutting the barn door . . .
   > age before . . .
   > clear the . . .
   > cool as . . .
   > bringing home the . . .
   > last but not . . .
   > sick as . . .
   > without a shadow . . .

   List five more overworked expression from your own experience.

3. Find three more vivid, concrete substitutions for each of the following words:
   > house
   > road
   > vehicle
   > garment

   > to take
   > to travel
   > to think
   > to put

4. As the teacher of a high-school course in public speaking you must give a ten-minute lecture on one of the following subjects: why predictable language is boring, how to develop an effective style, or the pros and cons of abstraction. From the material in this chapter and any other sources you can find, develop a complete outline for that lecture.

Chapter **9**

How to Deliver Your Speech

We have just been examining the *words* you will use to communicate your ideas. But what about all those ways you communicate with your audience apart from words? How do they fit into the picture? In this chapter we want to examine the *nonverbal* aspects of public speaking.

Nonverbal and Verbal Communication

We operate according to two different codes when we communicate with one another. The first is the *verbal* code. The basic elements in the verbal code are *words* (Latin, *verbum*). We choose our words in accordance with what is generally agreed upon as their meaning (or else redefine them for our audience), and we arrange them together according to the accepted rules of grammar and syntax. These rules are written down and taught to every grammar-school child (or at least they should be). Such rules and meanings together constitute the primary aspects of our linguistic or verbal code.

However, we also operate according to a second code, the much less understood *nonverbal* code. (Actually it would probably be more accurate to conceive of it as a conglomeration of codes, but for our convenience we will speak of them as one.) The nonverbal code does not govern any discrete element such as the word. Rather its rules deal with such things as the way we move, how we hold ourselves, what we look at and for how long, and how close we approach one another in our conversation.

As you might imagine, the behavior covered by the nonverbal code is extremely complex and difficult to define in any final way. It is almost infinitely variable as conditions and combinations of conditions change. Thus there are very few ironclad rules within the nonverbal code. Furthermore, our understanding of how we communicate nonverbally is still in its infancy. There is much yet to be studied and described. But we do know enough to permit us to state some broad principles of what tends to promote effective communication and what tends to get in its way.

The verbal and nonverbal channels of our communication can work together or they can work against one another. When they work together, what we communicate nonverbally serves to repeat, complement, substitute for, or in some way regulate what we say verbally. For example, if we say, "Get out!" and point to the door, we are *repeating;* if we spread our hands and arms while describing a panorama in front of us, we are *complementing;* if someone asks us a question and we merely shrug our shoulders in reply, we are *substituting;* if we avoid eye contact because we do not want to speak to someone (or vice versa, if we catch his eye because we do), we are *regulating.*

But our nonverbal cues can also *contradict* what we are saying verbally. There is truth behind the old adage, "Your actions speak so loud I can't hear what you say." A husband says, "I love you," but his wife does not really believe it; a pastor preaches on "love" but exudes hostility toward his people by browbeating them; you say, "I'm not frightened," but both your voice and your hands are shaking. In such cases the nonverbal messages are contradicting the verbal messages.

Usually we try to coordinate what we say verbally and nonverbally, so much so that it is sometimes difficult to force our verbal and nonverbal messages to contradict each other even when we want them to. Try this, for example: Shake your head yes but say aloud, "No." Did you have to concentrate for a moment to do it? That is because you are so used to making the verbal and nonverbal aspects of your messages work together.

However, sometimes the two work against one another when we least want them to. We can control our words easily enough (we can *say* anything we want), but the nonverbal cues we give off are much more difficult to control. We often give ourselves away quite unintentionally.

It is precisely because the nonverbal cues are so difficult to control that we come to trust them more than words. When a person's verbal and nonverbal messages contradict one another, we tend to trust the message which is more difficult to control. This is the principle of the polygraph, or lie-detector, test. The suspect says he was at home that night, but his body (via his heartbeat, respiration, galvanic skin response, etc.) says otherwise. Since few can control these bodily clues, the examiner accepts them rather than the suspect's words and declares the man to be lying. So do we all come to trust those messages we pick up from nonverbal cues when they give the lie to a person's words.

Keep in mind, too, that we usually do not communicate the same messages through verbal and nonverbal channels. Ideas— subjects and complements—are very difficult to communicate nonverbally. That part of your message will no doubt be communicated primarily by your words. But how you *feel* about your ideas, about yourself, and about your audience—these messages will be communicated largely through your nonverbal cues. This is because nonverbal communication channels are especially well adapted to communicating attitudes, feelings, and relationships rather than cognitive information.

Channels of Nonverbal Communication

How do we communicate nonverbally with our audience? Let us examine six channels of nonverbal communication which are especially relevant to public speakers: proxemics, kinesics, eye behavior, physical appearance, facial expression, and paralanguage.

Proxemics

Proxemics is the study of how we perceive and use the space around us to communicate nonverbally. It is an involved and complex area of study, and one of the most fascinating aspects of nonverbal communication. However, we will not go into the entire area of proxemics in detail since only certain facets of the subject are useful for our present discussion.

Distance

The basic principle behind proxemics is that physical distance is related to psychological distance. The further we are from someone physically, the further we are psychologically. This basic observation is susceptible to variation with the addition of complications. For instance, are you above your listeners (as, for example, on a stage or platform) or below them (as in

---

Demosthenes, when asked the three most important things in oratory, replied: "Delivery, delivery, and delivery!"

---

an amphitheater)? Are there other physical features such as a railing, podium, or desk between you and your audience?

As a general rule you will want to get as close to your audience as possible. The larger the audience, of course, the greater will be the distance to the first row; the smaller the audience, the less distance to the first row. But positioning yourself *unnecessarily* distant from your audience may communicate that you want to keep them at arm's length and that you are unfriendly or standoffish.

Because audiences often gravitate toward the back of the seating area, you will sometimes face speaking situations where two or three (or more) empty rows of chairs separate you from your listeners. If you can, either bring the audience forward or move your speaking position toward the first row of your listeners, thus decreasing this great gulf fixed between you and your listeners. If you can do this without antagonizing them, the dividends in increased intimacy will usually be worth the effort.

Elevation

Another feature of distance has to do with your elevation. Unless the audience is quite large, you will not need to mount a stage or platform, and you should avoid doing so if possible. The increased height puts you above your audience in more ways than one. It increases the likelihood that you will talk down to them. Keeping yourself on the audience's level communicates that you do not see yourself as better than your audience but rather as one of them, a friend speaking to friends.

In this connection, amphitheaters, in which the speaker is actually below the audience, create the opposite impression. In such arrangements the audience feels subconsciously that they have the upper hand, and therefore they feel quite safe. They may also feel more inclined to reject your ideas precisely because of this psychological safety, and you may find yourself feeling a bit more threatened (sort of a Daniel in the lions' den). When the audience is elevated over the speaker, the psychological scales tip in their favor. This is not necessarily bad if you as the speaker can handle it, but it is something you need to consider.

Obstructions

Another rule of thumb is to eliminate any physical objects between you and your audience. Objects blocking the audience's view of your body, especially if they are large and bulky, tend to block communication as well. They encourage a psychological wall between you and your listeners which will inhibit your communication. If you must use notes and therefore need something on which to lay them, or if you are doing some form of exposition (see chap. 10) and have your Bible open before you, try to use a small music-stand-type lectern. It should be as light and compact as possible. Stay away from large, bulky podiums if you can. They work against your efforts to communicate effectively through nonverbal channels.

Kinesics

Kinesics, otherwise known as "body language," refers to the way we communicate through the gestures, postures, and other movements of our body. While it is possible to overstate the case for body language, claiming that what people communicate via their bodies is much more powerful and specific than in fact it is, it is altogether true that we tend to read other people by the way they stand, move, sit, and gesture. So also do they read us.

This observation has significant implications for public speakers. From the first moment you come into the view of your audience, they are beginning to make inferences about you on the basis of what they see. Do you appear to be in control of yourself and the situation, or do you appear frightened and nervous? Do you stand tall, or are you slouching? Is there a certain dignity to the way you sit, or do you sag into your chair like a sack of flour? When you walk to the podium, do you do so with strength and vigor, or do you move with reluctance like someone facing an execution? Do you hold your head high, or let it droop low as if you are fearful of catching someone's eye? All of these things and more are eagerly examined by your listeners to see what sort of person you are. Indeed, you do the same thing, perhaps unconsciously, when you are sizing up a speaker to whom you are about to listen.

What you do with your body while you speak is even more important. Your posture, movement, and gestures should be orchestrated so as to serve your message. All of your body movements should complement what you are saying at the moment. Are you making a point forcefully? Perhaps your body should be leaning forward, muscles tense, with dynamic gestures jabbing the air. Are you at some point in your speech where the ideas are much more low-key? Perhaps a more relaxed and loose posture would be appropriate. Take a step back from your audience, maybe even put a hand in a pocket.

You see, there are no laws when it comes to using your body to help communicate your ideas. In past times, particularly during the "elocutionary movement" of the last century, speakers were taught in a very detailed way what moves to make, what gestures to perform, and what postures to strike. But today we shy away from such a rule-oriented approach to delivery because modern audiences enjoy a much more natural and relaxed style. The only rule is that what you are doing physically should complement and reinforce what you are saying verbally.

As the great English preacher Charles Haddon Spurgeon once told his students, "Let the gesture tally with the words, and be a sort of running commentary and practical exegesis upon what you are saying."

What this means is that there is hardly anything—within the bounds of good taste, of course—which should be arbitrarily ruled out. Sometimes teachers of public speaking have instructed their students not to put their hands in a pocket, not to hold on to the podium, not to slouch, and so forth. But is it not possible that even such things as these might conceivably reinforce certain kinds of ideas so that they would be appropriate in certain situations?

To be sure, a problem arises when a speaker places her hands on the podium or in her pockets and *leaves them there*. This should rightly be criticized because to do so is to eliminate the

---

Many a person gets a reputation for being energetic, when in truth, he is merely fidgety.

---

hands and arms as channels of nonverbal communication. Since the hands are, after the face, the most expressive part of the body, the loss is a significant one. So, while there is no law that says one must never put one's hand in a pocket or grasp the podium (since such actions might be entirely fitting at certain points in a speech), there is a solid principle which prevents us from planting our hands there permanently. We ought to use our hands, arms, and bodies to reinforce what we are saying at the moment.

Following this principle means that you will want to avoid *distracting mannerisms*. Distracting mannerisms are those which call attention to themselves and away from what is being said. Playing with a button on your coat, repeatedly pulling at an earlobe or brushing aside a lock of hair, drumming your fingers on the lectern, nervously shuffling a card in your hands—these all tend to draw attention away from what you are saying and should be avoided. Remember: The principle is that you should use your hands, arms, and body to help you communicate your ideas, not to get in the way of your ideas.

Another typically distracting use of our body comes when, either from a desire to be dynamic or from plain nervousness, we begin to pace back and forth. This is a common fault which conjures up in the mind of many listeners a caged lion or tiger padding repeatedly back and forth. Very quickly such pacing begins to wear on an audience. It draws attention to itself and away from the ideas.

Instead of pacing randomly, your goal should be to control your movement so that it reinforces your speech. Bodily movement can be very useful in a speech. It can add interest, vitality, and zest. It can help hold the attention of the audience, but only if it is the *right kind* of movement—movement *designed to reinforce* what you are saying. By contrast, random movement (that is, movement for its own sake) is of no virtue. It seldom adds anything and often detracts a great deal.

So move from side to side when you make a transition or from front to back when you want to emphasize or deemphasize a point, or step out from the lectern and move closer to your audience when you want to increase the intimacy of the setting. Be active as you speak. Move freely. Gesture widely and with vigor. But always be sure that your bodily movement is designed to serve your message, not get in its way.

Eye Behavior

The way we use our eyes is an important aspect of our nonverbal communication. Catching or avoiding one's eye, a steady stare, a hesitant glance—each contributes its share to the total nonverbal message we send.

One of the most important roles of eye behavior is its function as a *regulator* of our verbal communication. To establish a bond of communication with someone, we look him in the eye. To avoid communication, we avoid his eye. What is more, when we are talking with someone who refuses to look at us, we are frustrated, particularly if we are aware that she is focusing on other things around us. We want to look her in the eye, but she will not let us. This is why we dislike talking to someone who is wearing sunglasses. We can't see his or her eyes.

This regulating role of the eye is of crucial importance to public speakers. By looking at an audience we establish a bond of communication and say to them, in effect, "I want to talk with you." By refusing to look them in the eye, we say just the opposite.

It is for this reason that effective speakers place such a stress on good eye contact. Good eye contact between speaker and audience promotes effective communication; poor eye contact hinders effective communication. Since the choice of whether to have good or poor eye contact is almost entirely up to the speaker, and since the matter is such an important one, the practice of good eye contact deserves and receives a major emphasis.

How can you develop good eye contact? You probably will not be able to look every member of your audience in the eye, and

---

Eye Contact

Someday, someone might become rich and famous by authoring a book entitled *The Games Students Play*. The book will deal with such topics as Excuses Students Use, Courtship in the Classroom, and How to Cheat Creatively. But chapter one will have to be devoted to the Ostrich Game which takes place when the professor is looking for a response to his very convoluted and long-winded question. He looks around the room, searching for a student to call upon, but nobody will establish eye contact with him. The students are sanctimoniously scanning their notebooks, looking out the window, searching, gazing, staring everywhere *except* at the professor. Should our pedagog be offended by this mini-form of social isolation? Not at all. He should just be reminded that his students are playing the Ostrich Game, that well-entrenched, head-in-the-sand, classroom reaction that asserts: "If I can't see you, you can't see me, and hence, you can't call on me since I am not really here."

Roderick P. Hart, Gustav W. Friedrich, and William D. Brooks
Public Communication

---

probably should not worry about doing so even if you could. How then should you look at your audience? Do not try, as some advise, to look just over the heads of your listeners, avoiding true eye contact. Your audience will not be fooled. You will not be looking them in the eye, and they will know it. The indeterminate focus in your own eye will give you a glassy-eyed stare, which is easily picked up by your listeners. Rather, try to divide your audience into sections and then let your eyes range from section to section, looking at different people whenever your gaze turns to a particular section. Without choosing the same individual each time, do allow yourself to pick out individuals in the crowd. Look them in the eye momentarily and then move on. Once you get the feel of this, it will come naturally to you.

Physical Appearance

We constantly communicate to one another by the way we clothe and groom our bodies. We can present ourselves formally or informally, neatly or sloppily, modestly or provocatively, expensively or cheaply, in good taste or poor taste, or in any combination thereof. And as we do so, people who see us make inferences about our personality and abilities.

We may object that people ought not make such superficial judgments, but it will be futile to do so. People always decide about others on the basis of what they see ("Man looketh on the outward appearance . . . ," 1 Sam. 16:7). In fact, their decisions are often more accurate than we might guess. Research has shown that if we place an ordinary stranger before a group and then ask the people in the group to draw conclusions about the stranger on the basis of appearance alone, the conclusions of the group members tend to agree and, what's more, they tend to be accurate. Over the years of making such judgments and then testing them when we get to know a person better, we become rather adept at guessing about people on the basis of their appearance. Our judgments are by no means infallible (see the rest of 1 Sam. 16:7), but they may be more often right than wrong.

The implications of this are obvious for public speakers. How will you appear to your audience? What inferences will they draw from your appearance? Is what you are saying to them by the way you appear what you want to say, given *this* speech, on *this* occasion? Will the message you send through your appearance serve your speech or get in its way? Build your credibility as a speaker or hamper it? Antagonize your audience or reassure them?

There are few rules about how you ought to present yourself on specific speaking occasions, or at least few that you should follow. Beyond the obvious things like dressing formally for formal occasions (and the opposite), you will have to analyze each speaking situation individually. But remember: You will inevitably communicate something about yourself by the way you appear. The only real issue is, What will you communicate, and is it what you *want* to communicate?

Facial Expression

The face is perhaps the most expressive part of our bodies. Some researchers estimate that the face is capable of over a quarter million different expressions and that over half of the nonverbal messages we send to others come from the face. Moreover, certain facial expressions are common to all people (happiness, sadness, fear, etc.), while many others are taught by one's culture.

The closer you are to your audience, the more important your facial expression will be. At a distance the listeners can see only the major features of your expression (a frown, a smile, a grimace), but from up close they can tell whether your smile is real or false, whether the frown is from anger or concentration, whether the grimace is from pain or stage fright.

Since nonverbal cues are the primary way you will express attitudes and feelings about your subject and your audience, and since such a large proportion of your nonverbal messages emanates from your face, you should give serious consideration to what you are communicating through facial expressions. As a general rule, try to maintain a relaxed, pleasant expression. Sometimes you will be lighthearted and humorous; at other times you will be quite serious, depending on what you are saying at the moment. But through all of the kaleidoscopic changes of facial expression, try to allow your facial muscles to remain relaxed, unstrained, and pleasant to look at. Tight jaws, narrowed eyes, flared nostrils, furrowed brow—all of these typically represent forms of hostility, anger, strain, and frustration, none of which should characterize the speaker (except on certain limited occasions).

Paralanguage

The term *paralanguage* refers to all those things we communicate with our voice apart from the words themselves. For instance, a man may say to a woman, with an admiring tone, "You look *great!*" Or, with sarcasm fairly dripping from his words he might say, "*You* look great." Note that the two messages are diametrically opposed, the one approving and the other disapproving. Yet the words remained constant! Only the paralanguage changed, but this change was enough to reverse the entire message of the sentence.

Using Your Voice Correctly

There are three concerns you must face with regard to the use of your voice in speaking. The first, and most basic, is that you *speak correctly*—that is, that you use your vocal mechanism in a healthy and maximally effective way.

The production of the human voice, though seemingly such a simple thing, is actually a rather complex process involving three major areas of the body: chest, throat, and head. In the chest the lungs function like bellows, drawing air in and forcing it out as the abdominal muscles and the diaphragm expand and contract the rib cage in which the lungs are set. When we exhale, air from the lungs is forced up through the *trachea,* the tube in the upper chest and neck connecting the lungs to the oral and nasal cavities. At the upper end of the trachea is a voice box called the *larynx.* The larynx contains vocal cords stretched across the opening. When we want to make a sound, we allow the air to vibrate the vocal cords. To make a higher sound, we stretch the cords tight; to make a lower sound, we loosen the cords; to whisper, we loosen them still more. This process of sound making is called *phonation.*

Figure 13
The Vocal Mechanism

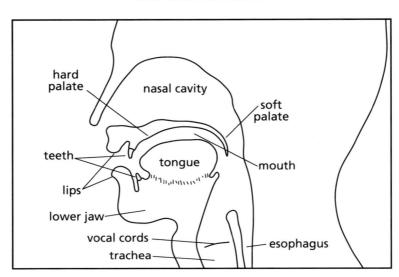

Once the sound is produced by the vocal cords in the throat, it travels up into the head where it *resonates* in the oral and nasal cavities, transforming it into recognizable sound. In addition to being resonated, the sound is also given shape by the tongue, soft palate, teeth, lips, and lower jaw. This is the process of *articulation*. In this way the mere noise of the vocal cords is fashioned into the syllables and words we use to communicate to one another.

Problems in speaking can occur at any point in this process. For example, some people do not produce enough air, and therefore their voices lack force. Others use mainly their chest muscles for breathing rather than their diaphragm; this tends to tighten the throat and restrict the vocal cords. Sometimes the vocal cords (or the nerves which control them) become diseased or damaged resulting in a loss of voice. Some people allow too much air to pass through the vocal cords, which produces excess breathiness. Others produce poorly resonated sounds, which result in a voice that is too nasal. But probably the most common problems stem from poor articulation. All people slur or mumble their words sometimes, but for many people this is a chronic and serious speech problem.

If you suspect that you are not speaking properly, examine some of the suggested reading at the end of this chapter. Better yet, seek out an instructor who can diagnose your problem and give you exercises to correct it. Such problems are often fairly simple to remedy, but can be troublesome if left untreated.

Using Your Voice Fully

A second concern about your voice is that you *use it to the fullest extent.* The human vocal mechanism is a marvelously flexible instrument and is capable of a spectacularly large array of sounds. To be an effective speaker, you need to use as much of this vocal range as possible. Why? Because a variety of intonation and inflection gives color, texture, and meaning to your words.

Unfortunately, many speakers unnecessarily bore their listeners by using such a narrow band of their vocal range that they come across in what is commonly called a monotone. There is little variety in their intonation or inflection. They use only a small proportion of what is potentially available to them in their voices. This is unfortunate mainly because a monotone is extremely difficult for an audience to listen to for any length of time. People need vocal variety to renew their attention and interest regularly, variety that a monotone fails to supply.

Effective speakers are usually characterized by the use of a wide range of vocal inflection. They make maximum use of their vocal facilities, refusing to settle for a droning monotone which puts people to sleep. The fullest natural use of your vocal apparatus should be your goal when you stand up to speak.

Using Your Voice Attractively

A third concern about your voice is that it be attractive to your audience. They should ideally find it interesting and pleasant to listen to. Whether or not they do will depend largely upon five important factors: articulation, rate, loudness, pitch, and quality.

ARTICULATION. It is important that you speak distinctly enough for your audience to understand your words. If you mumble or slur the words, your audience will have to struggle to understand you. Very quickly they will tire of the effort, become frustrated, and cease trying.

Practice pronouncing each syllable of each word. In ordinary conversation, "regular" all too easily becomes "reg-lar," "practically" becomes "prac-tic-ly." Such slurring of entire syllables is usually the product of a "lazy mouth," that is, an unwillingness to make the muscles of the mouth work hard enough to pronounce the words properly. To be a good speaker, you will want to overcome any tendencies toward a lazy mouth by speaking deliberately enough to be understood clearly.

It is possible, of course, to speak so deliberately that your speech seems stilted and unnatural. Moreover, some slight slurring of syllables is natural and not necessarily detrimental. But you will find that a style of distinct articulation is generally attractive to the ear and will enhance your credibility with the audience. Mumbled words or lazy articulation will do just the opposite.

RATE. The rate at which you speak will, of course, tend to affect your articulation. The faster you speak, the more difficult it is to articulate clearly, and the opposite is also true. Thus an appropriate rate of speech will be one that allows you to speak clearly, on the one hand, without drawing out the words unnecessarily, on the other. This will usually fall into the range of 120 to 160 words per minute.

Of course your rate of speaking ought not remain uniform throughout the speech. You will need a variety in your rate so as not to sound boring and monotonous. Often a speech will start out fairly slowly, allowing the rate to increase as it builds toward a climax. Then, too, within the speech itself there may be points of forcefulness and emotion which will call for a quicker pace, juxtaposed with other points where the rate will be more relaxed. Such changes in your rate of speaking add

Determination Pays Off

Demosthenes's first success as a speaker came when he made a claim against his guardian, who had defrauded him. The fortunate outcome prompted him to embark on the career of an orator. When he first took part in the public debates, his speech was so tortuous and feebly delivered that the audience could not understand him and laughed him out of the assembly. The actor Satyrus caught up with him as he was going disconsolately homeward and then and there gave him a lesson in how to deliver a speech. Demosthenes thereupon made himself an underground study where he stayed for weeks at a time, practicing his oratory. To protect himself against the temptation of going out into society, he shaved one side of his head so that he would be too embarrassed to show himself in public. He cured his stammer by speaking with pebbles in his mouth and his shortness of breath by declaiming poetry while running uphill. Thus he eventually acquired the skill to hold an Athenian audience spellbound.

Clifton Fadiman

variety and interest for your audience and are sorely missed if you maintain a uniform rate throughout.

Another aspect of rate is the use of pauses. Pauses provide much of the punctuation for oral discourse. As you speak, your audience has no periods, commas, semicolons, or dashes before them. They depend largely on your pauses to tell them what is to be distinguished from what. Thus pauses are not to be avoided or filled with "ers," "ums," or "ahs." They should be used to punctuate your speech; to separate clauses, phrases, and sentences from one another; to indicate stress or emphasis; to provide the natural rhythm so necessary to effective speech.

Loudness. Loudness refers to the force with which the sound produced by your voice vibrates the eardrum of your listener. Such force is in turn the result of three factors: (1) how much energy you have put into producing the sound; (2) the distance from you to the listener; (3) the acoustics of the situation in which you are speaking, including the presence or absence of any competing sounds.

Obviously, to be an effective speaker you must speak loud enough to be heard by your audience. But it is also true that you must avoid speaking so loudly that people become uncomfortable or distracted by the loudness. This is especially the case if you are using a microphone. It is a good practice to examine the speaking situation beforehand to determine how loud you will have to speak to be heard by all. Remember this, however: Once your audience is in place, their bodies will actually soak up some of the sound. Thus you will need to speak louder in a full auditorium than in an empty one.

As in most other aspects of public speaking, variety is important here. Both loudness and softness are useful ways of indicating emphasis. Thus there will be points in your speech when you may want to speak more forcefully, and other times when you may want to lower your voice. A wide range of variation in loudness (short of becoming false and overly dramatic) will add measurably to the interest of the audience.

PITCH. The difference between a tenor and a bass voice, or a soprano and an alto voice, is largely a matter of pitch. Some voices are pitched higher, others are pitched lower, but everyone has a natural pitch somewhere on the musical scale. Actually, most voices are capable of ranging about two octaves on the scale, but we use this range only when singing. In ordinary conversation most people seldom use more than a single octave.

Speakers with unusually high voices (whether male or female) face a hardship in public speaking. Shrill, highly pitched voices are generally less attractive to the human ear than lower-pitched voices. Speakers with high voices, however, can be taught to lower their pitch somewhat to make it easier on their listeners. If you feel you have this problem, consult a teacher or some of the books at the end of this chapter.

The primary goal should be to find your natural range and then use it fully. This variety in the pitch of your voice is the *vocal inflection* we have already discussed. Too much vocal inflection produces a false, overly dramatic impression, but the failure to use enough inflection is surely the more common error. It produces a dry, boring, monotonous style of speaking. Since

The 14 Worst Human Fears

"What are you the most afraid of?" a team of market researchers asked 3,000 U.S. inhabitants. Many named more than one fear. The results may surprise you.

	Biggest Fear	% Naming
1.	Speaking before a group	41
2.	Heights	32
3.	Insects and bugs	22
3.	Financial problems	22
3.	Deep water	22
6.	Sickness	19
7.	Death	19
8.	Flying	18
9.	Loneliness	14
10.	Dogs	11
11.	Driving/riding in a car	9
12.	Darkness	8
13.	Elevators	8
14.	Escalators	5

The Sunday Times (London)

varied inflection is probably the single most important contributor to an interesting and attractive vocal style, you should try to use as much of your natural vocal range as you can.

QUALITY. Vocal quality relates primarily to the timbre of your voice. Is it thin or resonant, breathy or full, nasal or clear, harsh or mellow? Such words are inevitably vague, but that is because vocal quality is very complex and difficult to define.

The most common problems with vocal quality are excess nasality, breathiness, and huskiness. Each is caused by different faults in the use of the vocal mechanism, and each must be treated differently. For help in remedying such faults, consult a teacher or some of the publications listed at the end of this chapter.

Stage Fright

"Have you ever been driving at night and come upon a deer frozen in the beam of your headlights? Here's my theory. The deer thinks the lights are spotlights, and what has it paralyzed is stage fright. It imagines the worst: it has to give a speech."[1]

Thus does CBS commentator Charles Osgood put into words what many people feel: stark terror at the thought of having to get up in front of an audience to speak. If it is any consolation, almost everyone experiences stage fright at this prospect, experienced speakers as well as neophytes. It is only when the apprehension becomes incapacitating, however, that it poses a problem. Within limits your stage fright is actually a positive (though uncomfortable) thing. It is your body's way of preparing you to speak. The adrenaline begins to flow; the heart rate steps up; your breathing quickens a bit. All of these are positive symptoms.

Unfortunately, you may also experience some negative symptoms. Your knees may become wobbly, your mouth dry, your throat tight, and your head empty. These symptoms are undesirable, and you need to learn how to combat them.

The best way to stave off the negative aspects of stage fright is to be fully prepared. Speech anxiety usually grows out of a fear of failure, or at least an uncertainty of success. If you were completely sure of yourself, you probably would not become nervous. It is only because you are unsure of yourself that you become filled with fear. Thus the best way to fight off debilitating stage fright is to be sure of yourself and of your speech.

If you think such advice sounds easy to say but difficult to put into practice, you may be right. But it is also not as difficult as it may seem. It simply requires some diligent work on your part. First, you must work hard to develop a good speech, one which will be interesting, relevant, and informative, and one that you can look forward to delivering. And, second, you must so control the material of the speech that you are confident you will not forget it. Both of these steps require much hard work and practice, but they are major contributors to keeping your stage fright within manageable boundaries. Then, when you have given your best effort, you must rely confidently upon the Lord

---

Public speaking is no more difficult than using chopsticks or tying a bow tie. The mysterious becomes simple once you know how to do it. **Charles Osgood**

---

for the rest. It is amazing how hard work and a solid faith can dispel anxiety!

Exercises

1. Observe three people whom you know well when they are engaged in conversation. Analyze each one for facial expression, gestures, and posture. Itemize the similarities and differences you find. Try to correlate what you have observed with each person's personality.
2. Listen to two speakers addressing live audiences. Examine each speaker's voice: Is it being used correctly, fully, and attractively? Analyze the strengths and weaknesses of the speaker's vocal style, giving special attention to (a) articulation, (b) rate, (c) loudness, (d) pitch, and (e) quality. Then compare and contrast the two speakers.
3. Do a study of three church auditoriums which have stationary pulpits. Compare and contrast the pulpits. Note all similarities and differences, including height and elevation. Then try to interview one person who uses each pulpit and one person who listens to others using the pulpit. Ask each interviewee what he or she likes and does not like about the pulpit. Then rank the pulpits

from best (1) to worst (3). Finally, list the qualities of a good podium or pulpit.

4. In the high-school public-speaking course you teach, you must give a ten-minute lecture on one of these subjects: handling stage fright, how the voice works, or the importance of good eye contact in public speaking. Using the material of this chapter and any other sources you can find, design a complete outline for that lecture.

For Further Reading

Anderson, Virgil A. *Training the Speaking Voice*. 3d ed. New York: Oxford University Press, 1977.

DeVito, Joseph A., Jill Giattino, and T. D. Schon. *Articulation and Voice: Effective Communication*. Indianapolis: Bobbs-Merrill, 1975.

Hahner, Jeffrey C., et al. *Speaking Clearly: Improving Voice and Diction*. 3d ed. New York: McGraw-Hill, 1989.

Kenley, Joan. *Voice Power*. New York: Henry Holt, 1989.

Mayer, Lyle V. *Fundamentals of Voice and Diction*. 9th ed. Dubuque, Iowa: William C. Brown, 1991.

McCallion, Michael. *The Voice Book: For Actors, Public Speakers, and Everyone Who Wants to Make Best Use of Their Voice*. New York: Theatre Arts, 1988.

Rizzo, Raymond. *The Voice as an Instrument*. 2d ed. Indianapolis: Bobbs-Merrill, 1978.

Van Riper, Charles, and Lon L. Emerick. *Speech Correction*. 8th ed. Englewood Cliffs, N.J.: Prentice-Hall, 1990.

Chapter 10

How to Prepare
a Bible Message

Most Christians—not just preachers—have the opportunity from time to time to speak before a group on a subject related to their faith. Some are asked to do so regularly. Only a relative few accept the challenge, of course, but many more could if they only had confidence in their ability to do a credible job. The purpose of this chapter is to provide some direction as to how to approach such speaking situations.

Purpose of the Message

There are really only two purposes for a religious talk: evangelism and edification.

Evangelism

If the audience is a group of non-Christians, in the end the most important religious subject to discuss with them is their eternal destiny. In some way they need to be confronted with the claims of Jesus Christ. To be sure, there are times when you will want to refrain from giving the entire gospel in favor of what Francis Schaeffer called "pre-evangelism."[1] On these occasions your goal is simply to plant or water seed (1 Cor. 3:6–8) which may later spring into full-fledged faith and which may be harvested by another. This is perfectly legitimate. Even the apostle Paul used this approach sometimes (see Acts 17). But even though you settle for limited objectives, your ultimate purpose remains an evangelistic one.

It is tempting sometimes to talk to non-Christians about the Christian faith in such a way that the gospel is entirely left out of the picture. Few are offended and many are soothed by a vague discussion of God and his love for us. By contrast, the gospel of "Christ and him crucified" (1 Cor. 2:2) offends; it confronts; it demands a verdict. But it is also "the power of God unto salvation" (Rom. 1:16 KJV), and as such, it is precisely what your audience needs most. Never allow yourself the luxury of bypassing the offense of the gospel in favor of a batch of sentimental words about God. Such a comfortable evasion is offensive to the Savior who gave himself as a ransom for all (1 Tim. 2:6). It also shortchanges the people in your audience who desperately need Christ.

Edification

The second broad purpose for a religious speech is edification. This is appropriate when you are speaking to Christians, whose greatest spiritual need is to grow closer to and more like their Savior, Jesus Christ. In such cases your task is to help them somehow see him more clearly and follow him more closely.

Sometimes, of course, your audience will be mixed. You will face both Christians and non-Christians together. What then? You really have only these options: either (1) you can attempt to speak to one group or the other, or (2) you can try to bridge the gap and speak to both at once.

The first option is the easier, but it requires you to ignore partially the spiritual needs of a segment of your audience. This is unsatisfying but sometimes necessary. On these occasions you will usually want to address the spiritual needs of the non-Christians in the group since theirs are the more critical of the two. Most of the Christians present will be understanding toward this tactic and will probably applaud your choice. Moreover, even Christians can profit from a retelling of the good news of Jesus Christ, "the old, old story."

On other occasions you may want to address the needs of both groups together. This is not easy but it can be done. Generally it requires you to make two separate applications, one for non-Christians and the other for Christians. In most cases you need not hesitate to distinguish quite explicitly between the two groups ("You may be here today and not know Jesus Christ as

your Savior. If so, I would like to say to you. . . . Others of you have no doubt been Christians longer than I have. For us, . . .").
But be careful not to put people on the spot. Discomfort produced by the conviction of the Holy Spirit is a positive thing; discomfort produced by a thoughtless speaker is not.

Types of Religious Speeches

We could no doubt list a wide variety of typical religious speeches one might hear or give. However, there are probably only a couple that are worth your audience's time. They are (1) your personal testimony and (2) an exposition of a passage of Scripture.

Personal Testimony

Every Christian has a personal testimony, including you. It is the account of what God has done in your life. Such stories are not only interesting; they are also worthwhile. They focus the audience's attention on the activity of God as seen in the life of one individual. As we have already observed, people are interested in other people; and when a personal testimony of even a very ordinary individual is done well, the result is a fascinating and profitable speech.

When we prepare a personal testimony, we must be sure that it is *Christ*-centered. It should be designed to praise and honor him above all. It is not difficult for testimonies to become *self*-centered, focusing mainly upon ourselves, our feelings, our responses. Though most testimonies will contain some of this, the main object of the speech ought to be to lift up Christ, to show his grace, his mercy, and his love as demonstrated in our life. Keeping this goal firmly in mind will prevent our speech from becoming unduly "I-centered."

Be sure also that you do not abandon the principles discussed in this book when preparing a personal testimony. Since the content of your testimony is so personal and familiar, you may be inclined just to "wing it," bypassing a more rigorous preparation. But this would be a serious mistake. Even a personal testimony needs the unity, order, and progress that a central idea contributes; it also needs to be well organized, to have interesting supporting material and vivid wording, and to be well delivered. In other words, all of the ideas of this book apply as much to personal testimonies as to any other type of speech. In fact, a rigorous preparation is the best way to prevent yourself from producing one of those rambling, disjointed, self-centered personal testimonies that seem so common.

Bible Exposition

An exposition of a passage of Scripture is probably the best kind of religious speech one can give. While many other kinds of religious talks can be a waste of time (that is, pious words which have little importance or impact), a truly scriptural message never is. What is more, the Bible addresses an extremely wide variety of theological, moral, and practical subjects, all of which are relevant to life and can be shown to be interesting and informative.

Most important of all, however, Scripture is *authoritative*. A religious talk merely conveys the speaker's idea on some topic. But biblical exposition is unique in that it lays out God's views.

Using the Bible

A man speaks with more or less wisdom as he is the more or less versed in the Holy Scriptures—I do not mean in the very copious reading and memorizing of them, but in the true understanding and the careful investigation of their meaning. For there are some who read them, but indifferently; they read them in order to memorize them, but they are indifferent to understanding them. There can be no question but that they by far deserve the preference who know them less, word for word, but who look into the heart of the Scriptures, with the eyes of their own hearts. But he is better than either of these, who both quotes them at will, and understands them as he ought.

Saint Augustine
On Christian Doctrine

Of course, an ugly dogmatism is inappropriate even (especially?) for an expositor; yet when the ideas of your speech are based solidly upon Scripture, you can and should take an unapologetic, "thus saith the Lord" stance. Such speeches may be the most important ones you will ever deliver.

Perhaps at this point you are thinking that only preachers should attempt to deliver such messages. Not so. The Bible is accessible to all of God's people. Every Christian is capable of understanding it and applying it to his or her own life. What's more, with a bit of thought and direction, and a lot of hard work, most Christians are also capable of helping others understand Scripture, too. Seminaries train preachers professionally to do just this, but that in no way rules out others from the field. There is nothing in the Bible which bars nonprofessionals from handling the Word of God. In fact, there are many audiences that will not listen to a professional, but will give a layperson a full hearing. You need not hold back from preparing and delivering a Bible message as long as you are willing to put forth the necessary effort to do the job well. The remainder of this chapter will explain a step-by-step procedure for preparing an expository message.

Before we can proceed, however, we must define exposition and underline how it differs from the other kinds of speeches we have discussed previously in this book. Bible exposition is *the communication of a biblical truth (which is derived from and transmitted through a study of a passage of Scripture) in such a way that the audience is able to see its relevance for their lives.* Note three important things about this definition:

First, the main ideas of an expository message come from the Bible. They are not derived from our own experience or generated independently. They are derived from a study of the passage we have chosen as our text. This represents a major departure from other kinds of speeches we have been discussing.

Saint Augustine was the first to make this distinction. He had been a teacher of rhetoric before he became a Christian. After he was converted, he began to think through the application of his rhetorical training to the proclamation of Christian truth. He was particularly interested in the part of the process called invention *(inventio)*, which deals with the gathering of the materials for the speech. It seemed to Augustine that a major change was called for. Thomas Benson and Michael Prosser describe Augustine's concern:

> With the beginning of the Christian era, the classical doctrine of *inventio* needed rethinking. Now the homiletician had to decide what he was responsible for and what God would supply, whether as a preacher and teacher he was an interpreter or a creator of ideas. Augustine's reformulation of classical doctrine to meet the needs of a preacher who had at hand, if he could only read it correctly, the certainty of the Word of God, in distinction to the probabilities available to earlier Greek and Roman rhetors, marks a major change in the relation of the speaker or writer to his materials.[2]

Bible exposition, then, is distinguished by the fact that the speech's ideas stem mainly from a study of the certainties of the biblical text, in contrast to the probabilities which we might discover elsewhere. Any so-called biblical message in which this is not the case is not an *expository* message.

Second, note that the ideas of the speech are not only *derived from* a study of the text; they are also *conveyed to* the audience through a study of the text.

This is one of the great strengths of an expository message. It plugs the audience into the Word of God. They do not have to take the speaker's word for it; they are helped to interact directly with the truth of the Bible itself. The speaker merely singles out a text and then shows the audience what it teaches. In this way, by the time the speech is finished, the audience has had a direct experience with Scripture.

Third, note that application is always a part of good exposition. An expository message should never be merely a historical or grammatical lecture. We must always ask the question, Why does God want me (and my audience) to know this?

The apostle Paul explained how the Scriptures are to be used: "All Scripture is inspired by God and profitable for teaching, for reproof, for correction, for training in righteousness; that the man of God may be adequate, equipped for every good work" (2 Tim.

3:16–17 NASB). What is clear here is that the ultimate goal of Bible study or exposition is to equip people to live for God. No expositor can afford, therefore, merely *to inform* an audience. The purpose of Scripture is not merely to satisfy our curiosity or to provide us with a glimpse of something that happened long ago. It is designed to transform lives *today*, and the expositor acknowledges this by always helping the audience to come to grips with the relevance of the passage for them.

Seven Stages of Preparation

With these features of Bible exposition in mind, we want to outline seven phases or stages in the development of a speech which explains a passage of Scripture. It is important to remember that these stages may not occur in chronological order, however. They may occur out of order or even simultaneously. The important thing to note is that they represent the steps a speaker must travel, one way or another, in the development of an expository message on the Bible.[3]

Select a Passage of Scripture

Choosing a passage is one of the most critical steps in the entire process of preparing an expository message. It will color everything else you do, from beginning to end.

Suppose you are assigned a topic for the speech. Your task will be to find the central passage in the Bible on that topic. In some cases you will have to use several texts for the speech (this is called *topical exposition*), each of which addresses your topic, but none of which is sufficiently exhaustive. If you are to do exposition, you must stick with these texts in such a way that the speech's ideas are derived from and conveyed through a study of these passages. The more passages you must cover, the more difficult your task will be; so try to limit your message as much as possible. Ideally you should have to treat only one central passage while perhaps citing others as support.

Where can you find central passages on a given topic? The best place to look is a good topical index to the Bible.[4] You might also try looking up key words in a concordance.[5] Or seek out the topic in a good systematic theology text, Bible encyclopedia, or Bible dictionary.[6] Each of these will probably direct you to pertinent passages of Scripture.

Usually, however, you will not be assigned a topic. You will be free to choose your own passage and therefore your own subject matter. How do you go about discovering a passage under such circumstances? Unfortunately, there are no easy answers to this question.

Sometimes you will already have a passage in mind. You have been intrigued and blessed by it in the past and would like to share it now with others. It is just the right passage for this occasion. In such cases you need look no further.

More often, though, you will come up blank and have no ideas at all. What to do? You have no alternative but to begin a search.

Determine first whether you want to speak from the Old Testament or the New Testament. After you have narrowed your speech this far, zero in on some particular book or books of the Bible. Read them through or at least skim them. Ultimately the Lord will direct you to an appropriate passage for your needs and those of your audience.

When you have settled upon your passage, it is crucial that you be certain that the passage represents a unit of discourse. The reason for this will emerge as we proceed through the following steps. For now, remember that by definition a "unit of discourse" has a central idea. It is this central idea which makes it a unit and sets it off from other units around it. Whether your passage is a story, a parable, a psalm, or a paragraph from an epistle, be sure it is in fact a unit.

In this regard, do not overly trust the chapter and verse divisions of the Bible. They were put there, not by the Lord, but by men, and they are in some cases quite misleading. They will often correspond to divisions between units, but there are also many exceptions. The paragraph divisions in a good translation are also useful, but not infallible. Check a series of good translations if you have serious questions. Usually this will lead you to a workable division of the text into units.

Study the Passage and State the Author's Central Idea

Now that you have selected a passage, your next task is to study it thoroughly to determine its central thought.

How to study the Bible is a complex subject in itself. We cannot provide a thorough discussion here. Instead we will have to assume a knowledge of Bible-study methods on the part of the reader. If you do not yet feel capable of studying the Bible on your own, consult some of the helps listed at the end of this chapter. There is no reason why any reasonably intelligent Christian cannot be a competent student of the Bible if he or she is so motivated.

Begin your study broadly. Try to determine the purpose and the broad outline of the book of the Bible in which you are studying. Then begin to narrow your focus to that portion of the book in which your passage is located. Try to determine how your passage fits into the flow of the book as a whole.

Next, examine your passage in detail. Why was it included? What are its several parts? What are the relationships among the parts? What is the author talking about in this passage? (In other words, what is his *subject?*) What is the author saying about his subject? (In other words, what is his *complement?*) What is the author's central idea (the combination of the subject and complement) in this passage?

Once you have stated the author's central idea (called the *exegetical* idea), test it to be certain it is inclusive enough to cover the several parts of your passage. Always adjust the idea to fit the passage, never the reverse. If the idea is too broad, narrow it so that it exactly fits the passage. If there are parts of the passage the idea does not cover, broaden the idea.

Next, outline how the author develops his idea through the passage. This outline is called the *exegetical* outline. (Note: The exegetical outline is *not* an outline of your message to your audience; rather, it is purely an outline of what the biblical author has said to his audience. Your audience is not yet in the picture.)

When you construct an exegetical outline, be sure to use full sentences for *each point*. This is an important rule because it forces you to think yourself through to a complete understanding of the author's thought.

Determine Your Audience's Need for This Idea

Now you can begin to think about your audience. According to 2 Timothy 3:16, all Scripture is profitable. Thus, there are no passages of Scripture which are without value (although some will obviously be more pertinent to a given audience than will others). You may be assured that if you have understood the passage accurately, it will speak *somehow* to the needs of your audience.

It is crucial that you pinpoint this area of need. Your task as an expositor is to help people incorporate the Word of God into their lives. In order to do that you must first understand where this truth touches their lives and what they will need to hear in order to see its relevance.

You will recall that your audience's needs will fall roughly into three broad categories: (a) the need for *explanation,* (b) the need for *proof,* and (c) the need to see *implications.* Let us think about each of these in turn.

Explanation

Suppose the biblical writer explains something in detail that your audience understands fully. In such cases you will not need to belabor the point. More likely, however, the biblical writer will touch upon something which his audience understood fully, but which is foreign to yours. In these instances you will have to pause to explain the meaning of the terms or concepts to your audience. They will have a need for *explanation.* Since the Bible was originally written by and for a people who were very different from most audiences you will address, the need for explanation will be a common one.

Proof

On the other hand, the biblical author may attempt to prove a point which his original audience found difficult, but which your audience readily accepts (for example, the humanity of Christ). If so, proof is not one of your audience's needs. But, again, it will also sometimes happen that the biblical writer merely mentions something his readers accepted unquestioningly, but which your listeners will find difficult to embrace. In such cases you may want to depend upon your audience's willingness to believe the Bible, or you may want to provide some additional supporting material which reinforces the author's point and thereby helps the listener see its truthfulness.

Why use a battering ram on an open door?

Implication

What difference should this truth make in the lives of your listeners? Why does God want them to know this? These are the questions you need to answer for your audience.

None of the Bible was written directly to your audience; each of its many parts was written to some other group of people, a long time ago. Yet it is also true that all of the Bible is relevant *somehow* to the contemporary individuals who make up your audience. The only question is *how* the truth of your passage applies to them.

As we have said, these concerns about application are the bottom line for the expositor. You cannot ignore application without ignoring the fundamental purpose of Scripture: changing lives. You may have to explain or prove a great deal in your message, but both should be viewed, not as ends in themselves, but as *means* to the end of applying the truth to life. This is the pattern we see repeatedly in the epistles of Paul: explanation and proof, followed by application (see, for example, Eph. 1–3 and then 4–6). To be sure, there are times when the application will be so obvious and powerful that it need not be explicitly stated. But this does not alter the fact that sound application is the ultimate goal of exposition.

Sound application is not always easy to accomplish. You will need to compare the original situation with your audience's situation to discover commonalities and differences. You will need to think hard about concrete situations in life today where these ideas will be helpful. You will have to think carefully about specific situations in which your listeners' thoughts and actions should be affected by hearing this truth. In all of this you will have to follow sound principles of hermeneutics (consult some of the sources at the end of this chapter if you do not understand the meaning of "hermeneutics"). If you can accomplish these things, first for yourself and then for your audience, you will discover that the Word of God is able to transform lives, both your own and those of the people to whom you speak.

State Your Speech Idea

You have your exegetical idea. It is a statement of the author's point to his audience. What is more, you have also given thought to the *relevance* of that idea for your own audience. In the light of this, you must now state the idea that you will attempt to communicate to your audience. This will be your *speech idea.*

The speech idea in an expository message always involves two ingredients: (a) the exegetical idea combined with (b) the needs of your audience. It is as if these two factors represented two lines plotted on a chart. The point at which the lines intersect represents your speech idea.

Many times the *exegetical idea* and the *speech idea* will be virtually identical. This occurs when the relevant characteristics of both the original audience and your audience are identical. For example, suppose your passage is Proverbs 21:23: "He who keeps his mouth and his tongue keeps himself out of trouble" (RSV). In this case the exegetical idea and the speech idea are basically the same. The fact that this bit of wisdom was originally addressed to ancient Hebrews, but you are addressing a twentieth-century American audience, has little effect on the statement. The same would be true of a passage such as John 3:16 or Ephesians 2:8–9. These passages state ideas which are universally true, so the statements will change little in translation from the first century to the twentieth. Many of the passages in the epistles of the New Testament will follow this pattern.

It would be a mistake, however, to assume that *all passages* apply so directly to your audience. Consider, for instance, a passage such as 1 Corinthians 8, where Paul discusses how his readers should deal with meat which has been offered to idols, so as not to hurt a fellow Christian. In this passage the exegetical idea is obviously stated in terms of the particular cultural problem Paul is addressing: meat offered to idols. As such the idea does not speak directly to the needs of a group of contemporary American listeners, who could not find meat which had been offered to an idol if they tried.

Yet, behind the exegetical idea about meat offered to idols is a broader *principle* about how to deal with questionable matters, a problem which contemporary Christians must face regularly. Thus, you would want to state your *speech idea*, not in terms of meat offered to an idol, but in terms of questionable matters generally. In the exposition of this idea you would first examine the application of the principle as it is presented in your passage, showing how the principle applied to Christians who faced the issue of meat offered to idols; then you would move to a contemporary application of the principle as your audience might confront it today.

What we need to see here is that the *exegetical idea* and the *speech idea* in a passage such as this are different (but closely related) ideas. The exegetical idea deals *strictly* with the author's point to his audience (in this case, meat offered to idols). But the speech idea must take into consideration the needs of the contemporary audience as well as the truth of the text, and seek out the point of intersection between the two. This would probably lead us in our example to state the speech idea in terms of the broader category of "questionable matters."

In this way the speech idea always grows out of the exegetical idea, but is often significantly different from it. The reason for this is rooted in the differences which exist between the original audience and your audience. The more divergent the audiences, the further the two ideas will diverge. The more alike the audiences, the more similar will be the two ideas.

Decide How to Develop the Body of Your Message

In the exposition of Scripture remember that it is important to teach the passage of Scripture, not just the idea you have derived from that passage. That is why your idea must not only be drawn from, but also *communicated through,* a study of the passage in its context. This priority, along with the needs of your audience, will shape the entire body of your message.

Here we may note a common difference between an expository message and an ordinary speech. In an expository message you may want to add a *fourth major division* to introduction, body, and conclusion. The fourth section might be labeled "background."

The reason for this addition is plain. In an expository message you are drawing upon a passage which is part of a larger whole. In order for your audience to comprehend the passage, they will commonly need to know something about the purpose and meaning of this larger whole. In the background section you provide them with this vital information. You may be able to incorporate this sort of material into the introduction or body of the message, of course, but a section entitled "background," inserted between the introduction and body of the speech, is a common way of meeting this need.

Whenever you can in your exposition, stay with the development of the idea as it is found in the passage. The closer you keep the speech's pattern of development to the pattern of development of the exegetical outline, without sacrificing the understanding of the audience, the better off you and your audience will be.

Often, however, you will not be able to stay exactly with the exegetical outline. You may have to explain or prove something that the biblical author did not. Or you may have to deal with areas of application which the text does not treat. Thus you may have to add ideas and supporting material to the speech outline which do not appear in your exegetical outline. Sometimes in your speech you will even need to arrange the ideas in an order different from that in which they appear in the text. This is not necessarily bad if it will help the audience understand the passage and its ideas more clearly. But do not choose this option unless you have to—if it is not done well, it can be very confusing to the audience.

In designing the outline of the speech, be sure to follow the directions on outline, transitions, and supporting materials discussed in earlier chapters of this book. The principles of sound speech development are as applicable to an expository message as to any other.

In particular, however, note that you should always try to state the main ideas of the outline in terms of *your audience* rather than in terms of *the text*. You will immediately need to turn to the text to support each major point, of course, but the point itself should be stated in terms of here-and-now principles for your audience.

For example, in a message on Daniel 3, the story of the fiery furnace, one of your main points might be based upon the observation that the three young men of God trusted God in the face of trial. But you would want to state the main point, not in terms of the three young men, but in terms of a here-and-now idea: "We ought to trust God in the face of trials." Then you would turn immediately to the experience of the three young men to demonstrate the point. Wording your main points this way will keep your treatment of the passage focused on the needs of the audience.

Expository speeches are as varied as the passages they represent and the audiences to whom they are directed. They can be organized along the lines of patterns as diverse as inductive, deductive, question-answer, problem-solution, symptoms-disease-remedy, cause-to-effect, theology-to-practice, or any one of a large number of others. Thus there is no way we can deal with all possibilities here. Nevertheless, we can suggest two standard patterns for handling at least the stories which are so prevalent in Scripture.

In dealing with narrative, or stories, in the Bible, the simplest approach is to tell the story, delineate the principle it teaches, and then apply the principle. Thus the basic outline of the message would be:

    I. Story

   II. Principle

  III. Application

Here is a sample outline of such a message, based upon Luke 10:38–42:

I. Story

    A. Mary and Martha each responded to the Lord in a different way.

        1. Mary focused all her attention on the Lord.

        2. Martha focused her attention on serving.

    B. Jesus reproved Martha's action and commended Mary's choice.

        1. He lovingly exposed Martha's problem.

        2. He gave approval to Mary's choice by using her as an example for Martha.

II. Principle: The key to discipleship is preoccupation with Jesus.

    A. Martha's ministry as hostess was important, commendable.

    B. But Martha allowed the good to crowd out the best.

    C. Mary may have neglected the good but focused on the best.

    D. Preoccupation with Christ is always the best for a disciple.

III. Application: As disciples, we must always keep Christ in focus in all that we do.

    A. As worshipers we must recognize that all the books and tapes and seminars are only means to an end.

    B. We must make sure that we have not substituted the good for the best.

A variation of this pattern occurs when you break the story into components, each of which is treated according to the same threefold pattern. In this case your outline takes the following shape:

I. Principle

    A. Story

    B. Principle

    C. Application

II. Principle

   A. Story

   B. Principle

   C. Application

III. Principle

   A. Story

   B. Principle

   C. Application

When you use this pattern, the principles should all work together to support one central idea. Here is a sample of this pattern based upon Daniel 1:

I. God disciplines his people for disobedience.

   A. Story: God delivered Jehoiakim, king of Judah, into Nebuchadnezzar's hand to discipline Judah for its disobedience.

   B. Principle: God will discipline his people for their disobedience.

      1. God disciplines in his own time.

      2. God will discipline whether we believe he will or not.

   C. Application: God will discipline us for our disobedience.

II. God honors his people for obedience.

   A. Story: God rewarded the four young men for remaining faithful to him.

      1. The school was a complete training program.

      2. Daniel, Hananiah, Mishael, and Azariah were selected for the school.

      3. The four young men chose not to defile themselves with the king's food.

      4. God rewarded them by granting them favor with the commander of the officials.

   B. Principle: God honors his people for obedience.

   C. Application: God will honor us for our obedience.

The central idea in this message is the multiple-complement idea: "God always disciplines his people for disobedience, but just as surely honors them for their obedience." The subject of this idea is "How God deals with his people." The complements are "(a) He disciplines their disobedience and (b) honors their obedience."

Develop Your Introduction and Conclusion

Now that you know what you want to say to your audience from this passage of Scripture, decide upon how you want to introduce and conclude the message. Remember that a good introduction is designed to capture attention, build rapport, point out a need, and orient the audience to the subject. A good conclusion is designed to tie the entire message together and drive the main idea home one last time. All of the instructions about introductions and conclusions in previous chapters directly apply here.

Write Out Your Manuscript

In exposition your goal is to communicate the ideas of the speech to your audience through a study of the passage itself. Your object is to so direct the attention of your listeners that by the time you are through they have understood the passage and seen its relevance to their lives. Thus, you need to guide their thinking back to and through the passage continuously throughout your speech. Writing out a good manuscript can help you do this.

It is quite startling to see how often writing a manuscript can reveal problems with the speech we might not have seen otherwise. As we attempt to write out the speech in advance, gaps in our understanding and holes in our thinking emerge. Blind spots slip into view. Weaknesses in our grasp of the passage, or soft spots in our presentation of it, make themselves known. Without the step of preparing a manuscript we perhaps would not discover these problems until too late.

Work hard to make the wording of the speech vivid and interesting. To bore people with the Bible is tragic. Use the principles of effective word choice discussed in chapter 8.

Exercises

1. Listen to three Bible messages. Analyze in each case to what extent the speaker (a) derived the message *from* and (b) communicated the message *through* an examination of the text. On a scale of 1 to 5, evaluate each message as to whether it was strongly expository (1) or not expository at all (5).
2. Choose at random three paragraphs from the epistles of the New Testament. Once you have checked to be sure each paragraph really is a true unit of thought, determine the author's subject and complement(s). Then list the main points of the exegetical outline.
3. Design a ten-minute version of your personal testimony for a non-Christian audience. Be sure it is Christ-centered and that it incorporates each of the features of an effective speech we have discussed in this book.
4. You have ten minutes to address a high-school Sunday-school class in your church on one of the following subjects: how to give your personal testimony, communicating the gospel to non-Christians, or keys to effective Bible study. Using the material in this book and any other resource you can find, construct the complete outline of that lecture.

For Further Reading

Allison, Joseph D. *The Bible Study Resource Guide.* Rev. ed. Nashville: Thomas Nelson, 1984.

Braga, James. *How to Study the Bible.* Portland: Multnomah, 1982.

Conyers, A. J. *How to Read the Bible.* Downers Grove, Ill.: Inter-Varsity, 1986.

Fee, Gordon D., and Douglas Stuart. *How to Read the Bible for All It's Worth.* Grand Rapids: Zondervan, 1982.

Mears, Henrietta C. *What the Bible Is All About.* Ventura, Calif.: Regal, 1983.

Traina, Robert A. *Methodical Bible Study.* Wilmore, Ky.: Robert A. Traina, 1952.

Ryken, Leland K. *How to Read the Bible as Literature.* Grand Rapids: Zondervan, 1984.

Wald, Oletta. *The Joy of Discovery in Bible Study.* Rev. ed. Minneapolis: Augsburg, 1975.

Warren, Richard, with William A. Shell. *12 Dynamic Bible Study Methods.* Wheaton: Victor, 1981.

Endnotes

Chapter 1: *An Introduction to Effective Public Speaking*

1. Quintilian *Institutio Oratoria* 12.1.1, trans. H. E. Butler, Loeb Classical Library (Cambridge: Harvard University Press, 1919), 4:355.

2. Roderick P. Hart, Gustav W. Friedrich, and William D. Brooks, *Public Communication* (New York: Harper and Row, 1975), 11.

3. Ibid., 12.

4. Karen Feld, "Lecturers: Their Talk Isn't Cheap," *Parade,* 30 September 1979, 23.

5. C. S. Lewis, "Christian Apologetics," in *God in the Dock,* ed. Walter Hooper (Grand Rapids: Eerdmans, 1970), 93.

Chapter 2: *How to Analyze Your Task*

1. Donald R. Sunukjian, "Patterns for Preaching: A Rhetorical Analysis," Dallas Theological Seminary, 1972, 184.

2. Ibid., 194.

3. George Eldon Ladd, *A Theology of the New Testament* (Grand Rapids: Eerdmans, 1975), 404.

4. Henry C. Thiessen, *Introductory Lectures in Systematic Theology* (Grand Rapids: Eerdmans, 1949), 268.

5. Frank E. Gaebelein, *The Pattern of God's Truth* (New York: Oxford University Press, 1954).

6. See Paul C. Vitz, *Psychology as Religion: The Cult of Self-Worship* (Grand Rapids: Eerdmans, 1982), for a discussion of the shortcomings of modern psychology (but especially the third-force psychologists) from a Christian point of view.

7. Abraham H. Maslow, "A Dynamic Theory of Human Motivation," *Psychological Review* 1 (1943): 370–96; idem, *Motivation and Personality* (New York: Harper and Row, 1954).

8. Maslow, "A Dynamic Theory," 372.

9. Maslow, *Motivation and Personality,* 91.

10. For a full treatment of this subject, see Chester A. Insko, *Theories of Attitude Change* (New York: Appleton-Century-Crofts, 1967); Shel Feldman, ed., *Cognitive Consistency: Motivational Antecedents and Behavioral Consequents*

(New York: Academic Press, 1966); Charles A. Kiesler, Barry C. Collins, and Norman Miller, *Attitude Change: A Critical Analysis of Theoretical Approaches* (New York: Wiley, 1969).

11. Leon Festinger, *A Theory of Cognitive Dissonance* (Stanford, Calif.: Stanford University Press, 1957); idem, *Conflict, Decision, and Dissonance* (Stanford, Calif.: Stanford University Press, 1964).

12. M. Farber, "English and Americans: A Study in National Character," *Journal of Psychology* 32 (1951): 241–49.

13. Wayne C. Minnick, *The Art of Persuasion*, 2d ed. (Boston: Houghton Mifflin, 1968), 218–20.

Chapter 3:   *How to Discover an Idea for Your Speech*

1. H. Grady Davis, *Design for Preaching* (Philadelphia: Fortress, 1958), 243–44.

2. Ibid., 70.

3. Ibid.

4. John F. Wilson and Carroll C. Arnold, *Public Speaking as a Liberal Art*, 3d ed. (Boston: Allyn and Bacon, 1974), 69–70.

5. Adapted from Wilson and Arnold, *Public Speaking*, 79. This list of topics is an elaboration of Roget's system for generating ideas. The ancient rhetoricians of Greece and Rome used a much more complex system of topics *(topoi)*, and found it immensely helpful!

6. Alfred Glossbrenner, *How to Look It Up Online: Get the Information Edge with Your Personal Computer* (New York: St. Martin's, 1987).

Chapter 4:   *How to Focus Your Idea*

1. Wayne C. Booth, "The Rhetorical Stance," *College Composition and Communication* 14 (October 1963): 139–45.

2. Ibid., 139.

3. Ibid., 141.

4. Ibid., 144.

5. Douglas Ehninger, Alan H. Monroe, and Bruce E. Gronbeck, *Principles and Types of Speech Communication*, 8th ed. (Glenview, Ill.: Scott, Foresman, 1978), 59.

Chapter 5:   How to Develop Your Idea into a Speech

1. Plato *Phaedrus* 264C.

2. H. Grady Davis, *Design for Preaching* (Philadelphia: Fortress, 1958), 12.

3. Ibid., 169.

4. This is a very technical subject, but for those who might wish to pursue Chomsky's ideas, see *Aspects of the Theory of Syntax* (Cambridge, Mass.: MIT Press, 1965). See also John Lyons, *Noam Chomsky* (London: Viking, 1970); and Eugene A. Nida, *Toward a Science of Translating: With Special Reference to Principles and Procedures Involved in Bible Translating* (Atlantic Highlands, N.J.: Humanities, 1978).

5. For an application of this approach to biblical messages, see Faris D. Whitesell and Lloyd M. Perry, *Variety in Your Preaching* (Westwood, N.J.: Revell, 1954), 83–91.

6. Adapted from Whitesell and Perry, *Variety*, 84–88.

7. See John Dewey, *How We Think* (Boston: Heath, 1933).

8. For a full discussion of the Motivated Sequence, see the text by Douglas Ehninger et al., *Principles and Types of Speech Communication*, 10th ed. (Glenview, Ill.: Scott, Foresman, 1986). This book is the descendent of Monroe's original text of the same name.

9. Adapted from Ehninger, *Principles and Types*.

10. Davis, *Design for Preaching*, 165.

11. Wayne C. Booth, "The Rhetorical Stance," *College Composition and Communication* 14 (October 1963).

Chapter 6: *How to Support the Ideas of Your Speech*

1. Ernest L. Boyer, "Communication: Message Senders and Receivers," *Vital Speeches of the Day*, 15 March 1978, 334–37.

2. William Wearly, "The Bureaucratic Babylon," *Vital Speeches of the Day*, 1 November 1977, 45.

3. Ernest L. Boyer, "A Universal Measurement Language," *Vital Speeches of the Day*, 15 January 1979, 203.

4. Newton N. Minow, "Television: How Far Has It Come in Thirty Years," *Vital Speeches of the Day*, 1 July 1991, 555.

5. Louis T. Hagopian, "Giving Impact to Ideas," *Vital Speeches of the Day*, 15 December 1977, 154.

6. Oliver Wendell Holmes, *Autocrat of the Breakfast Table* (New York: Hurst, n.d.), 7–8.

7. Robert Jastrow, *God and the Astronomers* (New York: Norton, 1978), 116.

8. John McKelvey, "An Overview of Where Solor Energy Stands," *Vital Speeches of the Day*, 1 January 1978, 167.

9. Donald P. Regier, "A Survey of the Old Testament Prophet's Use of Visual Communication Methods" (Master's thesis, Dallas Theological Seminary, 1969), 17.

10. Ibid., 10.

11. John Skinner, *The Book of Ezekiel* (New York: Hodder and Stoughton, n.d.), 61.

12. Gene A. Getz, "The Bible and the Eyegate," *Sunday School Leader,* April 1966, 19.

13. George L. Gropper, "Learning from Visuals: Some Behavioral Considerations," *Audiovisual Communication Review,* Spring 1966, 59.

14. Ibid., 60; see also Robert M. Gagne and George L. Gropper et al., *Studies in Filmed Instruction* (Pittsburgh: American Institute for Research, 1965).

15. Gene A. Getz, *Audiovisual Media in Christian Education,* rev. ed. (Chicago: Moody, 1972).

16. The following sketch of where to find supporting material is adapted from Theodore Brewer, "How to Develop Effective Sermon Illustrations" (Master's thesis, Dallas Theological Seminary, 1976), 40–51. For further help, see L. P. Lehman, *How to Find and Develop Effective Illustrations* (Grand Rapids: Kregel, 1985).

17. For example, for help with anecdotes and illustrations see: Michael P. Green, ed., *Illustrations for Biblical Preaching* (Grand Rapids: Baker, 1989); *The Oxford Dictionary of Quotations,* 3d ed. (Oxford: Oxford University Press, 1979); Clifton Fadiman, gen. ed., *The Little, Brown Book of Anecdotes* (Boston: Little, Brown, 1985); Ruth A. Tucker, *The Christian Speaker's Treasury: A Sourcebook of Anecdotes and Quotes* (New York: Harper and Row, 1989); Paul Lee Tan, *Encyclopedia of 7700 Illustrations* (Rockville, Md.: Assurance Publishers, 1979). For help with quotations see: Dennis J. Hester, comp., *The Vance Havner Quotebook* (Grand Rapids: Baker, 1986); Frank S. Mead, compiler and ed., *12,000 Religious Quotations* (Grand Rapids: Baker, 1965); Croft M. Pentz, *The Complete Book of Zingers* (Wheaton: Tyndale, 1990); William Neil, *Concise Dictionary of Religious Quotations* (Grand Rapids: Eerdmans, 1974); Tony Augarde, *The Oxford Dictionary of Modern Quotations* (New York: Oxford University Press, 1991).

18. Charles E. Little, *10,000 Illustrations from the Bible* (Grand Rapids: Baker, 1977).

Chapter 7:   *How to Introduce and Conclude Your Speech*

1. Aristotle *Rhetoric* 3.14.9, trans. W. Rhys Roberts (New York: Random House, 1954).

2. Wayne C. Booth, "The Rhetorical Stance," *College Composition and Communication* 14 (October 1963): 140.

3. H. Grady Davis, *Design for Preaching* (Philadelphia: Fortress, 1958), 187.

4. Aristotle *Rhetoric* 3.13.3.

5. Davis, *Design for Preaching,* 192.

6. Waldo Braden, "In the Heads of the Listeners: Principles of Communication," *Vital Speeches of the Day,* 1 November 1977, 42–44.

7. Newton N. Minow, "Television: How Far Has It Come in Thirty Years," *Vital Speeches of the Day,* 1 July 1991, 552.

8. Kenneth Mason, *Vital Speeches of the Day,* 15 January 1979, 204.

9. William H. Webster, "The Lincoln Assassination: Its Investigation," *Vital Speeches of the Day,* 15 March 1979, 3.

10. Samuel L. Becker, "Tolerance Is Not Enough," *Vital Speeches of the Day,* 1 July 1991, 575.

Chapter 8: *How to Word Your Speech*

1. William Shakespeare, *A Midsummer Night's Dream,* act 5, sc. 1, lines 14–17.

2. Aristotle *Rhetoric* 3.12.2–3, trans. W. Rhys Roberts (New York: Random House, 1954).

3. H. Grady Davis, *Design for Preaching* (Philadelphia: Fortress, 1958), 276.

4. Aristotle *Rhetoric* 3.2.1.

5. Ibid., 3.2.8.

6. Quoted by Sue Spencer, *Write on Target* (Waco: Word, 1976), 83.

7. Spencer, *Write on Target,* 105.

8. George Williams, *Creative Writing for Advanced College Classes,* rev. ed. (New York: Harper and Row, 1954), 96.

9. Aristotle *Rhetoric* 3.7.2.

10. Ibid., 3.2.

11. Sue Nichols, *Words on Target: For Better Christian Communication* (Richmond: John Knox, 1963), 13–15.

12. Ernest L. Boyer, "Communication: Message Senders and Receivers," *Vital Speeches of the Day,* 15 March 1978, 335.

13. For a helpful discussion of these points, see the books by Sue Nichols (Spencer), *Words on Target* and *Write on Target.*

14. Aristotle *Rhetoric* 3.2.4.

15. Nichols, *Words on Target,* 64.

16. For example, see Wilfred Funk and Norman Lewis, *30 Days to a More Powerful Vocabulary* (New York: Pocket, 1970); Norman Lewis, *Instant Word Power* (New York: Signet, 1981).

17. Davis, *Design for Preaching,* 12.

18. Quintilian *Institutio Oratoria* 10.3.1.

19. Ibid., 10.3.4.

20. Ibid., 10.4.1.

21. Ibid., 10.4.2.

Chapter 9: *How to Deliver Your Speech*

1. Charles Osgood, "Speaking Easy: Seven Steps to Pain-free Public Speaking," *Reader's Digest,* January 1990, 145.

Chapter 10:   *How to Prepare a Bible Message*

1. Francis A. Schaeffer, *The God Who Is There* (Downers Grove, Ill.: Inter-Varsity, 1968), 135ff.

2. Thomas W. Benson and Michael H. Prosser, eds., *Readings in Classical Rhetoric* (Bloomington, Ind.: Indiana University Press, 1972), 180.

3. The process we are about to examine is a homiletical process, but not purely so. It also has a spiritual dimension. When you handle the Word of God, you are dealing with spiritual issues. You are influencing the hearts and minds and, to some extent, the eternal destiny of the men and women you address. Thus you need to bathe the entire process of your preparation in prayer, first for yourself and then for those to whom you will speak. The matter of prayer is not addressed in the following steps because it is not technically *a stage* in your preparation. But make no mistake about it: the lack of a discussion of prayer is not because it is unimportant, but because its importance is taken for granted. Its role in the process is assumed to be crucial to the successful outcome of an expository message.

4. For example, Orville J. Nave and S. Maxwell Coder, *Nave's Topical Bible* (Chicago: Moody, 1975); *Zondervan Topical Bible*, ed. Edward Viening (Grand Rapids: Zondervan, 1969).

5. For example, James Strong, *The New Strong's Exhaustive Concordance of the Bible* (Nashville: Nelson, 1990); Robert Young, *Young's Analytical Concordance* (Nashville: Nelson, 1986).

6. Encyclopedias: Walter A. Elwell, gen. ed., *Baker Encyclopedia of the Bible*, 2 vols. (Grand Rapids: Baker, 1988); Geoffrey W. Bromiley, gen. ed., *The International Standard Bible Encyclopedia*, 4 vols., rev. ed. (Grand Rapids: Eerdmans, 1979–88); Merrill C. Tenney, gen. ed., *The Zondervan Pictorial Encyclopedia of the Bible*, 5 vols. (Grand Rapids: Zondervan, 1975). Dictionaries: R. K. Harrison, gen. ed., *The New Unger's Bible Dictionary* (Chicago: Moody, 1988); Merrill C. Tenney, *Zondervan Pictorial Bible Dictionary* (Grand Rapids: Zondervan, 1967); J. D. Douglas, gen. ed., *New Bible Dictionary*, 2d ed. (Wheaton, Ill.: Tyndale, 1982).

Index